Nobody Saw This Coming

Nobody Saw This Coming

How a Privileged Elite
Bankrupt a Nation

Dara MacGabhann

Published by Left-Field Publishing Ltd

A CIP catalogue record for this book is available from the British Library.

ISBN 978-0-9572048-0-5

Book and cover design by Clare Brayshaw

Cover photograph 'Correfoc', by Dara MacGabhann. (Correfoc means 'The Fire-Run' in Catalan)

Prepared and printed by:

York Publishing Services Ltd
64 Hallfield Road
Layerthorpe
York YO31 7ZQ

Tel: 01904 431213

Website: www.yps-publishing.co.uk

I gcuimhne mo thuistí,

Tomás agus Treasa.

Do Marian

is

do mo mhac,

Marcus.

They say that patriotism is the last refuge
To which a scoundrel clings
Steal a little and they throw you in jail
Steal a lot and they make you King.

(Bob Dylan)

Acknowledgements

Ten years ago it was my fortunate pleasure to watch an edition of The Money Programme, produced by David Strahan, entitled 'Inside the Enron Scandal'. This forty minute gem of a programme provided all the evidence that was required to question the viability of the very system of finance upon which countless billions of people worldwide were so thoroughly dependent. I have deliberately adhered quite closely to the brilliant account of the Enron scandal provided in David Strahan's excellent piece of work in an attempt to illustrate how easily it should have been to forecast that the collapse of capitalism was an inevitable outcome of the malpractices and fraudulent behaviour that were highlighted in the case. This programme also highlighted the invaluable benefit which public service broadcasting, in its truest sense, can be to society and I would like to add my voice to all those others who have congratulated David Strahan and his team on their wonderful programme of which they are undoubtedly and deservedly proud.

In a similar vein I would like to mention Adam Curtis's The Century of the Self, in particular, for the manner in which it enlightened me with regard to John Nash's significant influence on Margaret Thatcher's political ideology.

To all at YPS publishing, many thanks, especially Duncan Beal and Clare Brayshaw.

To Henry Ettinghausen, whose expert help in editing my initial efforts went far above the call of ordinary friendship, moltes gràcies, el meu amic.

I dedicate this book to the memory of my late parents, Tomás and Treasa, to whom I remain eternally indebted for the profound influence they had on me and whose guiding hands I have sensed so often at my shoulder, never more so than on the 30th of September 2008, the night I attended the parliamentary session in which the parliamentarians of Ireland effectively voted to bankrupt the nation.

If it was, indeed, their hands that guided me on the journey that lead me to Dáil Éireann on that fateful night for our nation, and I sincerely believe if was, then it was the influence of the two other most important people in my life that has ensured that I completed the written account of those experiences in this book. My wife, Marian, was a constant source of encouragement, support and good council in the initial stages of writing and then a brilliant, thoughtful and measured critic who patiently read and re-read the script, providing invaluable advice along the way. All this whilst taking on all the extra responsibilities which were left to her to complete in the nine month period it took me to complete the book.

My son, Marcus, made sacrifices too. During that period from January 2009 to October of the same year he was sent away disappointed on many an occasion having come to me in the reasonable expectation, for a five-year old, that his father would choose to play with him rather than sit in front of a computer screen writing a book, or that goddamn book as it became know. His only consolation was the promise I made him that when it was finished I would never undertake the writing of another and that 'book writing' would never again come between me and the fantastic, treasured times we spend together as a family. Well, Marcus, with the completion of this sentence, that's it!

Prologue

Nobody saw this coming!

Jan 18th 2009

The year was 2001. The Enron scandal had not just rocked
the financial system of the USA but had sent shock waves
reverberating around the world. The scandal had leapt
from the business and financial sections of the print
media and made its way into mainstream headlines, from
where it was always more likely to attract the attention
of someone with an inquisitive mind and an eye for an
interesting story. As one who had studied economics for
a short period in my school life – as the classes meant
staying in after normal classes, I gleefully abandoned
matters economic after three weeks, if I remember rightly
– this was possibly the first time since then that my interest
in the subject had been reawakened. I had heard that the
BBC intended to broadcast a programme about the Enron
Corporation and the fraudulent practices it had engaged
in, and had resolved to watch it. With hindsight, I realise
that my interest must have been whetted to quite an
extent, as I decided to record the programme, a decision,

I believe, that was to have a profound effect on the course of future events in my life.

'The Money Programme', produced and directed by David Strathan and presented by Rajan Datar, proved indeed to be riveting viewing. It provided a thought provoking insight into the fraudulent practices which had been employed to underpin the creation of one of the world's largest energy trading corporations before its eventual collapse. The programme also, shockingly, revealed the extent of the collusion between politicians, boards of directors, regulating authorities, chief-executives and auditors and accounting firms which facilitated the biggest financial scandal the world had witnessed to date. It was this cosy cabal of the most powerful elements of the financial system, aided and abetted by a political consensus which propagated the benefits of the unfettered and deregulated market in the pursuit of iniquitous profits, which alarmed me most. That, together with a public that was completely unaware of the dangers inherent in precisely such a system, having been misled by privately owned media that were in thrall to, and indeed an integral part of, this financial fraud for its own capital gain. I believed all the elements were in place for a complete collapse of the world's financial system as we knew it.

Were it not for the fact that I had recorded that particular 'Money Programme' and watched it repeatedly in the intervening years, it might not have had the sustained effect on my thinking that it was to have. Being a teacher in a south Dublin secondary school, I decided to show the programme to senior classes, as a means of instigating discussion on the merits of requiring an adherence to a stricter code of conduct and morality in business. As a result, I would have occasion to watch the programme at least twice a year with different classes and partake in the exchanges of views and analyses with the students that would inevitably ensue. This would keep the issues, which the scandal raised, very much to the forefront of my mind and develop in me a keener awareness of the issues involved. It also encouraged me to question features of our society which I believed people unthinkingly assumed were to our collective benefit. What with further instances of financial corruption that were emerging at ever more regular intervals around the world, I became ever more convinced that my initial prognosis was correct. My convictions were supported on occasions in the intervening period when I read or listened to the insights of such commentators and economists as David McWilliams and George Lee in Ireland and, perhaps more relevantly, the work of Will Hutton and Ruth Sunderland in 'The Observer' in England.

However, these commentators, particularly those in Ireland, were a very conspicuous minority in a journalistic profession which will undoubtedly emerge from this disastrous period with its reputation damaged immeasurably. Indeed very few sectors of society will, I believe, emerge with reputations intact after this thirty-year long orchestrated attempt by vested interests to deconstruct the basic tenants of organised society so that free unregulated economies could flourish and thereby benefit the few to the detriment of the many. The fact that outrageously inflated house prices were proffered to the public in general by those self-same vested interests, as bearing witness to their ever increasing wealth in society was but one example of this elaborate fraud. It is simply baffling to witness how the transformation, from the position of a moderately salaried public servant requiring two and a half times their salary in the eighties to buy a modest home in a middleclass area over a twenty year period to the same person requiring ten times their salary over thirty years in the early years of this century, could be put forward as an example of the economy's success. Yet this is what occurred, and it is but one example of the deceit which all but the very few became willing disciples of, resulting not in an improvement in their standing in society but in a decrease in personal wealth vis-à-vis the correlation between income and mortgage, but also in a monumental deterioration in personal freedom as a result of enormous and extended debt.

It was this aversion to over-indebtedness, instilled in me from a young age, which I believe made me sceptical, from the outset, of the raging philosophy of free market capitalism. The day I watched that instalment of 'The Money Programme' in 2001, I inadvertently began a journey which has ended now with the writing of this book. Little did I know, at that time, that the journey would end with me seated no more than a few yards away from Ireland's Minister of Finance, Brian Lenihan TD, privy to his private conversations and witness to his demeanour on the night of 30 September 2008.

That was the night that the Government of Ireland proposed the legislation which would see them guarantee the Irish Banking System – a decision that was unquestionably the most calamitous piece of legislation in the history of the Irish Republic. This guarantee, I was convinced at the time, would have disastrous consequences and would eventually condemn the Irish people to years of crippling indebtedness that will dim the prospects of generations of our children. What struck me as most alarming on that night in the Irish parliament, Dáil Éireann, was the complete lack of appreciation or concern as to the consequences which could result from this action. What drove me to go to Dáil Éireann to protest that night was my belief that the Government's decision to guarantee the banks was provoked by the chronic cronyism that had bedevilled Ireland for years. However, it was the total ignorance that was apparent amongst the politicians present, across the political divide, as to the prevailing dire financial situation worldwide and the disastrous consequences which would inevitably result from their decision that night that beggared belief. The question that arises from the events thus far described is that, if I appreciated the precarious state of Ireland's finances, and indeed those of the world's financial system at that moment, then why on earth did nobody else seem to?

Chapter 1

Enron – the canary in the coalmine

When, in the year 2000, Enron, one of the world's largest corporations, collapsed the tremor rocked the financial system in the USA to its core and sent shockwaves that reverberated around the world. No one could believe that this colossus of the stock market, which had seen its share price trade, only a few months previously, at the dizzying heights of ninety dollars, could have collapsed so ignominiously, leaving a trail of destruction in its wake that included thousands of loyal employees and shareholders. These victims' anger was, initially at least, primarily directed at the chief executives of the company, Kenneth Lay and Jeff Skilling, who, they believed, had reaped huge personal financial rewards by fraudulently inflating Enron's share price and then selling their personal shares just before the inevitable collapse.

However, in the course of the subsequent investigation the wrath of those most adversely affected was to turn to an ever increasing group of individuals who contributed to Enron's eventual downfall. This group included the Board of Directors, the auditors and accountants and the politicians and regulators who had all benefited to some extent from the fraud. They would also have cause to criticise the role which Wall Street itself had in Enron's affairs and, significantly, the blind eye which the journalistic profession turned to events.

The Enron story begins in 1985, when Kenneth Lay, the boss of a local gas pipeline company in Houston, Texas, bought one of its rivals. He named the new entity Enron. Within fifteen years Lay, the son of a Baptist minister, had, with the help of Harvard business school graduate Jeff Skilling, turned that small local concern into an energy trading giant which claimed sales worth hundreds of billions of dollars. They were undeniably helped in this regard by the fact that the gas industry was in the process of being deregulated, and they were perfectly positioned to take advantage of this fact. Deregulation recurs in the Enron story and should have been an alarm signal in the years after its crash. But at that time it was a primary tenet of an economic doctrine which claimed that business should be left free to create previously inconceivable wealth and that the fruits of that success would be enjoyed by the whole of society. Politicians worldwide, including the Minister for Finance in Ireland, Charlie McCreevy, became leading disciples and propagandists for deregulation, exalting its virtues at every opportunity, unrestrained, it must be noted, by much, if indeed any, dissention.

Enron was to benefit from deregulation on a notable occasion when Wendy Gramm, chairwoman of the authority which regulated commodities trading, ruled that speculative trading in gas and electricity did not need to be regulated. Wendy Gramm subsequently joined the Board of Executives at Enron and personally benefited by reaping the rewards of years of directors' fees. She also happened to be the wife of Republican Senator Phil Gramm who, it transpired, had received one hundred thousand dollars in contributions from Enron. He was, to be fair, but one of the seventy-five percent of all members of Congress, across the political divide, who had received such contributions from the corporation. As we shall see, Enron was greatly to benefit from this gift of deregulation which the political world had so kindly bestowed on them in that it enabled them to continue their fraudulent practices away from the prying eyes of independent government regulators. The unfortunate victims of this shameful deceit, of which there were thousands, would doubtless become far less less enamoured of their political representatives who colluded with the business world in this elaborate sham.

Angelina Lario was one such unfortunate victim. After working for Enron for some twenty-eight years, she had been rewarded with bonus shares and had been encouraged to purchase more as a means of supporting her pension fund. On 'The Money Programme' she recounted how she had put much of her personal life on hold as she concentrated on her professional career in the belief that she would eventually become financially secure, at which point she would indulge herself and her young daughter on the rewards of her lifetime of commitment to work. Unfortunately for Angelina Lario, the collapse of Enron left her unemployed and out of pocket to the tune of five hundred thousand dollars as her pension pot of share funds disappeared in a puff of smoke. From a position of relative financial security she was now, at the age of fifty-five and with a teenage daughter to support and educate, wedded to a half-million dollar mortgage which she could see no way of repaying. Her scorn for those responsible, particularly the Chief Executives Lay and Skilling, was understandable. These were the men who had promoted Enron on every possible occasion as a company of repute which valued honesty, integrity and truthfulness. It is quite possible that Kenneth Lay's upbringing as a Baptist minister's son enhanced his credence in this respect. Jeff Skilling, on the other hand, was generally considered to possess one of the finest minds ever to have emerged from the renowned and respected Harvard Business School.

It was Skilling who introduced staff performance reviews, a system that is now common practice worldwide, whereby employees are ranked against each other in an end of year review. At Enron this was seen generally as dividing employees into 'winners' and 'losers', or 'rank or yank', as it was commonly referred to. This system saw the top twenty percent of employees very generously rewarded with excellent bonuses and share options, whilst those less fortunate, the bottom twenty percent, were 'yanked', i.e. fired., One can easily imagine the levels of stress that this brutally effective annual process created amongst the employees. In the opinion of the Wall Street analyst, John Olsen – one of very few people to emerge from this fiasco with his integrity intact – Skilling took an already adrenaline-driven competitive culture and supercharged it. The company quickly developed a reputation for being arrogant and dogmatic. The employees from top management down were incentivised to make the company, and therefore themselves of course, as much money as possible. Skilling soon received his own personal incentive package. Kenneth Lay appointed him boss of the company's main trading division. He would be rewarded under the review system with a slice of the market share of the company. The bigger the company grew, the fatter his pay packet would become. Skilling now had a splendid financial incentive to ensure that the market share price continued to grow. The concern surely should have been that, with a system such as this, in which people could be tempted by the allure of accumulating previously unimaginable personal wealth, there was an inherent danger of corruption flourishing. When taken in conjunction with the previously mentioned fact that the politicians had deregulated the industry, all the components of the impending disaster began falling into place.

The year 1990 saw Jeff Skilling and his co-executives begin to reap the huge personal rewards that the business culture he helped to create encouraged. With the Gulf War raging, gas prices rocketed and Enron made vast profits, somewhere approaching two hundred billion dollars. Skilling, his co executives and all other employees ranked as being in the top twenty percent of achievers by the performance review system were rewarded with enormous salaries supplemented by massive share options. These share options greatly enhanced the bonuses they were being awarded, as the stock market acknowledged the continued growth of Enron by hugely increasing its share value. Everything appeared rosy for all associated with the company. Bumper profits had been announced, thereby increasing the share value, which in turn benefited the executives, the members of the Board of Directors and indeed all associated with Enron. But the vagaries of the stock market demand that a company should demonstrate on-going growth and, as we all know, the value of shares can go down as well as up.

The following year, with the Gulf War a distant memory, oil and gas prices came down to more reasonable levels. The problem for Enron now was that it had pledged an earnings growth rate that could simply not be achieved on existing operations. Skilling's vast bonus, to which presumably he had become accustomed, was in grave danger. He would have to turn his respected business mind to the challenge of finding a new way to create profit, thereby ensuring continued share price growth and so protect, or indeed further inflate, his enormous salary.

His solution to the problem came in the form of some very creative accounting. The practice of 'mark to market' accountancy was, and remains, an accepted and legal method, both in the USA and worldwide. It was created to enable companies involved in business contracts that would not begin to show profits until possibly the second or third year of the contracts, the means to show earnings in their trading book from the first year. Skilling and Enron took this accountancy manoeuvre and manipulated it to allow them to distort facts and fraudulently inflate their share price.

In 1991 Enron signed a deal to supply oil to a power station in New York State for twenty years. The profit from the first year of the deal would not have been enough for Enron to claim an increase in profits. Skilling's master manoeuvre was to use 'mark to market' accounting to claim the expected profit of the twenty years of the complete contract in the first year. This enabled Enron to announce that earnings had been boosted and that there was ongoing growth, and this resulted in the share price continuing to grow, thereby guaranteeing Skilling's salary and bonuses. In 'The Money Programme' this ruse was described as being as if Enron had placed a huge bet on the roulette table and then announced to everybody that they had won, even though the wheel had not yet even started spinning. It was also revealed that the company had misled regulators on this point. Enron claimed in a letter to the regulators that the use of 'mark to market' accounting in this instance would not have 'any material impact' on the company's earnings that year. In fact it was a complete misrepresentation of the company's true earnings that year and resulted in an unjustified and fraudulent increase in share price.

Of course, certain individuals would benefit greatly from this corrupt practice, though thousands of unfortunate others would eventually pay an enormous price. It was later demonstrated that the use (or, rather, abuse) of 'mark to market' accounting amounted to fifty percent of Enron's profits that year. This misuse of accountancy procedures was not noticed or, if it was, it was not deemed to be a corruption of accountancy practice by the auditors of the company or by its Board of Directors. The auditors, Arthur Anderson, one of the top five accountancy firms at the time, approved the accounts, thereby allowing the deceit to proceed unchecked. The results, needless to say, impressed Wall Street, and the required boost in share price naturally occurred. Some of the top staff gained twice over: through their bonuses and through the stock options issued to them.

Naturally, the bonus system for rewarding staff, and the ever increasing demand to demonstrate continued growth in share price as the only commonly accepted method for valuing a company, were in themselves contributory factors to the financial and human disaster that would later unfold. The conflict of interest which arose from the fact that Arthur Anderson were both advisers and watchdogs to the company, in their role as consultants and auditors, was also significant. As auditors, they were supposed to be keeping an eye on the company and ensuring that its business was conducted in accordance with the law. However, at the same time, they were employed by the company to help it dodge costs and to contribute to its aim of announcing strong profit growth, in order to impress Wall Street and so boost its share price. The astronomical retainer fees that the auditors earned – twenty-five million dollars as consultants, and a similar figure for its role as auditors – were themselves inextricably linked to the profits announced annually by Enron and to the consequent rise in its share price.

All of those involved in the Enron story were deeply compromised. The executives, whose salary, bonus and share options depended on supposedly rising profits; the directors, such as the aforementioned Wendy Gramm, the consultants and auditors Arthur Anderson, or indeed the vast majority of the employees: all were exceedingly well remunerated, as long as the share price continued it relentless climb. This very fact contained within it the seeds of the corporation's inevitable downfall. It was in the financial interests of those concerned, in particular the executives, to employ every possible means to ensure that the gravy train sped onwards and upwards. Almost inevitably, the system created a culture of self-delusion amongst those charged with the responsibility of ensuring that the company's business practice was above board, be that the members of the Board of Directors or the auditors.

Another fine example of the business culture which had developed within Enron was provided nearer to home when, in 1993, Lord Wakeham, the former UK Energy Secretary, approved the opening of a giant power station by the company in Teesside. Not long afterwards, Lord Wakeham was invited onto the board of Enron as a non-executive Director. The power station soon announced that it had contracted to buy gas from the North Sea for twenty years. This meant that, to transport the gas to the British mainland, Enron would have to pay three million pounds a month for the use of an undersea pipeline, so the company turned to previously successful accountancy manoeuvres which would allow it to hide costs and thereby inflate profits once more. As an accountant employed at Enron explained on 'The Money Programme', the method employed was as follows. Of the three million pounds a month represented by the hire of the pipeline, only one million was recognised in the company's accounts. This, they claimed, was on the basis that they did not intend to use the pipeline for the twenty years of the contract and that they would eventually sell on the remaining years' use of the pipeline, making a profit in the process.

This was considered by some to be aggressive accounting and by others a very optimistic guess, but the fact is that it allowed Enron to continue its practice of announcing profits and inflating share price. Once again the auditors reviewed and approved the accounts. By now, however, trouble was brewing for Enron. The company had expanded its portfolio and become a global trading house, buying and selling anything to do with energy. But, in the meantime, gas prices had tumbled, and this had the effect of sharply decreasing profits. The company was tied into the pipeline deal and subsequently lost five hundred million dollars. It was too late to increase profits in any legitimate way, or even by having recourse to their previously trusted methods, so on this occasion the crude order was sent out to Enron's European offices to "get us more fucking money". It was almost possible to hear the appendage "or my fucking bonus and share option will be hit". However, only the first part of the order was attested to by the employee of Enron's European office, the former director of Ocean Freight Trading, Pierre Aury, who declared on 'The Money Programme' that he had refused to comply with the order but intimated that others might not have been so principled and might have simply rewritten the books in a more favourable light, a practice referred to within the company as 'tweaking the knob'.

By the late 1990s, however, Enron was finding it increasingly difficult to conjure up ruses that would artificially inflate its share price. Lurking behind the illusion of vast profits were in fact enormous debts, the result of years of fraudulent reporting. But just when it seemed that Jeff Skilling was running out of means to deceive the stock market and thereby maintain his huge salary, along came a more than willing accomplice in the person of Andrew Fastow. This young associate was the brains behind another complex web of accounting manoeuvres which would be employed to hide away debts or create questionable profits. The trick consisted in exploiting a company law which illustrates once more the prevailing attitude amongst politicians that the business world should be left to carry out its function of creating wealth unhindered by requirements to abide by sound practice as wealth could be relied upon to create more wealth and everybody benefited in the long run.

The loophole, which Andrew Fastow cynically exploited to help maintain the great illusion of continued growth in Enron's profits, lay in the regulatory rules in the USA which, incredibly, allowed a parent company that sold as little as three percent of a subsidiary to outside investors to then claim that that subsidiary was independent and that therefore the parent company was not required to show its debts in its accounts. This scheme was ideal for Enron, as it happened to dispose of huge debts which were in danger of harming its share price. Fastow set up an extraordinary complex of subsidiary companies into which he piled Enron debt, which he proceeded to sell on to supposed outside investors. Not only did this relieve the company of the debt, which would not need to be reported, but he also claimed that Enron had received highly inflated prices for these deals which they proceeded to claim in their accounts as profit! By these means Fastow and Enron managed to conceal twenty-seven billion dollars in loss making businesses. Not one of these deals, which numbered over four thousand, matched any real business purpose. In the opinion of Economics Professor Robert McCollough, who was quoted on 'The Money Programme', they were simply a sham. However, these fraudulent deals were discussed and approved by Directors on the Board, directors who were exceedingly well remunerated for executing their functions, which included the duty of ensuring that the company's business was above board. Is it just possible that their huge rewards – salaries of over three hundred thousands dollars being commonplace – distracted them from fulfilling their moral responsibilities?

'The Money Programme' also addressed the role of the media in connection with the Enron fraud. As with the consensus which was apparent in the political world, it was obvious that the media in general had succumbed unreservedly to the deregulated, free-market ideology. In fact they became flag bearers for the principle, all the more so as much of the media, now privately owned, was an eager participant in the stock market. This would have the effect of spreading the Gospel, unchallenged by and large, throughout the world. In the case of Enron the media in general and the financial media in particular, were in thrall to the dizzying successes of the corporation. Unabashed and unqualified praise was lavished on the organisation, as practically everybody bought into the extraordinary success story that was Enron. 'Fortune Magazine' included Enron, year on year, in its 'most admired' list, and Andrew Fastow was recognised for his brilliance with an award for 'capital structure management' from 'Chief Financial Officers' magazine.

Enron was the emblem of the age, with practically everybody associated with it enjoying lavish lifestyles on the seemingly endless fruits of its success. Executives were earning tens of millions of dollars as they cashed in their shares as they rose exorbitantly in value on the stock market. One executive, Lou Pai, earned – if that is the right word – two hundred and fifty million dollars from one such share sell off. The fact that these shares were effectively being parked, like other bad debts from the company, only for someone else to pick up at a future date, would only emerge with the passing of time. This, it appeared, was not the time to question where the outrageous profit was destined, the common economic consensus being that it would remain in the system and 'trickle down' to all in society. Time would, unfortunately, prove that no such benefits would accrue to society in general.

Enron's continued success was, as we have seen, dependent on a continually rising share price. A major contributory factor in this process was the role played by analysts who recommended share acquisitions. Kenneth Lay and Jeff Skilling were well aware of the need to keep analysts on board who would manipulate the system to ensure that they would continue to receive 'strong buy' recommendations for Enron. These analysts were required to be independent and should have had a duty of care to the thousands of investors who might heed their advice. However, they were employed by the major investment banks, and these were paid enormous fees from corporations such as Enron.

There existed, once again, the conflict of interests in the business world which rewarded those who were predisposed to corrupt the system in order to garner immense personal wealth. Kenneth Lay maintained an account of the 'strong buy' recommendations issued by the financial analysts and rewarded their employees, the investment banks, in accordance. In 2000 Enron announced profits of one billion dollars. Investment banks competed vigorously for a share of these vast spoils. Kenneth Lay, and Enron, unsurprisingly received their 'strong buy' recommendations, and so another part of the financial system was indelibly corrupted. Moreover, Lay insured that his company would continue to receive positive recommendations by ensuring that analysts who refused to comply lost their jobs. One such example was the aforementioned John Olsen, a financial analyst, who was hounded from his position on not one, but two, occasions with major investment banks, as he was unwilling to issue 'strong buy' recommendations for Enron. On the second of these occasions he was asked 'to consider his position' with the giant Wall Street investment bank Merrill Lynch. The evident compliancy of a major institution, such as Merrill Lynch, with Lay in the fraud that Enron was committing was further evidence of the complete corruption of the financial system and should have been a warning that the Enron example was not an isolated incident but was indicative of the generally accepted business climate at the time.

More evidence was to be found, for those who wished to acknowledge it, in the next sham which Enron, in conjunction with the pillars of capitalism in both the USA and Europe, decided to launch on an unsuspecting world. Though the corporation had announced a one billion dollar profit in 2000 and Andrew Fastow had been rewarded to the tune of thirty million dollars, the continued success of the ruse could only be assured by a further rise in share price the following year. To achieve this, Andrew Fastow proposed setting up another dummy subsidiary into which bad – or, to use the current term, toxic – debt could be dumped. Merrill Lynch was awarded the contract for drumming up support amongst investors for this shambolic enterprise.

At a meeting in Florida, arranged to encourage financial support for the project, those in attendance were informed by Fastow and Skilling that the intention was to create a company that would again hide debts and thereby inflate Enron's profits. Those in attendance, who included representatives of the major USA and European finance houses – amongst them, Morgan Stanley, Chase Capital, JP Morgan Capital and Dresdner – were obviously aware of the corrupt nature of the proposal before them, but they were offered such unbelievable rates of return on their initial investment that many not only invested on behalf of their banks but also chose to lay out millions personally. Many of these self same institutions were to survive the collapse of Enron only to arrive back on the public radar in the past few years as the banking crisis took hold. Little wonder, as no corrective action was to follow Enron's collapse. The pursuit of profit continued apace, with neither politicians, the media nor the public apparently aware of the need to totally reconstruct this ailing system if collapse on an even greater scale were to be avoided in the future.

By then Enron's own inevitable demise was only a matter of time. The company was never again to achieve the heady heights of its success in 2000 when share price reached the ninety dollar mark and the company had an overall market valuation of one hundred billion dollars! It was at that point that executives started leaving the company and a massive sell-off of shares took place. Within a year Enron executives had in fact disposed of shares to the tune of over £750 million. The corrupt business practice was beginning to unravel, as it always inevitably does, and these executives, and others who enjoyed the privileged position of foreseeing its decline, took advantage and disposed of their shares at their highest value. Lay, Skilling and Fastow, the three primary players in the fraud, banked nearly two hundred million dollars between them in the sell-off.

The corollary of this despicable action was, of course, that those innocent shareholders who did not have access to inside information were left financially ruined and emotionally shattered. It is worth pausing to consider that shares of this nature would primarily be acquired by pension funds. The plight of those who had toiled throughout their lives in the reasonable expectation that they would live out their remaining days free from worry, only to discover that they had been the victims of a colossal hoax is not hard to imagine. The encouragement of employee participation in the philosophy of driving share price inexorably higher, and then benefiting from the outrageous profits that would inevitably accrue, was central to the success of this sham. As the share price rose they were, understandably, seduced by the possibility of acquiring riches beyond their wildest dreams. Of course, a scenario that envisaged a decline in share price and a shattering of this beguiling illusion was obviously not even considered. This form of entrapment was an essential element of the fraud that was committed by Enron.

Angelina Lario, one of the many employees who had been encouraged by the company to buy shares to provide for her retirement and had been rewarded with bonuses in the form of shares, lost five hundred thousand dollars when Enron collapsed. At fifty-nine years of age, she also had seventy-five thousand dollars outstanding on her mortgage. It must have been just a little galling for her to hear Jeff Skilling testify to the House Senate Committee that he had been unaware of the impending collapse of the company when he sold his shares for upwards of sixty million dollars.

Enron's collapse was to send shock waves around the world. A company that had previously enjoyed a market valuation of one hundred billion dollars and been a jewel in the crown of the business world had effectively disappeared into thin air. Its business model was, to all intents and purposes, a fraud perpetrated on the stock market, and thereby on the unsuspecting public who acquired its shares. Most of the creative energies of the brightest and best business minds in Enron were directed towards means of fraudulently inflating share price and subsequently reaping the rewards for themselves. This culture of exclusively focussing on the boosting of share price, to the exclusion, on many occasions in Enron's case, of any real business purpose had within it the seeds of its own destruction which would result in the decay of the financial system as a whole. The stock market itself appeared to become beguiled by the riches which were to be accumulated by those who participated in this fraud. Politicians, regulators, boards of directors, consultancy and auditing firms, investment banks, the media, and indeed the public in general succumbed to the allure of the fortunes on offer. This cosy consensus became the breeding ground for a growing complacency which would further increase the chances of this fraud's initial success. Possibly the greatest cause for concern was that there was increasing evidence to suggest that this, rather than being an isolated incident, had in fact become the model for modern business practice, not just in the USA, but worldwide.

Chapter 2

The Pennies Begin to Drop!

Anyone who was predisposed to even the most minimal levels of scepticism could not help but be concerned by the issues raised by the Enron scandal. If one of the most powerful corporations in the world had employed such a fraudulent business plan over such a lengthy period without being detected by the regulating authorities, why couldn't others? If the huge investment banks, such as Merrill Lynch and Morgan Stanley, had not only condoned but also collaborated in the swindle, wasn't this evidence that Enron's business culture was not confined to that company alone but was in fact common practice? If the auditors Arthur Anderson, one of the top five auditing and accounting practices, were compromised by their joint roles as consultants and auditors, wasn't it more than possible that the other top four – and indeed all auditors – would succumb to the very generous temptations that were on offer? Couldn't the effectiveness of the boards of directors in safeguarding the interests of the shareholders be called into question, seeing as these self same directors reaped the rewards of the rising stock market valuation? Wasn't the composition of boards of directors, often comprising of former politicians, indicative of a consensus between the business and political worlds which facilitated further the expansion of this corrupt corporate mentality? Would this be one reason we saw the promotion of the free market ideology, and particularly the clarion call of 'deregulation', echo almost unopposed throughout the political world? Were these former politicians, and other pillars of this common consensus of acceptable business practice, really being chosen for these generously rewarded positions as directors to protect the interests of shareholders and ensure that company practice was above board, or as a reward for previous or future favours? Whatever the absolute truth of the matter was, there was surely ample evidence of the emergence of a consensus amongst the political and business worlds which unreservedly accepted the ideology that creation of profit in ever increasing and excessive amounts was beneficial to all in society, and indeed to society itself. Was the fact that this view of the economy was always taking precedence not potentially devastating for modern society itself?

These were but some of the questions which came to mind as a result of my initial viewing of the 'Money Programme' back in 2001. Frequent subsequent viewings served only to reinforce my view that these failings in corporate and political practice were in danger of irrevocably damaging the very fabric of the system to which, by that time, nearly the whole world was wedded. This assessment was to be reinforced by a growing number of examples of similar deficiencies which were beginning to arise in the system applied closer to home, in Ireland. One of the first examples was the case of National Irish Bank and the methods it employed to boost profits which first came to light in 1998. As a result of an investigation conducted by George Lee and Charlie Bird, on behalf of

RTE News, it was to emerge that very doubtful practices were endemic within the bank as a means of increasing profits. The investigation which ensued was to uncover methods of boosting earnings within the bank which those employed in Enron to perpetrate fraud would, I believe, have blanched at, so outrageous were they in their nature.

National Irish Bank, like its competitors, had introduced a policy of remuneration based on performance and on bonuses linked to results. The local branch managers recounted how they were continually being bullied and coerced into finding new ways of increasing monthly returns. This supercharged competitive culture was supplemented by regular regional meetings at which managers were ranked against each other on the basis of overall monthly returns to the bank, a practice that closely resembled the scheme that Jeff Skilling had introduced at Enron. Of course, it was to prove highly successful in its aim of boosting annual profit returns for the bank and would have the required effect of increasing its share valuation on the stock market. Everybody benefited. Everybody, that is, except the account holders within the bank. As with the case of Enron, the bank was to discover that there was a finite number of ways to legally increase profits. However, the continued rise of the stock market valuation was contingent on just such an increase being annually announced. The local bank managers came under increased pressure and, since their bonuses, if not their very positions, were dependent on their success in this regard, little wonder that the temptation to indulge in elementary chicanery in the accounting department became too much to refuse. With a little help from central management, who at the very least turned a blind eye to the proceedings, it was recommended at the monthly managers' meetings that they could countenance the withdrawal of varying amounts of money from depositors' accounts.

Even at some twenty years' remove, it is hard to comprehend how this could have been regarded as acceptable business behaviour, but it is a perfect example of the manner in which people could be seduced into performing extraordinary acts in the pursuit of wealth. The bank managers had become the bank robbers in this business model, in which the employees became accomplices in chief to the executives who demanded ever-rising share price valuation, as their personal financial remuneration was inextricably linked to it. In fact, the report which emerged six years later from the commission set up to enquire into the affair maintained that "systematic overcharging and bank sponsored tax evasion was practiced in order to boost profits and bankers' salaries". A prominent member of parliament for Fianna Fáil Beverly Cooper Flynn, who had worked for the bank for a period before entering the Dáil, was found "to have encouraged customers to avail of offshore schemes to avoid paying tax".

This fraud within National Irish Bank was to increase my scepticism towards the prevalence of corrupt practice within business and my suspicion that these practices were greater in number and more widespread than generally thought – all the more so since it actually predated the revelation of Enron's malpractice by some years. There was also the worrying concern that not one employee of National Irish Bank was to lose their job as a result of the investigation into this outrageous scam. A promise that they would not repeat that particular fraud appeared to be enough for our regulators and politicians to accept that not one executive, not one board member, not any auditor nor anyone charged with regulating the industry, should take responsibility for this audacious bank robbery. The message seemed to be, however inadvertently it was portrayed, that their only real crime was that of being caught!

However, the most alarming aspect of the National Irish Bank story was the revelation that the 'performance related pay' and 'bonus culture' had become an established and accepted practice in the corporate culture of Ireland, well before the Enron scandal was to illustrate the dangers inherent in precisely such a culture. That nobody saw fit to correct or even challenge the assumption that these unseemly remuneration packages encouraged fraudulent business practice was also a cause for concern. Indeed, far from challenging this potentially destructive element of corporate culture, economic analysts, as well as government ministers, aided and abetted by an unquestioning media, formed a dangerous consensus of opinion that became its loudest and most fervent propagandists.

So efficient was 'performance related pay' deemed to be in the private sector that it was pronounced imperative to construct a similar product that could be foisted on the public sector, a sector which was unanimously derided by economic analysts as being ineffective and unproductive. Unlike the private sector which was, according to these economists, generating vast wealth in the general economy, the public sector was a drain on our financial resources. In the words of one of the leading apologists for the free market project, Jim Power, chief economic advisor of Friends First Life Assurance Company, the public sector "contributed nothing to the economy". This comment, I believe, perfectly illustrated the mindset of the prevailing economic ideology. Profit took pre-eminence over every other consideration in business, to such an extent that in the end, as was the case with Enron, it became the exclusive motivation, relegating the product or service provided to an ever more inconsequential and immaterial role in comparison.

So the greatest economic minds joined together and conceived the public sector version of remuneration related to productivity: benchmarking. Again, no issue was taken with the fact that previous examples from private industry had revealed that indeed profits were increased substantially but at a substantial cost in terms of actual business practice. Benchmarking was designed by economists as a means of substituting deserved traditional inflation-related pay increases with the new model of incentive-related increases. Public servants would be required to demonstrate increased performance and productivity in order to qualify for a pay rise. This made perfectly good sense to those economic boffins who held sway at the time, but unfortunately it would have the same devastating effect on our public services as it had in the private arena. Though benchmarking was lauded as the mechanism by which the perceived under-performing public sector would be reformed and become more efficient, it would in fact have the totally opposite effect.

The policy of ' performance-related pay' did not take into account the fact that, far from under-performing, the public sector is in fact populated by an over whelming majority of people who take their commitments to 'public service' very seriously and were already committing one hundred percent of their energies and abilities to the performance of their duties. How were these people to earn their bonuses or benchmarked pay increases? They would have to take on the numerous new duties which were invented in order to create the illusion of increased productivity and which would allow politicians to claim that there policies had been successful. Unfortunately, in real terms, what actually occurred was that nurses, teachers and gardaí, for example, now found themselves committing only eighty percent of their time to their previously essential work, whilst twenty percent of their time was allotted to onerous inconsequential paperwork, with the consequential diminution in the very services which the public rightly demanded of them and were entitled to.

It is worth noting that the small minority of under-performing staff in the public sector were not in the least discommoded by benchmarking. If the aim of the policy had been to ensure that this group would contribute more, then it failed abysmally on that score also. Lazy and unproductive workers continued to abdicate their responsibilities, as is their wont. This in turn contributed to a further increase in the amount of time that the responsible public servants had to designate to completing the new duties which had been assigned to their less motivated colleagues. These new benchmarking duties, mainly report filling and box ticking, which had no worthwhile contribution to make to the service being supplied, were, nonetheless, compulsory. The slack was taken up by the motivated and professional workforce, but this resulted again in a diminution of the service provided, as the percentage of time committed to ancillary and needless duties increased further. Economic theory, especially one so flawed as the model provided by Enron, could and should never have been employed in the public sector. This, I believe, is one of the reasons why our public services are in such a shambolic state.

Meanwhile, in the real 'otherworld' of corporate business, the pursuit of exorbitant and excessive profit continued apace. Entrepreneurs who boasted of previously inconceivable wealth as a result of their brilliance in the field of commerce were heralded as the new gods of our time. The consensus was that money grew money and that these untouchables of the corporate sector were the propagators of the flood of money into our system which would raise all our boats in due course. If the fuel that drove the engine on those boats was the 'performance-related bonus' then the annually announced profit statement was the super luxury yacht which these wealthy magnates owned and ostentatiously paraded for mere mortals to gasp at in admiration. Yet it should have been noticed, as was seen with Enron, where a hundred billion dollars suddenly went missing, that unthinkable events could occur which could result in profits disappearing into thin air in the corporate world's version of the Bermuda Triangle. But these were considerations that nobody seemed willing to take on board as more and more people fell under the spell of the allure of money.

We need only consider a few instances of how greed made people abandon their critical faculties and become dangerously complacent. The global aspect of this corrupt business culture, which had been witnessed in Enron's American and European dimensions, was to be corroborated by a further example of corporate corruption that set alarm bells ringing in the minds of those who suspected that this business model could end up in a devastating crash. That example was to come in the year 2004 in the form of the Parmalat crisis in Italy, which was to be described as Europe's Enron. This giant corporation had undergone rapid expansion from a small dairy concern to one that employed thirty six thousand people. In October 2004 it emerged that the company, which enjoyed a market share valuation of nearly four billion euro, was having difficulty making a one hundred and fifty million euro bond payment. Its share price began to fall rapidly, and the company moved to quell rumours that they were in trouble, claiming that they had nearly four billion euro in an account in the Cayman Islands and producing a letter, on paper that boasted a Bank of America

letterhead, which seemed to c[...]
an account. As their auditors[...]
and as Bank of America wa[...]
America at the time, this a[...]
the claim. This contract wa[...]
raise cash which was subs[...]
to day losses in the compa[...]

By October 2004 the t[...]
Company executives had simply [...]
the Cayman Islands, and ten billion dollars [...]
almost overnight from the company's accounts. Another
giant corporation came crashing down, providing further
evidence that this was a worldwide phenomenon and
that the result was invariably the same, wherever this
fraudulent model of business madness was employed. The
involvement of auditors such as Deloitte and Touche and
the third largest bank in America in the affair gave further
cause for concern. The names of two more seemingly
reputable companies could now be added to the ever
increasing list of those which were implicated in financial
fraud being committed worldwide.

In Ireland one example of the ludicrous situation in
which excessive profit was lauded and countenanced,
even though it actually did irreparable harm to the
economic wellbeing of the country and its citizens, was
the case of the M50 motorway. This was an example of
such economic folly that it simply beggared belief. The
clamour for private interests to take over the management
of public affairs, because of the perceived ineptitude of
public service management, had reached a crescendo
amongst the economic commentators at the time. This
constant refrain of the pre-eminence of private over public
was to gain in momentum over the years and was a huge
contributing factor to the crisis we now face. It is worth
noting that the chief apologists and propagandists for this

...logy continue to this day to be blind to its ...ute failure.

...0 motorway was rightly proposed as a means ...ting the chronic traffic disruptions which were ...ring the development of Dublin City, and it was ...gested that it would be best to place the task of ...ilding it in the hands of private industry. A deal was agreed between the minister Padraig Flynn, father of the aforementioned Beverly Cooper Flynn, and a foreign company to build the motorway at a cost of €38 million euro, and a contract was signed which would see the private company continuing for twenty years to collect a toll from all citizens who availed themselves of its use. When completed, in 1990 a barrier was placed across the motorway which resulted in enormous traffic disruptions, the alleviating of which was the reason it had been built in the first instance.

If this nonsensical outcome wasn't enough to put into question the decision to use a private builder, then the fact that this piece of wood remained across the capital city's main transport artery for twenty years, requiring our citizens to pay close to 1.2 billion euro in tolls before it could be removed, surely was? Sixteen years after its completion we witnessed the farcical, not to say immoral, situation of the government spending €600 million euro to remove the piece of wood in order to facilitate the movement of citizens freely within their own land. The detrimental effect which this toll barrier had on economic development was enormous and further highlighted the stupidity and ineffectiveness of the system, which eulogized profit over product.

The awarding of the second mobile phone licence in 1995 to Esat Digifone was another example to arouse suspicion. This licence to print money, as it was generally regarded at the time, was awarded to businessman Denis

O'Brien for what was considered the very reasonable sum of €19 million. When if came to light that this had not even been the highest amount offered in the bidding process, suspicions were raised. Further doubts were cast on the validity of the award when it was alleged subsequently that payments of €100,000 were made to the minister charged with awarding the contract, Michael Lowry TD. When Denis O'Brien sold the company only seven years later for €2.4 billion, questions were asked about the excess profit he had made on what was, or rather should have been, a state asset. When Denis O'Brien then belligerently refused to pay a cent in tax on his own, not inconsiderable, personal profit of €317 million from the sale, it only served to compound the injustice which had been committed on the citizens of the state. Another to benefit greatly from this private sale of public assets was the financier Dermot Desmond, who profited to the tune of €110 million, and of whom more will be heard presently.

Another financial scandal which was to rock the state in the nineties was that of Greencore. This particular scandal bore remarkable resemblance to those that preceded it, and indeed followed it, even to the extent of the primary characters involved. In this instance the same deficiencies in corporate governance resulted in a major fraud within the company going undetected. The audit committee, the chair of which earned €21,000 euro annually and whose members were awarded bonuses of €10,000 euro every year for fulfilling their duties in safeguarding the interest of shareholders, failed to detect a €21 million euro fraud at the company's Scottish mineral water division. The company's auditors, Price Waterhouse Coopers, carried out the handsomely remunerated duty of clearing the accounts each year. During their tenure as Greencore's auditors it is estimated that they extracted fees approaching €10 million euro, yet they failed to provide the service for which they were employed. In the final year before the colossal fraud was spotted the four chief executives in the company were awarded 'performance-related bonuses' amounting to €1.8 million. Although they were obviously based on profits that were illusionary, and in fact fraudulent, none of the directors were to subsequently return these payments. Meanwhile the share price plummeted and the honest shareholder was left in possession of valueless pieces of paper as the real money exited the company in the hands of those complicit in the sham that had been perpetrated.

In 2005 and 2006 the Greencore executives would avail of the opportunity that EU sugar policy reform would provide and close the last two remaining sugar processing plants in the country. By agreeing to shut down the eighty year old industry completely the producers and processors were entitled to over 100 million euro in compensation from the European Union. The executives were also swayed in their decision by the fact that the land banks on which the factories sat were by this time vastly more valuable than the long term production of sugar. Ireland, an island nation, had been asset stripped of one of its vital and traditional resources. Sugar production, a fundamental element of any society's economy, a traditional cornerstone of this country's agriculture and industry sectors for the best part of a century, had been scattered to the winds in the avaricious scramble for the new found wealth. Unfortunately it would of course prove to be yet another example of those who knew the cost of everything and the value of nothing. There is no question or doubt but that the government will have to invest vast quantities of taxpayers capital into re-establishing sugar processing in Ireland and overturning the decision of the executives of Greencore to destroy a perfectly viable, profitable and sustainable traditional industry that provided gainful, honourable employment to thousands and an essential service to the citizens of this State. How unfortunate that the executives, hand-picked by the peoples representatives in government, were following a different, far more self-serving agenda than this.

The company had in fact been mired in controversy for years, beginning with accusations that its original floatation as a private entity from its previous incarnation as a semi-state sugar company had been subject to undue influence from the Taoiseach Charles Haughey. Amongst those whom he selected from his golden circle of friends to serve on the board at Greencore was the afore-mentioned financier Dermot Desmond, a long-time associate of the ex-Taoiseach, who was elected chairman, and two other interesting characters, Seanie Fitzpatrick and Ned Sullivan, who would subsequently re-emerge in another scandal as members of the board at Anglo Irish Bank. Another Haughey acquaintance, Jack Stakelum, sat on the board at Greencore for many years. Nearly all these highly paid members of the audit committee and of the board of directors were later shown to have invested minimally, if at all, in shares in the company. Their guaranteed financial remuneration was in stark contrast to the massive losses incurred by the innocent shareholders in the fraud perpetrated under their watch.

The existence of the golden circle of privileged citizens of this state whose concerns took precedence over all others has long been an established fact. Its existence is to be evidenced by the frequency with which the same names keep recurring in preeminent positions within Irish society. They also have a tendency to appear as players in the country's major financial scandals. The Ansbacher scandal, another major fraud committed on the citizens of the State, uncovered once more by some fine investigative journalism by George Lee in RTE, was to bring some of these names to the public's attention. The aforementioned Jack Stakelum, friend to our ex-Taoiseach Charles Haughey, was to crop up in association with this bank scandal, which saw the richest and most affluent in our economy avail themselves of the services provided by Ansbacher Bank to spirit money out of the State to off-shore accounts so that they wouldn't have to pay taxes. Duty to their State was, once again, deemed to be beneath them: that could be left to the ordinary hardworking people, many of whom they had fleeced already with fancy financial products.

The list of those who possessed these tax evading and tax avoiding off-shore accounts would make for interesting, indeed shocking, reading, as it included names from the top echelons of Irish society. Unfortunately, it would never be deemed sufficiently important to be published for wider public appreciation, as the government of Bertie Ahearn, supported by their coalition partners The Labour Party under the leadership of Dick Spring, decided that an amnesty would be declared for all those who willingly came forward and admitted to holding such accounts. Yet the names of account holders that were to become public knowledge were stellar and illustrated the levels of Irish society that were involved.

A final example of how the general public were being duped on a regular basis into providing the real money, through share acquisition, for the privileged few at the top of the business pyramid is provided by Eircom. This was possibly the finest example of the ruse which Enron encapsulated, as it was attempted on a major scale. The public at large were invited by their political masters to join in the sure-fire guaranteed success that would ensue from the privatisation of yet another state asset: the telecommunications company Eircom. The Eircom share issue was the most widely talked about passport to unimaginable riches in the history of the state, the first occasion when nearly the entire population became excited by the idea of acquiring shares. Ordinary working people became enthralled by the promises made to them of cast iron rewards on their investments.

The Taoiseach, Bertie Ahearn, the Minister for Finance, Charlie McCreevy and the Minister for Public Enterprise, Mary O'Rourke, led the posse in promoting and sponsoring this racing certainty which would result in a guaranteed windfall for all those involved. But, as with all previous cases recounted thus far, the shareholders, of whom there were 600,000, were merely the unfortunate suckers who provided the pool of cash deposits from which the perpetrators of the sham drew their premium profits. This they did by a variety of methods: by the executives and company directors – such as former politicians Ray McSharry and Dick Spring, or political appointees such as a leading member of the Progressive Democrats, Paul McKay – receiving huge bonuses of stock options on foot of floatation; or by the decision of initial large investors, such as KPN and Telia, who had representatives on the board, to sell their stakes in Eircom at its early high valuation; or by the exorbitant remuneration packages which executives annually awarded themselves.

The result was always the same. The small people, those generally deemed worthy only to provide succour to our genial political and business classes, were left holding worthless shares as they witnessed the real capital leaving the building. At its first Annual General Meeting, in September 2000, seven thousand ordinary shareholders were left incandescent with rage as it was revealed that Chief Executive, Alfie Kane, and Finance Director Malcolm Fallen had been awarded nearly £1 million in bonuses, even though they had presided over the company the year in which share value had dropped by more than a third in value. They also watched helplessly as the Chairman of the meeting, former Minister for Finance Ray McSharry, used almost 1.2 billion proxy votes to secure the adoption of a lucrative stock option scheme which would permit executives to buy shares at a price substantially lower than that set at floatation. It was to emerge also, at a later date, that the former Tánaiste, Dick Spring, had not acquired any shares in Eircom, even though he sat on its Board of Directors.

The floatation of Eircom is now generally accepted as having been a disaster. Not only were hundreds of thousands of Irish people to lose out financially as a result of this disastrous floatation, but the public in general were to suffer once more as the private company failed to deliver the service for which it had been contracted. Not only have we witnessed, yet again, the flight of capital from the system, leaving the inevitable paper trail of valueless shares in its wake, but also the spectre of the re-nationalisation of the company, at huge cost to the taxpayer, so as to ensure that the tasks which it was commissioned to complete, such as the provision of broadband on a national basis, will be completed. Eircom has declared that the profit margins would be insufficient for them to proceed with the provision of broadband in remoter parts of the country. The economic development of these regions will undoubtedly be retarded by such a decision, but again we witness the pre-eminence of exorbitant profit, which takes precedence over any issue of duty to provision of service to society, or indeed to the economy on which that society depends. But, of course, the imbalance between society and economy had long since been skewed outrageously in favour of the latter. Indeed, the tendency for those in position to dictate public policy or to sway public opinion in this regard had long been to dismiss totally the requirement for decision making to include a social element to it. When challenged about their decisions or when asked to comment on government policy the refrain, from politicians, economic commentators and of course the pillars of our business society, is generally that, "for the sake of the economy", or "the economy requires", or even, more worryingly "the economy dictates" that certain actions should be taken.

As these recurring examples of the seemingly endemic nature of corruption within, not alone, Irish political and corporate systems, but throughout the world, came to light my scepticism towards the viability of such a system continued to grow, leading me to the conviction that the financial system of the world was fatally flawed and would eventually collapse entirely.

Chapter 3

The Paper Trail

In 2005 another event was to have a profound effect on my
thinking with regard to the vagaries of the financial system
as was being practiced on a global scale. While watching
the BBC News my attention was drawn to a report on
the annual financial results that had been announced by
the Marks and Spencer Group for that year. During the
course of a particularly gloomy account by the Business
Correspondent it was revealed that the group's results
were down considerably on previous years and that it had
'only' made profits of some £610 million that trading term.
My attention was grabbed and my scepticism reawakened
when the question was put to the Business Correspondent
by the news anchor in studio that 'this possibly spelt the
end for Marks and Spencer'?

The incongruity of a company which provided not only
a perfectly good service to society but also thousands of
jobs being in danger of financial failure, even though it had
announced profits for the year totalling over half a billion
pounds, was to my mind absurd in the extreme. But then
this was the accepted currency of the stock market, where
a company's financial fate and trading future depended on

the ever rising share price valuation. As we had witnessed with Enron, and countless other examples, the moment shareholders, particularly large investment funds managers, lost faith in a company's ability to continue to increase its stock market valuation, it ceased to be a viable concern and was consigned to the scrapheap. Very little consideration seemed to be taken of the valuable service this entity offered to society in terms of the product it provided or the vast contribution it made by way of the thousands of people employed. Stock market valuation took precedence over every other concern and seemed again to be the exclusive driving force of commerce. It appeared once again that the demand for a constantly rising share price valuation was increasing strain on the financial system and having a further negative effect on the society it was supposed to serve. If, on the other hand, the share price was not of such a vital and over-riding concern, would companies not be in the altogether more financially, and structurally, sound position of being able to trade free from the onerous burden of stock market demands and comfortable in the knowledge that any profit announced would leave them in the happy position of being able to continue trading, thereby providing a double service to society in terms of product delivery and employment provided?

The requirement to increase profits year on year had corrupted the financial system to such a degree that it had negated the need to even provide a service in return for monetary reward. The system that was becoming ever more evident on a global basis was one in which excessive profit was the only consideration. This, of course, resulted in the ludicrous situation where companies were forced either into ensuring that their share price valuation rose, through fair means or foul, or accept being consigned to the scrapheap, due to the fact that, although they had made huge profits in the trading year, their fate had been sealed because the amount was less than in the previous years. It was becoming ever more evident that this absurd and ineffectual system would have a devastating effect on our society in due course.

The moment I heard the report on the BBC News regarding the Marks and Spencer group my thoughts inevitably returned to the Enron programme. With every new scandal that was revealed, be that Nick Leeson at Barings Bank or John Rusnak at Allied Irish Banks, my scepticism would invariably be increased. A pattern was beginning to emerge which deviated little from the one which the Enron model provided. Having initially reached the conclusion that Enron was a harbinger of doom for the world's financial system, further consideration convinced me that this would in fact be its inevitable outcome. The core of the Enron fraud, and increasingly the exclusive reason for the company's existence, was the boosting of stock market valuation, by whatever means possible. One would have to admit that Lay and Skilling were undeniably successful in this regard, if we take into account that the company was valued at $100 billion dollars at one point, but a question which continually arose amongst my pupils was: Where had all that money gone? The answer came in the form of another question: Had it ever been there in the first place?

Consider the facts. Enron demonstrated unbelievable year on year growth usually by the use of the bluntest of instruments. It simply made up the numbers. As long as this inexorable growth was demonstrated and its continuation believed in, there would be ample interest in the acquisition of the shares. Enron was in fact availing itself of the opportunities that the deregulated stock market provided by, in a fashion, replicating the methods that Andrew Fastow had initially employed to boost the company's profits. It was Fastow who had developed the ruse of parking bad debts in subsidiaries, which could then be removed from the company's accounts, thereby increasing overall profits. It was adaptations of this plan which Enron, and thereafter many other corporations, employed when manipulating the stock market and consequentially defrauding millions of innocent shareholders worldwide.

In effect, what occurred was that, as the share price was driven relentlessly higher, executives would continuously sell off shares, garnering vast profits for themselves and effectively 'parking' the bad debt in the form of a share or, as it would later transpire, an IOU for the amount concerned. These shares created an illusion of wealth and bestowed considerable comfort on those who held them that their financial futures were guaranteed, when in reality the real money had exited the system in the hands of the fraudsters. This was in fact a double accounting manoeuvre that was based on the real capital being effectively withdrawn from the financial system and being replaced by a paper trail which was effectively claiming the existence of this money within the system again. The beauty of this particular fraud, for its authors, was that this worthless paper share value was dumped on the stock markets, where it was enthusiastically purchased by innocent shareholders mesmerised by its seemingly unrelenting rise in valuation. A further attraction and benefit to the fraudsters responsible for the scam was the fact that, as share values continued to increase, there was little or no chance that shareholders would dispose of shares, thereby giving them enough time to implement their plan.

The fact that shares were acquired by investment institutions and indeed private individuals as a means of providing for people's future pension needs also considerably benefited this financial fraud, as by their very nature they were only drawn down or cashed in over lengthy periods and in relatively miniscule amounts. Shamelessly, all the while that ordinary people were honestly trying to provide for their own, and in most cases their families', futures the executives were busy withdrawing the real money from the system. This process was completed without a second thought, it would appear, for those unfortunate people they were perpetrating their business crimes against. One executive in Enron, Lou Pai, when asked how he was feeling in the aftermath of the company's collapse and in light of the fact that he personally had sold shares worth $250 million dollars in the period immediately preceding the fall, replied that he was "feeling nothing at all". The fact that hundreds of thousands of people were left facing a very uncertain financial future and that upwards of fifty thousand people lost their jobs did not seem to register on his moral radar. This abdication of any real sense of moral responsibility in the conduct of commerce was and is, I believe, another element of the business mindset which contributed to the decay of the economic system as we know it.

The general consensus, amongst economic commentators and their political allies, was that vast quantities of money were generated, primarily, by releasing the constraints which the regulated market placed on the entrepreneurial free spirit. This, it was argued, was beneficial to all in the economy, as some of the great wealth being created would inevitably trickle down to all others, thereby raising all boats. This was a popularly perceived definition which would gain common acceptance. The reality, I believed, was quite different. What appeared to be happening, as evidenced by the examples of Enron and other scandals, was that the real money in the financial system was being sucked up to the top by fraudulent means and thereafter exiting the system completely. Not only that, but the system itself was being left propped up by incalculable amounts of paper shares which were no more that an illusion. Where the real money, which had been created by the sale of those shares, disappeared to was the final part of the financial system fraud jigsaw which had to be put in place.

The answer to that particular puzzle was to arrive with a better understanding of the latest developments in the practices employed in the increasingly deregulated stock markets themselves. If one was to consider the traditional stock markets as no more than a higher class of bookmakers, where share price could rise as well as fall, like horses in a steeplechase, then the new unregulated stock markets was the super casino, the playground for ultra-rich investors, most likely those same executives who had defrauded the original stock market in the first instance. They were now being invited to cash in their chips in the local amusement arcade and to join the big guns at the roulette wheel in the exclusive club which allowed unlimited and unregulated betting. This was in effect, a newly created luxury casino, employing a restrictive membership policy designed to accommodate only those of nigh-on unlimited reserves of cash. This money, though originating in the world economy, had now been elevated to the new casino of the rich and shamelessly wealthy where it was used to create even further obscene profits, but with an ever more tenuous link to the real economy.

The practices which were indulged in by these super gamblers, or hedge funds as they are called, can be confusing when first encountered. In essence, however, they were a means of permitting money to be gambled outside the real economy in order to create outrageous quantities of wealth. One of the simplest ways of illustrating what went on, and the resultant effects it would have, can best be achieved by reference to the following examples.

A hedge fund, which was *de facto* a private investment fund with recourse to a huge pool of unregulated capital, would avail itself of the increasingly unregulated and diverse range of new products on the money markets to maximise returns. One such technique, which the British Government attempted to ban at the height of the credit crunch in 2008, was short selling. This was an investment technique whereby, quite simply, investors bet that the price of a certain share would fall. The investors, incredibly, could and still can borrow a share from another financial institution, which in turn charges a fee. The hedge fund then sells those shares into the market hoping, and in fact betting, that the price will fall, allowing them to then buy back those shares at the lower price, pocketing the difference when they are returned to the original investors. Other techniques included the use of Credit Default Swaps. These products were a means by which investors protected themselves from the risk of companies defaulting on their loans. They were originally intended as insurance policies which investors would buy that would cover them in the event of a company failure. But CDSs, which were unregulated, were manipulated by speculators who, by the time of the credit crunch, were using them as a means of betting on which companies might go bust. It was estimated that by the middle of 2008, when it had long since become apparent to the most knowledgeable hedge funds that the financial crisis would cause the collapse of many companies, that the value of credit default swaps stood at $30 trillion.

The final ignominy for the real economy perhaps came in the form of other derivatives which were used by the hedge funds to take bets on anything from the future direction of currencies and markets to the weather! Derivatives are products which crucially can be invested in without the investor having to acquire shares, thereby allowing hedge funds to bet on any eventual outcome. Warren Buffet, considered one of the investor geniuses of his age, proclaimed that derivatives were 'financial weapons of mass destruction'. George Bush's administration, which encouraged more than any other the policy of liberalisation and deregulation of the world's financial system, would therefore have more reason than most to regret ever having encountered the term 'weapons of mass destruction', seeing as they resulted in two disasters occurring during his term in office.

So there it was: evidence, it if was required, for those who wished to acknowledge it that the world's financial system was on the brink of an inevitable crash that would have disastrous human consequences long into the future. The money markets had evolved to such an extent that capital, garnered initially from the real economy, was now being used to create further capital by betting on companies which were supported by shares that these executive gamblers knew were worthless and would collapse. It seemed clear to me that the finite amount of real capital which resided in the world's real economy was being relentlessly sucked upwards into a surreal playground for the immorally rich. What was being left in its place was a paper trail of worthless shares or IOUs which would cause unknown harm and suffering when the inevitable collapse of the fraud which was underpinning it occurred. Wasn't this precisely what had happened in the case of Enron and all the other shams we have looked at? Wasn't the world's entire financial system now nothing but a carbon copy of the model employed by Enron's executives? I was convinced that the answer to both questions was yes and that it was only a matter of time before we witnessed an economic crash, the likes of which the world had never before witnessed.

Chapter 4

Ireland Inc.

In 1994 my wife and I, both secondary school teachers with seven years service completed, decided to purchase our first house. The previous year we had placed a deposit on a three-bed starter home in one of the newly developing suburbs in Sandyford, in the foothills of the Dublin Mountains. However, nagging concerns that this development was just too far a commute from our workplaces in Dublin's Southside, and also as to how well it would eventually be serviced, led us to redouble our saving efforts so that we could afford the mortgage for a home nearer the city centre where we could avail ourselves of the facilities which were, to our minds, an essential element in the choice of a family home for life.

Having been brought up in Dundrum, an area populated predominately by middle class civil servants at that time, it naturally appealed to us, and our search was eventually to lead us to a three-bed semi detached house in the adjoining, but crucially, slightly more affordable area of Churchtown. After saving assiduously for the previous couple of years and possessing the princely sum of £19,000, we set about acquiring the loan, a task we assumed would not be that onerous, as we had nearly a third of the total value of £67,000 already accounted for. However, we were refused a mortgage in the Bank of Ireland, even though we had permanent and pensionable state jobs and a creditable savings record with a building society. Thankfully we acquired the loan from this building society, the EBS, when they agreed to lend us the maximum allowed by the criteria of the day, which was two and one half times the first salary and one and one half times the second. As my wife and I were on the same salary of £15,500 we qualified for a mortgage of £55,000, a loan which would be repaid over a twenty year term. We bought the house in Churchtown, where we continue to live happily to this day.

The above account is related for a few good reasons. It is a reminder of an era when, although house prices had begun to escalate steeply, it was still possible for two young public sector workers to afford a reasonably comfortable house in a typical middle class area. It also highlights the extent to which the banking sector took reasonable and officious care in the awarding of mortgages, and it contains within it all the evidence one could require to illustrate how illusionary the wealth which the Celtic Tiger created really was.

If we moved on to the year 2006, and if we were to consider the case of a similar couple in a similar situation to our own, we can clearly see the fraud which was committed on the people of Ireland by the property developers, the builders and their propagandists in chief, economists, the media and the Government itself. A married couple, both teachers with seven years' service, would have been entitled to a mortgage loan of €160,000, if one was to adhere to the two and a half, one and a half banking criteria of the old school in the year 2006. The house which they might wish to buy in Churchtown was by that time valued at a staggering €650,000. This was an unbelievable *sixteen* times their basic salary, as opposed to the four to five times required just twelve years previously. The only way, of course, that people could afford this outrageous inflation in the cost of, what was generally accepted in this country as being a fundamental right, a roof over one's head, was to agree to an extension to the mortgage term. These terms saw increases, year on year, from twenty to thirty-five, and even forty, years. The people of Ireland, who had repeatedly been told that they had 'never seen it so good' and that financial rewards beyond their wildest dreams were theirs to enjoy, had, in fact, been enslaved to debt by an intricate fraud that had at its core the plan adopted by the executives at Enron. But, whereas Enron Inc had limited its effect to those unfortunate enough to become entangled in its web, the Ireland Inc. version of the fraud entrapped every single citizen of this state by dint of the fact that the share price which was being inflated by fraudulent means was the price of the very house that they lived in.

For this greatest of all scams' inception we must go back to 1981 and the period in office of one Charles J Haughey. It was his government which instigated the first steps, with regard to housing policy in particular, which would lead us to our inevitable disastrous outcome. When one considers how his tenure in office was subsequently to be indelibly associated with a cosy cabal of cronyism which enabled the chosen members of the golden inner circle to abuse their position in order to enrich themselves to previously unthinkable degrees, then this surely should come as no surprise. Haughey himself, more than anyone else, was a personal embodiment of the culture of performance-related pay. He was so completely wedded to this culture that it was a natural extension of his thinking that anything that he should be responsible for in his position as Taoiseach, democratically elected leader of the people of Ireland, which resulted in financial reward for the country should inevitably see a concurrent reward for him personally. It was Charles J Haughey, in particular, who embraced the culture of free market liberalism and trickle-down economics at that period. It was he who galvanised the political element which was such an important component in the fraud which would be committed on the Irish people. It would, however, be unfair to suggest that Haughey was alone in embracing this business culture. The predominant position of the economy over society was in fact becoming the generally accepted consensus during that period, and Haughey was but its most ruthless and devout supporter, his commitment to the cause undoubtedly reinforced by the considerable personal rewards which were to come his way as a result of his cooperation with, and patronage of, a privileged elite who were about to perpertrate the greatest deceit ever witnessed in Ireland.

In 1981 the first of the tax incentives were introduced by the Haughey Government to encourage the construction sector. Section 23 tax relief was first introduced, under section 23 of the Finance Act 1981, as a means of stimulating the construction sector by offering generous tax relief to investors. Of course, it would also have the obvious benefit of creating employment, a factor which is used frequently as an 'end of discussion' justification for the sanctioning of any given measure. I would contend, however, that, although laudable, the creation of employment should not be the sole justification for proceeding, and the totality of effects must be taken into account before sanctioning any given policy. As we would see, the long term effect of measures such as tax relief for investors would have disastrous consequences for not alone the construction industry but also every man, woman and child in the country.

This thinking was but one element in a government policy that reflected the increasingly accepted notion of a house, previously considered a near basic human right, being an economic product which could, as with all economic products, have its core or share value corrupted and inflated to an outrageous degree. This notion, of course, contained huge advantages for those who appreciated the possibilities it afforded. The very fact that every single citizen of the state would have to have recourse to the 'shares' being offered, by dint of the fact that everyone required a roof under which to live, the pool of innocent shareholders who could be taken advantage of was limitless. The fact that the Irish people's traditional loyalty to the concept of home ownership would make them eager purchasers of these shares made the construction industry very fertile ground for the sowing of the Enron seed on a massive scale. With Charles J Haughey as Taoiseach leading a political consensus which encouraged free market economics, and with that consensus extending to economic commentators and the media in general, a media which was increasingly privately owned and selfishly agenda driven, the conditions were ripe for the golden circle of bankers, builders, developers, entrepreneurs and politicians to reap the considerable rewards that were on offer.

By the mid nineties, so successful had they been in their mission that the first steps had to be taken to calm an overheated property market which was becoming ever more increasingly difficult for a whole generation of our young people to access. This was, of course, the first indication that this policy was imitating the business plan we witnessed with Enron. The share price of housing was being artificially inflated so as to economically reward certain sections of the populace, but to the detriment of a majority of the public and to society as a whole because they could no longer afford a home to live in. The economy was taking precedence over society, and this fact was becoming increasingly clear to the public in general. The resultant outcry saw the government forced to commission the Bacon report, with its principal objective being to alleviate the desperate plight of these first-time buyers. The report, published in 1998, suggested means by which to squeeze investors out of the market. These investors were by now considered by the public in general as fat cats who had been using the property market like a monopoly board. The Bacon report recommended that they be taken out of the market by the withdrawal of investment tax relief and by a variety of other methods, including changes to Capital Gains taxes and Stamp Duty, alterations which were primarily aimed at taking the excess profit available to investors out of the property market.

The success of Peter Bacon's report, which was implemented by Bertie Ahearn's government in 1998, can be gauged by the reaction it aroused amongst those whom it affected detrimentally. Within just a few months of its implementation, a dramatically improved position was created for first time buyers which included lower prices and greater availability, as speculators left the market. These property speculators, many of them members of the golden circle, were, however, never likely to take this challenge to their lofty financial positions lying down. Joining forces with the considerable clout and influence of other vested interests, such as bankers, land developers, builders and auctioneers, they succeeded in defending their right to make unseemly amounts of capital out of the housing market. Fortunately for them, by this time they were now bolstered by Fianna Fáil's new government coalition partners, the free-market capitalist party, The Progressive Democrats. Little wonder, then, that the Government repealed Bacon's recommendations, allying itself, once and for all, with the interests of corrupt commerce over the concerns of the public, which it was supposedly elected to represent. This marked, I would suggest, a crucial point in government support for free-market capitalism over sound economic public policy. Rather like Jeff Skilling in his role in the Enron scandal, the government, when confronted with the choice of reeling in the excesses of corrupt business culture, in order to benefit society in general, or running with the bulls of the stock market, decided to choose the latter option. Although initially this would appear a more financially lucrative option, it would eventually, as we witnessed with Enron and other comparable frauds, end in misery for all those innocently caught up in its web.

From 1998 on, the Government, with the Progressive Democrats as its ideological driving force and Fianna Fáil as willing executors and primary benefactors, unreservedly supported the free market, and the free housing market in particular. With implied support from the opposition, who were, after all, hewn from the same free market mindset – the original members of the PDs being to all intent and purposes Fine Gaelers trapped in Fianna Fáil clothing – a dangerous consensus began to emerge. When this was allied to consensus amongst economic commentators and a media which was by this stage controlled by and promoting the right wing economic agenda, little wonder that the public at large was to surrender to the prevailing mood. When, like the shareholders in Enron, the public also appeared to be gaining considerably in financial terms, few stopped to ask questions.

The lack of scepticism regarding the merits, or otherwise, of prevailing convictions was, as we have seen, a major factor in the success of Enron's fraud and should be a lesson to all with regard to the future. The Labour Party's inability to fill the political and ideological vacuum that emerged marked its failure, and particularly that of its leaders Dick Spring and Pat Rabitte, to rise to the challenge before them. The path was thus left clear for the political consensus to pursue with impunity policies which benefited the few to the detriment of the majority. In the housing market, which will be our major concern, as it was the greatest fraud committed on the Irish people; those policies took the form of countless methods of inflating house prices, including the repeal of major elements of the Bacon report and the countless initiatives proposed by vested interests in the sector, not least encouraging everybody possible into the property market. As we have seen with the other scams, the continued appearance that share values were rising was an essential element in the success of this sham.

This was achieved by a combination of factors, many instigated by the bankers, builders, developers and auctioneers themselves, but the role of government was crucial. Every constraint which could hamper the building sector was removed. Tax relief for investors, which Bacon had removed, was reintroduced. Increased levels of mortgage relief were introduced at budget time. Changes to Stamp Duties and Capital Gains taxes were implemented at various times. The speculators tax of two per cent, which Bacon had proposed, was removed. The first time buyers' grant was raised. Public-private partnerships were promoted. The list was endless and included the fact that a blind eye seemed to be turned to the tax implications for investors who were renting their properties.

In 2002 it was estimated that only 24% of landlords were registered as paying tax on rent. This, of course, had the added disadvantage of widening the gap between rich and poor and of exacerbating the tax burden on those who were tax compliant. Every possible thing was done to ensure, as the Irish Auctioneers and Valuers Institute (IAVI) demanded in 2000, "that the sector should be regarded as a business for taxation purposes." The provision of housing was to be considered a business, susceptible to all the same fraudulent abuses which were, as we know, commonplace in the business culture at the time, rather than a social requirement which had an important economic element to it.

With Government dutifully fulfilling its part of the fraud by creating the conditions in which business was, to all intents and purposes, completely deregulated and unburdened of even the moral duty to behave responsibly, the opportunities that arose for self-aggrandisement were, apparently, too great to be spurned. The banking institutions took full advantage of the situation which presented itself. Their pivotal role in this outrageous scam cannot be overstated. Their once former glorious reputation as pillars of society, a position which saw the local bank manager as a trusted and highly respected member of the community, was to be ruined by their reckless behaviour in the pursuit of obscene profits, both institutional and personal.

In the period between 1996 and 2006 we would witness the near complete abdication by bankers of any sense of duty towards the concept of responsible banking. As was the case with their counterparts in Enron, the executives in the Irish banking sector were to promote a supercharged culture of performance-related remuneration throughout the industry, the worst excesses of which we had witnessed in the model adopted by National Irish Bank. The chief executives awarded themselves outrageous basic pay packages based on percentages of profits, topped up by bonuses in the form of share issues which hyper inflated their personal fortunes. This also had the effect of seeing them doubly rewarded by the stock market valuation of their companies. But, as we have witnessed with the example set by Enron, amongst others, this method contained within it the fatal flaw of providing ample motivation for those not of sufficient moral substance to inflate those profits by all possible means. When we consider that this was the method of remuneration employed and sanctioned throughout the industry at all levels, little wonder, perhaps, that risk-taking (and not effective risk-management) became the order of the day. Irish banks – driven, it would appear, from the outset, by a very aggressive business culture employed by Anglo Irish Bank under the stewardship of Sean Fitzgerald in particular – adopted all the means at their disposal to increase business and inflate stock market valuation. The days when your local bank manager was respected as trustworthy and prudent, to the point of being parsimonious, were long since gone.

It is worth considering a little further my application for a loan in 1994. The fact that we were refused a loan by Bank of Ireland, even though we had demonstrated an impressive savings regime over a two-year period which resulted in us possessing nearly one third of the purchase price of the home we wished to buy, did not impress that particular lender. This conservative attitude towards risk assessment and the management of loans reflected the more traditionally prudent banking mentality of the time. Though harsh, many would believe, it was reflective of the generally accepted banking model and contrasted tremendously with the aggressive and reckless lending culture which we were to witness being adopted thereafter.

This new model was based on the overly simple idea that capital created and generated further capital and that the function of banks was simply to lend money to as many customers as possible, with little or no regard for the risk involved. Whether it was the international financial institutions of Germany, Britain and France that recklessly lent vast quantities of capital into the European markets, or Irish financial institution who availed of this easy money and liberally dispensed it into our economy like confetti at a wedding ceremony. The mindset was the same. The advertisement used by one such Irish banking institution at the time reveals the sea-change in the banking culture. This advertisement featured college students applying for loans from their local bank manager under a dizzying array of worthy guises, whilst the real, superfluous reason for their loan application was displayed in subtitles on the screen. It ended with these and indeed all students being addressed by the 'caring' and 'understanding' bank manager reassuring them that he had heard 'all the excuses' and that they had no cause for concern, because he and his bank 'understood' and were willing to lend because they 'cared'. The fact that the advertisement was cynically directed at enticing young people, in particular, to join in the rampant culture of indebtedness was bad enough, but it was revealing that they were also deliberately and publicly undermining the fundamental tenet of trust on which the system depends. It was ironical that this was the same bank that had refused to sanction our loan application only a few years previously.

However, soon mortgages of eighty per cent of purchase price were being offered and, inevitably, in the race to the bottom of market share and indeed market valuation that ensued, these rose to ninety, one hundred, and indeed over one hundred percent of purchase price. Again it was becoming apparent that stock market and share price valuation could only be increased year on year by indulging in what at Enron was referred to as 'tweaking of the knob'. A significant difference between this and the version employed within Enron, though, was that this particular 'tweaking of the knob' was a very public affair. As the advertisement described above shows, the recklessly inflated mortgages on offer were common knowledge. This policy helped house prices continue to soar, which in turn required people to take increasingly outrageous and unsustainable multiples of their wages as loans over ever expanding periods of repayment. Frighteningly, the connection didn't seem to register with the public. Whereas the Enron hoax was, by and large, covert, the fraud indulged in by the Irish banking sector was overt: so blatantly so, that the question inevitably arises as to how the public failed to notice it or, maybe more patently, why they chose to ignore it?

The dilemmas which these questions create, though unpalatable, must in all consciousness be faced up to honestly. If people are truthful to themselves they will be forced to admit that, as in all scams, once they perceive themselves to be benefiting personally or gaining financially from events, then an overriding principle of selfishness begins to take precedence over moral, or indeed rational, behaviour. An example taken from the Enron scandal of this kind of exuberant self-delusion, or 'irrational euphoria', is provided by the story of Margeret Sicone. An executive at Enron who had been headhunted from a rival competitor, she told of her disbelief at some of the methods practiced at her new place of employment. One of the eventual whistleblowers who brought the fraud to the attention of the relevant authorities, she was constantly amazed by the fact that her co-employees at the corporation, conditioned most probably by years of exposure to the increasingly corrupt methods promoted by the chief executives, seemed incapable of recognising the fraudulent nature of much of what they were being required to do. Her scepticism at the company's capability to announce profits year on year on the back of business practices which should not have yielded such results eventually got the better of her and she challenged some of her co-workers, though she was invariably met with the response that 'she just didn't get it'. Her own reply to this was that she certainly did 'get it' and that it was patently obvious that they were the ones who 'didn't get it'.

Perhaps the most revealing example of the lengths to which employees would go in order to satisfy their executives, who through their 'brilliance' were ensuring that everyone was sharing in previously unimaginable financial rewards, was the case of the fraudulent trading floor. The tale was recounted to Siccone of an occasion in 1998, before she joined the corporation, when Enron's Chief Executives, Kenneth Lay and Jeff Skilling, wanted to impress some financial analysts who were visiting its headquarters in Houston, Texas. Skilling and Lay were keen to show off their new dealing room but, as this trading division had not actually been opened at that point, they demanded that the company's employees find an open space and pretend it was a trading floor. Company secretaries and other non-traders were required to man the telephones and pretend to do deals as they acted out their roles in this particularly peculiar aspect of the overall Enron scam. These roles they unquestioningly assumed to the best of their abilities. When Margerat Siccone asked her assistant, who was charged by the executives with executing the plan, why she did it and if she had not seen anything wrong in 'pretending' to have a trading floor, she replied that she didn't think anything of it. She said that she had been asked to do it by the Chief Executives and she didn't see why they would ask her to do something that wasn't right.

This irrational behaviour, born of blind loyalty and resulting in dispensing of one's critical faculties and moral scruples, was surely facilitated by the very fact that one's own financial position appeared to be vastly improved through acquiescence and compliance. This 'irrational euphoria' contributes to the creation of an arrogant sense of 'financial invincibility' which easily results in the vulnerability that is exploited by the vultures who engage in financial fraud. It was certainly a significant contributory factor in the participation and entrapment of so many in the biggest and most extensive fraud which had ever been committed on the Irish people.

It was the banks, with the aid of their highly remunerated and populist economic analysts, that nourished this illusion of ever-increasing and previously unimaginable wealth through the acquisition of property. As with all the best shams, they propagated the idea that the ownership of house shares was the equivalent of a cast iron guarantee of previously undreamt of financial rewards. Not only did they recklessly encourage people to acquire these shares, but they shamefully engaged in a policy of scare-mongering by warning people that these house prices were dead certainties to continue rising, leaving them incapable of owning their own if they did not purchase at the earliest possible opportunity. Subsequent property purchases, using the collateral provided by the first, were recommended as a means of accessing even greater financial rewards – and thereby crucially creating further business for the banks, which continued to announce greater profits year on year, which in turn ensured that the pockets of those engaged in the execution of the fraud were stuffed with greater and greater quantities of bonus-related payments. And so the fraud at Ireland Inc. continued to ape the methods adopted by Enron Inc. in everything but scale. Every single man, woman and child in this country would ultimately pay a further, considerably more painful, price because of the selfishly motivated actions of the primary instigators of this nauseating hoax.

The consequences of their immoral actions would not just result in people paying mortgages for terms of thirty or forty years for houses they could have afforded over twenty-year terms just ten years previously, but, even more disastrously, would result in these peoples' children being lumbered with the enormous debts of these banks for generations to come when they eventually came crashing down.

Chapter 5

If it looks too good to be true...!

By 2006 Ireland Inc. was regarded by proponents of the liberal free market ideology as the jewel in the crown of that particular philosophy. Ireland's Celtic Tiger economy was the envy of the world, and the achievement of transforming the near-bankrupt state of the eighties into, officially, one of the richest countries on this planet was heralded as one of the economic wonders of the world. That year, a report published by Bank of Ireland Private Banking showed that, in a survey of the top eight leading OECD nations, Ireland was ranked the second wealthiest behind Japan – above the US, UK, Italy, France, Germany and Canada – showing an average wealth per head of €150,000.

A key defining characteristic of our wealth, according to the author Mark Cunningham, was that the vast bulk of it had been created in the previous ten years through gains in property investment and through a willingness to borrow to invest further. Taking its calculation of how a millionaire is defined – as total assets, excluding the principal private residence – the report concluded that there were 30,000 millionaires in the country. It also concluded that, if principal private residences were included, that figure would rise to an amazing 100,000!

Certainly Ireland Inc. was enjoying the fruits of the construction boom. The house building frenzy was fed by our banking sector, which was one of the primary benefactors. Irish banks regularly announced annual overall profits exceeding one billion euro. In 2006 house prices in Ireland reached a peak. A house on Shrewsbury Road fetched €56 million, making that address the sixth most expensive in the world, according to the Dow Jones Wealth Bulletin. An average three-bed semi-detached house in Dundrum would sell for over three quarters of a million euro.

This peak in house prices coincided with record pre-tax profits for our banks. Anglo Irish Bank, for example, announced pre-tax profits of €850 million for the year 2006, an increase of 38% on the previous year's record profits. The top six executives at that bank were rewarded with a combined total pay of €7.77 million. The Chief Executive, David Drumm, enjoyed a pay package worth €3 million, made up of a basic salary of €818,000, a performance bonus of €1.3 million, €600,000 in deferred bonus payments, and a €258,000 pension contribution. That same year non-executive director Sean Fitzpatrick, with an address on Shrewsbury Road, took a salary of €320,000 and a bonus payment of €533,000 as chairman of the group.

These performance-related salaries were of course linked to the bank's dealings in the commercial property sector. This, at the time, was enjoying particular success, as evidenced by the fact that commercial property leases for Grafton Street were recognised as the highest in the world. The number of houses built that year surpassed all previous records at 93,419, allowing the developers, builders and associated vested interests in the construction industry to acquire massive property portfolios in Britain,

Europe and indeed worldwide. With Bank of Ireland's share price at €18.65, Anglo Irish Bank's at €16.64 and Allied Irish Bank's at €23.95, in February 2006 the ISEQ index of shares rose to an all-time high of 10,041. Further good news arrived with the prediction published in the Bank of Ireland Private Banking report that, though the wealth in Ireland was entrepreneurial and more risk-orientated than in other developed countries, fears about rising debt levels were overstated, so net wealth was forecast to increase to 1.2 trillion by 2015. Ireland and its people were, it appeared, living in a dreamlike state of uninhibited euphoria and enjoying wealth the likes of which had been unimaginable only some twenty years earlier, when the country was generally regarded as 'a basket case economy'.

The reality, though, as it unfortunately tends to be, was somewhat different. In 2002 the number of vacant house units already stood at a worrying 140,000. By 2008 that number had risen to a staggering 350,000. A 'natural' peak in house price had, in fact, occurred some seven years previous, in 2001, when genuine first-time buyers had found themselves unable to access the market because of the dominant position of property investors in the sector. As was noted in a previous chapter, circumstances had become so dire for prospective first-time buyers that the government was compelled by the ensuing public outcry to take action, implementing measures that would have a stabilising effect on a property market that had all the appearance of spiralling out of control. It was becoming increasingly more difficult for people even in the middle income bracket to purchase their own homes. The Bacon Reports were commissioned and implemented with some initial success. The housing market began to cool, and prices even began to drop from their unrealistic levels, with beneficial effects for buyers who were purchasing homes as primary residences. The corollary of this, however, was that property investors, and indeed the vested interests of the property industry as a whole, began to foresee the value of their shares – that is, house prices – decrease. Simultaneously the dot.com bubble collapsed and the value of the ISEQ index of shares plummeted spectacularly.

It was at this time, and as a result of this particular set of circumstances, that the government chose to align itself totally and unashamedly with the vested interests of the property industry. The share price or market value of Ireland Inc., in the form of house prices, would not be allowed to collapse, and every conceivable measure would be taken to artificially re-inflate it. That these measures would have a disastrous impact on the welfare of the majority of the population was of little or no concern. All shackles were to be removed from the business community: the liberal free-market philosophy was to be given free reign, and any semblance of a balanced or co-ordinated attitude towards social and economic policy was dispensed with. The economy was king, a house was a commodity, and home ownership became for many couples a forty-year financial millstone which would have huge negative repercussions for society.

Three critical decisions from this period illustrate the manner in which the government of Ireland aligned itself completely with this artificial attempt to increase house prices. The first was the decision by the Minister for Finance, Charlie McCreevy, in 1999, to announce his intention of pursuing a policy of individualisation with regard to tax. This measure, introduced under the guise of attempting to remove taxpayers on average earnings from very high taxes, was in fact a deliberate policy of forcing women, especially married women, into the workplace. The measures, as introduced, could result in a one-income married couple with children paying as much as €6,000 more in tax each year than a two-income couple on the same earnings. This decision, combined with an increase in the tax exemption limit for childminders from €10,000 to €15,000 under the cynically titled 'Cherish Children, Cherish Childminders' campaign, was part of a concerted attempt by the government to encourage more women into the workforce. This was, in fact, a cornerstone of European policy at the time and constituted one of the major aims of the Lisbon Agenda which the Taoiseach Bertie Ahearn signed the same year as the government decided to pursue a policy of individualisation in the tax system. Amongst three primary aims which the Lisbon Agenda committed countries to was the achievement of an employment rate of 70%, and specifically 60% amongst women. Though the government, and minister McCreevy in particular, denied that this was their aim when introducing tax individualisation, claiming that it was designed to alleviate the burden of tax on average earners, it did in fact penalise parents who wished to care for their own child in their own home and encouraged the sending of children into care. Conor Lenihan TD admitted as much when he was quoted as saying, 'I'm glad the Minister, Deputy McCreevy, is an honest man.... He made no secret of his aims and objectives in the budget. He wanted to get more women back in the workplace'.

Lenihan's own unguarded moment of honesty revealed the true intent of the individualisation policy, which was to enable the property industry to vastly increase house prices, as prices would be set as ever-increasing multiples of two salaries, especially in the highest bidder system which was practiced in this country. We were now witnessing a sea change with regard to home ownership in the state. Whereas it was more than possible for one income families to afford housing up to the early eighties, there was now an inexorable push from the property industry with government support to set house prices as multiples of double-income families. This had a disastrous effect, allowing developers to push prices ever higher and therefore increasing the financial pressure on families, and also severely limiting the choices parents had with regard to childcare. The social cost of this economic policy, although already apparent, will, many believe, only be truly appreciated in the years ahead.

The government's penchant for implementing policy changes which greatly benefited vested interests whilst appearing to be in the public interest was to be revealed on several subsequent occasions. The best examples of this cynical corruption of democratic principles were to be seen in the years following the collapse of stock market valuations in 1999 / 2000. With the property sector facing decline, those who had invested huge sums in these particular shares, as housing units had been allowed to become, brought all their considerable clout to bear on government to ensure that house prices would continue to rise. In a pre-budget submission in 1999, the property industry, led by the Irish Auctioneers and Valuers Institute (IAVI) and the Construction Industry Federation (CIF), called for the implementation of countless measures, including stamp duty reform, changes to Capital Gains tax and an extension of mortgage interest relief. All of these were looked on favourably by the government.

It was, however, two other proposals by the property industry which were to have an even more profound and ultimately disastrous effect on the social and economic fabric of Ireland. The first had its beginnings in a suggestion by the IAVI and the CIF that "there should be some mechanism whereby first-time buyers are encouraged to save, so that they can afford to get into the market." The extent to which these property industry

lobbyists held sway over the democratically
members of the Dáil can be gauged by the fact that
all the measures suggested by those within the hou
industry were introduced *en bloc*.

The Minister for Finance, Charlie McCreevy, wh
was a major advocate of the primacy of the free market
over the considerations of society in general, acted at all
times to assist the re-inflation of house prices by every
means at his disposal. Whether by his championing of
the cause of deregulation, which he saw as essential in
enabling financial masters of the economy to indulge
themselves in an orgy of wealth creation unhindered by
an intrusive moral overseer, or in his shameless support
for the primacy of the economy over affairs of society,
everything possible was done to facilitate wealth creators
at the expense of every other member of society. In the
Finance Act 2001 he announced the introduction of a
new saving scheme, the SSIA, a five year saving scheme
in which the government would contribute an extremely
generous one euro of public money for every four euro
saved by the individual. According to the minister its
principal objective was to encourage regular savings by
individuals and to help reduce inflation, which was a cause
for concern at the time. No mention, once again, of the
real policy agenda which was, to all intents and purposes,
another attempt at collusion with the property market to
facilitate yet another artificially assisted hike in house
prices. All this, in a market which had been previously
recognised as dangerously overheated and which had, in
fact, by that point reached a natural ceiling.

Minister McCreevy refused to listen to those who
suggested that the generous financial support which the
government was committing to the SSIAs would have
been better spent in more needy areas, such as education
or health. These two areas, in particular, were suffering

ıly from the government's stated
ʳ at every possible turn in order to
ʰut also because both sectors were
free market, a fact that resulted
ᵥ capital that was being spent in
₋ppearing as private profit with little
₋ʟo the services provided to the public. The
₋ʟnent chose, recklessly, to rely more and more on
₋ʟcome from stamp duty and capital gains taxes from their
artificially created property boom to fund essential social
services. Now health and education were asked to make
further sacrifices, as the minister was adamant that the
citizens of the state were more deserving of the fruits of
the increases in taxes from the property sector. That this
money would invariably and inevitably make its way back
to the very source that had created it was, of course, rather
conveniently overlooked. No mention was made of those
who would ultimately gain from the generous rewards
of the SISAs, the property industry, benefiting from a
savings scheme which was created at their behest by a
government which was by this point in complete collusion
with them. It appeared, in fact, that the government's only
concern at this juncture was facilitating those who wished
to manipulate the people of Ireland's inherent right to
housing for their own financial gain. A subsequent report
issued in 2006 by IIB Bank/ESRI stated that SSIA's would
boost Irish house prices by 10%.

This artificial manipulation of market conditions
for the benefit of the economy but to the detriment of
society was taken a step further by the government's next
decision, which was also reminiscent of decisions taken
by the Enron management, to yet again artificially inflate a
share price which had reached a natural peak. A point had
been arrived at when it was realised that the share price,
in Ireland Inc's case the price of housing, was in danger

of flat lining or, heaven forbid, decreasing. The Minister for Finance's SSIA saving scheme for deposits for houses would only take effect five years after its instigation. A scheme was also required to boost the property industry in the more immediate short term. The man who provided this timely boost to proceedings was the Minister for Justice, Equality and Law reform, Michael McDowell.

The Irish economic boom, which had started in the early nineties, had come to an end in 2001 in the productive sectors of the economy. Capital at this point then shifted to more profitable sectors, such as construction. Easy credit from the banks allowed a housing bubble to soon grow out of all proportion. Rising property prices helped to prop up the Irish stock market after the previous bubble burst in 2000. Though property was selling, the number of vacant housing units was rising alarmingly year on year. The Construction Industry Federation proposed a number of schemes to increase the number of available workers in the industry. It wanted the government to encourage foreign contractors to bring labour forces with them when awarded contracts in Ireland and for the government to ease restrictions on work visas. Construction employers should also be allowed to pay a tax-free accommodation allowance to foreign workers.

The government, in its wisdom, decided that this was insufficient a measure to achieve the aim of stimulating the required increase in house prices. It therefore took the decision to go much further than even the CIF had dared to suggest. In 2001, only a few short months after the Irish people had rejected the Nice treaty, the government, it appears, without informing the Dáil or even discussing it with the Irish people, committed the state to adopting a totally open-door policy to the 75 million or so citizens of the EU applicant countries, which was one of the main tenets of the enlargement treaty. This door would be opened in Ireland from January 2004, even though citizens from the accession states would only acquire such rights seven years after that date from the other member states of the EU. Of course, not only would these new immigrants mean more mortgages being sold and more tenants for vacant housing units which property investors could benefit from, but they would also contribute to increasing the profits of developers and construction company chiefs by lowering their wage costs.

This was, of course, manna from heaven for all those with a vested interest in the property share price boom: the banks, the auctioneers, the builders, the developers, the government through stamp duty taxes, the media through the advertisements in their property sections, lawyers through conveyance fees, boards of directors, audit committees, accountancy firms – in other words, the usual suspects. The effect that this massive inflow of migrant workers would have through increased demands on health, housing, welfare, education and law and order services, which were already at breaking point, was blissfully ignored. Those who raised such concerns were branded as racist and xenophobic, a move which cynically cut short the rational debate that such a major policy decision would have warranted.

In fact, Michael McDowell, a man who had infamously declared that "a dynamic liberal economy like ours demanded flexibility and inequality in some respects to function" and that "It was such inequality which provided incentives", assumed the position of champion of the underprivileged. He chided those who argued that the state's health and education services, in particular, were in no position to cope with a sudden massive increase in population reminding them that we who had benefited to such an extent from the Celtic Tiger were morally obliged to extend a charitable hand to those less fortunate than ourselves. The blindingly obvious hypocrisy which McDowell indulged in when adopting a cloak of social responsibility whilst acting in reality on behalf of the masters of the economy leaves a bitter taste in the mouth to this day. The disastrous effects which this economic policy decision would have on the indigenous and immigrant populations of Ireland would only truly emerge when McDowell had shuffled off the political stage to pursue a lucrative career in private law practice. But his political, social and economic legacy should not be forgotten. As a result of this policy decision, the ordinary people of Ireland would remain enslaved to crippling mortgages over ever increasing terms whilst enduring the further disadvantage of downward pressure on their wage levels which the arrival of migrant labour inevitably brought to bear on the salaries of all concerned.

The case of the unfortunate employees of GAMA Endustri, a Turkish construction company working in Ireland, highlighted the issue of the obscene exploitation of migrant and guest workers in the country. The socialist TD, Joe Higgins, who investigated the case, claimed that many companies were paying migrant workers below the minimum wage, were refusing to pay overtime rates and that this was a shameful example of 'bonded labour'. The GAMA employees recounted how they had been forced to work, eat and sleep on site and, furthermore, due to the fact that the Irish government had allowed the company retain complete control of their work permits, workers lived under the constant threat of being repatriated should they object to their inequitable treatment. It subsequently transpired that it was Tánaiste, Mary Harney, who had originally travelled to Turkey to encourage GAMA Endustri to locate in Ireland.

However, these were but a few of the countless measures which were taken by successive ideologically like-minded governments which committed the state to a policy of unconditional support for affairs of the economy over concerns for the citizens. Ever since Charlie Haughey's audacious adoption of the right wing policies of Garret Fitzgerald in order to win the general election of 1981, followed by Alan Dukes 'Tallaght Strategy', which committed Fine Gael to support the government as long as it continued to implement these policies, Ireland – in common, it must be admitted, with most liberal democracies of the developed world – has suffered from a dangerous political consensus which threatens the democratic system itself. This formalised coming together of the traditional opponents within the political system in Ireland in the eighties did, though, create a vacuum in the political world which offered hope to those who argued that at least a second, if not exactly a third, way was essential for a vibrant liberal democracy to thrive.

It was a calamity for the state that this political vacuum was in fact filled by a party which offered not so much another option which would ensure that debate and discussion, two essential elements of democracy, were maintained to the benefit of all citizens of the state, but by a party which proposed an even more extreme right wing philosophy than that which was offered by the existing traditional parties. The leader of Fine Gael at the time, Garret Fitzgerald, has in fact admitted publicly that he considered extending an invitation to Fianna Fáil's Des O'Malley to join him in what was his natural political philosophical home in Fine Gael. It was to be to the country's eternal regret that Fitzgerald demurred from extending the invitation, as he recognised that O'Malley had committed himself totally to his third force option of creating the Progressive Democrats, thereby preventing the creation of a new and radically different political philosophy which could have transformed the political landscape. As it was, free market forces could now rest assured that a broad political consensus existed which accounted for an overwhelming majority in the Dáil. This would enable them to vigorously pursue their free market liberal agenda unburdened by even the remotest challenge through political debate which might have kept some of the more dangerous extremes of policy in check.

Whether by means of self-assessment in the area of tax, or the outrageously generous corporation tax brought in by Fine Gael's John Bruton, or the myriad of property-related tax relief schemes introduced by successive Fianna Fáil/ Progressive Democrat cabinets, the shackles preventing the accumulation of further obscene amounts of wealth were to be removed. A policy of light regulation or, more truthfully, non-regulation was adopted with regard to business by successive Ministers for Finance. In particular, deregulation became the clarion call of Charlie McCreevy when he assumed that position. This, in spite of the fact that many of those who were implicated in scandals, such as Eircom and Greencore, were now in positions of profound influence in the business community. Seán Fitzpatrick, who sat on the Board of Greencore, was now chief executive at Anglo Irish Bank, which would of course play a major role in the destruction of the state's economy, with all the disastrous consequences which that would have for her citizens.

The Irish Financial Centre was created on the back of the twelve and a half percent corporation tax and it was this, more than any other decision, which saw an influx of unregulated foreign capital which would eventually see the country baptised 'the wild west of the financial world' by economic commentators internationally. Banks and insurance companies, in particular, reaped the generous rewards from the corporation tax when relocating to the Financial Centre. Allied Irish Bank and Bank of Ireland announced billions in pre-tax profits year on year, generated mainly on the backs of the hard-pressed citizens of the state who were taking huge loans to purchase their homes and then suffering the double indignity of seeing these banks pay a miserly twelve and a half per cent tax on such extortionate profits. Insurance companies had the gall, year in year out, to brazenly announce similar billion pound profits and seemed to expect the public to applaud the fact.

The irony that pertained to advertisements by the insurance companies which scolded fraudulent insurance claimants for having the audacity to steal money from the public's pockets was obviously lost on the executives and directors of these institutions which were indulging in the self-same practise on a much grander scale. That insurance costs were contributing to ever increasing amounts of capital outlay, which was crippling the population with debt, exerting enormous hardship on small and medium enterprises and inflating our economy, thereby exerting a further increase in wages, was neither here nor there. As long as profits continued to rise and wealth continued to be created, this could only result in benefits for the economy as a whole, we were told by the proponents of the free-market ideology.

The creation of wealth was paramount. The economy was paramount. There was no other policy. And the decision had been taken that the best and increasingly, it appeared, the only way which wealth would be created in the Irish economy from the late nineties, in particular, was though the property industry. Cognizance need not be taken of the effects such economic decisions would have on society. This was to be a recurring and remarkable aspect of the economic strategy of the Celtic Tiger period. Income tax reduction became central to all political parties' political agendas. It was, of course, argued that this would result in a consequential boost to the economy, though the political pay-off in electoral terms surely had much to do with its adoption. How public services could be adequately supported was, it seemed, of little or no concern. Anyway, as long as the property sector continued to boom, the supply of indirect taxes from the likes of Stamp Duty and capital gains taxes would suffice, it was claimed, to provide a reasonable level of services.

That successive Ministers of Finance were following a common line of placing all our financial eggs in one basket, by depending nigh-on totally on indirect taxes to support government expenditure was a worrying sign that basic house keeping was being ignored by people who should, one would have thought, known better. This arrogant disregard for policies which have served communities well for centuries became another distinguishing feature of this generation of political leaders. This unquestioned self confidence laid the basis for an arrogant complacency which would play its part in creating conditions that would have a disastrous impact on the country as a whole.

These matters were of little concern to those who were in positions of power and influence in the state at the time. Money was frittered away on a succession of government initiatives with little regard for cost effectiveness. The payroll computer system, PPARS, which was supposed to cost €9 million and be introduced within one year in 1999 was finally halted after seven years, having cost €220 million and providing a flawed system which resulted in one employee infamously being paid one million euro. Over sixty million was spent on an electronic voting system which could never be employed, for fear of fraudulent manipulation. Aer Lingus, the state airline, was privatised by Minister Martin Cullen in such a botched manner that the state received far less for the company than had been offered only a year previously by another bidder. Moreover, the decision to publicly float the national airline left the country dangerously exposed to having air access monopolised by one carrier when Michael O'Leary, chief executive of Ryanair, launched a powerful bid to gain control. The same minister presided over cost over-runs on the Luas and port tunnel projects, which cost €620 million between them. This appalling wastefulness was but a fraction of the amount that this one minister cost the state whilst in government. The fact that he was never asked to resign, let alone be sacked, demonstrated the hypocrisy of a government that exalted the so-called 'professionalism' of the private sector and yet accepted far lower standards from its own ministers. The fact that much of the cost overruns, including the €3.2 billion overrun in Ireland's road building projects since 1999, was going to the government's friends in the construction industry, surely was of relevance.

The construction industry's concerns were in fact central to the government's policy initiatives at the time. The transport policy seemed to have been designed more for the benefit of that industry than for any significant improvement in the country's chronically underperforming transport facilities. How else could one explain the decision to construct two Luas tram lines simultaneously in the capital as major components of a proposed integrated transport system whilst the huge cost was sanctioned in the full knowledge that those two tracks would not meet! The actual construction of the projects seemed to justify the expenditure and satisfy those who proposed financing them. The policy with regard to road construction likewise implied motives other than the relief of traffic congestion. Here again, profit and wealth creation seemed to be the defining factor. The hugely detrimental effect of the M50 toll bridge on the business community, and indeed on the general public, was never addressed.

Since capping the profits of the company which ran the road would have seriously affected others in the wealth creation world, the toll bridge continued to create the very congestion it had been constructed to alleviate. Roads were being built, it appeared, primarily to accommodate the construction industry in its attempts to access lands for development. In 2005 a report on RTE News on the opening, by Transport Minister Martin Cullen, of the outer ring road in Waterford noted that, as well as helping to relieve congestion, the road would provide "access to vast tracts of land for potential development."

However, such co-operation with the construction industry through transport policy paled into insignificance when compared to the countless other initiatives which the government instigated in its all out-support of the building industry. A myriad of tax incentive schemes, such as Section 23 which was already in place, and Section 50, 'Urban, Town and Rural Renewal', and those covering hotels, nursing homes, private hospitals, childcare buildings and student accommodation, were all introduced to further supercharge construction during one of the most sustained building booms in post-Second World War Europe. These measures helped boost house prices, and they also helped create extreme levels of inequality by allowing the well-off the legally compliant option of avoiding and evading tax. In a study conducted by the Revenue Commissioners which examined the income tax affairs of the State's 400 top earners in 2008, it was revealed that people who earned the equivalent of €90,000 a week were thus enabled to pay income tax at 20%, the same rate as those who earned €500 a week.

In fact, many of the richest people in the country paid no tax at all, as a result of a decision taken by the Minister for Finance, Charlie McCreevy, in his Budget in 2001, which allowed people to be deemed non-resident for tax purposes if they spent less than 183 days a year in the country. They could also use another loophole: excluding from the calculation those days on which they left the country before midnight. By the stroke of a pen, McCreevy had legalised the tax avoidance and evasion which had been rampant in the eighties and nineties and created a situation whereby tycoons such as Denis O'Brien could refuse to contribute a single penny to the State's coffers. This was the same man to whom, remember, the government had awarded the mobile phone licence at a knock-down price and who then proceeded to amass an enormous personal fortune.

The public were to suffer a further indignity when O'Brien subsequently applied for the protection of the non-residency legislation so as to ensure that the wealth he had created in Ireland could be transported off-shore. None of the capital gains which he made on what was originally a State asset would therefore return to the citizens of that State in terms of direct tax. This, at the same time as health and education in Ireland were found, in a United Nations Report into poverty produced in 2008, to have been amongst the most under-funded in the eighteen developed countries which they had studied. This combination of tax incentives for the property industry and a manifold increase in tax evasion methods for the super-rich resulted in Ireland bizarrely being ranked in a Bank of Ireland Private Banking report as the second-richest country in the world in terms of wealth per capita, but also the second-worst in terms of poverty by that United Nations report into eighteen developed countries.

By 2008 it was estimated that there were over 5,000 individuals who claimed to be non-resident for the purpose of tax avoidance. Whilst private executive jets whisked business tycoons into and out of their palatial homes, many of our children were condemned to attending rat-infested and dilapidated schools and our older generation, in particular, suffered the indignity of attending hopelessly overcrowded hospitals where they were frequently left to suffer in silence on makeshift beds in cramped corridors. This was the legacy that these Celtic Tiger tycoons were bequeathing to their fellow citizens, a legacy one might have thought more befitting the corrupt controllers of some autocratic communist State. Ironically, Denis O'Brien, when publicly challenged over his unwillingness to contribute his fair share to the tax take, railed against those ungrateful begrudgers who failed to appreciate the contribution entrepreneurs such as he had made to our collective wealth, and declared that we were in danger of becoming a communist State. Little did he know how prophetic those words were.

Successive governments continued apace to facilitate the personal aggrandisement of their wealthy patrons in the property industry. Whether that was by the systematic corruption of the planning procedures, which has become the subject of endless tribunal investigation, or by allowing the banking sector to introduce products which contradicted all conventional wisdom with regard to safe business, no obstacle was to be placed in the path of wealth creation through house building. Some of the products which the regulator deemed acceptable included the ever- increasing amounts in loans, in both real and indeed percentage terms, which banks were prepared to offer. Of course, the performance-related remuneration culture, which commensurately rewarded those who loaned the most, must bear much of the responsibility for this irresponsible business practice. Though it is generally accepted that it was Anglo Irish Bank which started this supercharged competitive culture in the banking sector, it was not long before all were recklessly following suit. It was in fact Cormac McCarthy, chief executive of Ulster

Bank, who was credited with being the first to condone the practice of granting one hundred percent mortgages. These products were invariably introduced when it appeared to all intents and purposes that the market had again reached a ceiling point and a natural course of events would have seen a decline in the price of housing.

This would have had a calamitous effect on the earning potential of those involved in the property industry, and therefore could not be allowed occur. This would not be countenanced by the banking employees who were raking in huge bonuses, based on the products they were providing to the market. Nor would it be by the auctioneers who were still benefiting from the anomalous one percent of the purchase price in remuneration, no matter how high that price had risen in the boom years. Neither, indeed, by solicitors, who likewise received one percent commissions on overly-inflated house prices for conveyancy work. All three sectors were in fact being allowed to benefit from business practices which were bloating not just house prices, but general inflation too.

The systemic corruption of planning regulations was the primary means by which the property moguls gained access to sites for potential development, but it was by no means the only method employed by politicians to accommodate their wealthy patrons' every wish and command. Some of the more ingenious were undoubtedly concocted in the environs of the Fianna Fáil tent at the annual meeting of minds at the Galway races. One can but imagine the mirth and, indeed, the backslapping that ensued when the person who dreamt up the de-centralisation policy first announced it to his audience of like-minded cronies. This policy, made public for the first time in the 2004 Budget, was surely conceived in the convivial atmosphere of the champagne- fuelled racing weekend. Minister McCreevy proposed re-deploying

10,000 Dublin based public servants to new government offices around the country, and he set up a committee, to be chaired by the industrial relations expert, Phil Flynn, to assist him in completing this massive transformation before 2006. That there appeared to be little justification for such a policy was clearly of no concern for the Minister.

In a year when vacant housing units reached the alarming figure of 260,000, most of these built in rural areas and the result of the generous tax relief that had been granted to investors under the section 23 legislation, imagine the relief which this massive translocation of prospective purchasers to the countryside would provide to the rural property industry, which had been worrying that its generous property cash cow was in danger of drying up. As Jim Power, the Friends First economist, predicted, further spin-offs for the property sector would arise when the government offices in prime Dublin locations became available to the developers. At a period when sites, especially in the most expensive city in the world, were at a premium this could well have been the decisive factor in propelling the government down the dangerous road of decentralisation.

The political advantage which could be achieved by a minister relocating thousands of public service jobs to a location at the heart of his constituency also had a huge bearing on events. The policy has since then been recognised as an unmitigated disaster, with public services being neither centralised nor decentralised. This should come as no surprise, as the Progressive Democrats, under the leadership of Mary Harney and Michael McDowell, were vigorously opposed to the concept of 'Big Government', ideologically wedded, as they were, to the notion that wealth is generated by individuals conceived with the gene of entrepreneurship, entitled to hold onto the rewards of their superior talents. Ably assisted by champions of the cause such as Jim Power, they were remarkably successful in promoting their 'small government' agenda. Like their ideological guru, Margaret Thatcher, they did not believe in the concept of society and had no time for public services, such as universal healthcare and equal access to education, which they appeared to view as State-supplied handouts to economic losers, financed by economic achievers. Their contempt for public servants, in particular, was made evident on numerous occasions. Jim Power, who had considered running for the Progressive Democrats in the general election, was a leading supporter of the privatisation of all public services. In Power's narrow world view, nurses, teachers, gardai, those in the fire service, amongst others, were guilty of the unforgivable sin of not creating wealth and therefore were of no economic value.

These, unfortunately, were not the incoherent ramblings of one solitary free-market economist, but lay at the very core of the free-market ideology which the Progressive Democrats and their supporters subscribed to. The theory had its origins in the work of Professor John Nash, the schizophrenic mathematician whose life story was depicted in the Oscar-winning film *A Beautiful Mind*, in which Russell Crowe took the lead role. Nash developed a strategy, Game Theory, which, when applied during the Cold War, ensured that a balance of power would be maintained between the Soviet Union and the United States. Fear and self-interest, he reasoned, would prevent the Soviet Union attacking America, knowing that, if they did, they too would be devastated.

Its successful application in the Cold War encouraged Nash to develop the theory further, arguing that stability in society could be achieved through suspicion and self-interest. Game Theory proffered a dark few of humanity in which all people were assumed to mistrust each another.

In order to demonstrate his ideas, Nash developed a game called 'Fuck you buddy', in which the only way to ensure that you won was to betray your partners. Nash held that a society based on mutual suspicion did not lead to chaos, but equilibrium. Crucially, this system could only work if everyone behaved selfishly. In tests which Nash carried out, as soon as people began co-operating with one another, instability inevitably ensued.

Game Theory was adopted by a group of American right-wing economists, inspired by Friedrich von Hayek, himself an inspiration for Margaret Thatcher, who set out to prove that the concept of public duty was simply a sham. Using the example of the chaos, resulting from the general strike which brought down Labour leader Jim Callaghan and ushered in Margaret Thatcher as prime minister, the right-wing economists argued that the greed of public servants had made them turn on the very people they were supposed to serve. This, supposedly, proved the essential principle of Game Theory: that, in effect, all those involved were strategising against each other in order to gain some advantage. The very idea of public service was held to be a fantasy, because it assumed that there were shared goals based on self-sacrifice and altruism when, in fact, people were motivated solely by self-interest.

Professor James Buchanan, another major influence on Margaret Thatcher, convinced her that British institutions were full, not of people working for the public good, but of self-serving bureaucrats. When she came to power in 1979, she set about privatising as many of the State institutions as possible. When she realised that some of them would have to remain in State control, she decided to introduce a system based on incentives and self-interest. In 1986 she further adapted this right-wing philosophy in her attempt to reform the Health Service, enlisting a nuclear strategist, Alain Enthoven, who had devised mathematical models for nuclear war to incentivise the other side and who insisted that his technique, known as 'Systems Analysis', could be applied to any human organisation. Its aim was to remove any emotional or subjective baggage which could confuse the system, thereby rendering it less efficient, and replace them with mathematically defined targets and incentives.

Enthoven's system had first been employed by Robert McNamara when he was in charge of the Pentagon in the sixties. Against the wishes of the military, McNamara instituted a policy of performance targets and rational incentives during the Vietnam War. These were, unsurprisingly, a disaster and led to very large numbers of civilians being killed. Undeterred by this fact, Margaret Thatcher carried on regardless, introducing the principles of the free-market to National Health Service, adopting Enthoven's rebranding of 'Systems Analysis' as the 'Internal Market'. This resulted in self-interested people, whom John Nash had cynically envisaged in his original Game Theory, finding their way to the core of the health service, with all the disastrous consequences that would inevitably have.

It was this same philosophy which lay at the heart of the Progressive Democrat's ideology in Ireland, an exclusively economic perspective which relegated human beings to the role of digits in mathematical calculations which were formulated with the sole purpose of so-called wealth creation. Successive governments, and indeed the opposition parties, became followers of the PD's creed, which held that the country's wealth was created by an exclusively gifted group of individuals and that this self-generated capital was manifestly theirs to keep. This was the ideology that proclaimed deregulation an economic prerequisite and would remove any constraints that might limit the ability of the geniuses of the financial world to function to the full extent of their undoubted abilities.

This philosophy lay at the very heart of the consensus parliamentary mindset which appeared to condone tax evasion and tax avoidance to such an extent that, when the illegal avenues which could be pursued by the country's elite were closed, due to the sterling work of investigative journalists such as George Lee, the government proceeded to implement policy which effectively legitimised the previously illicit methods.

The fact that the Progressive Democrats were ideologically opposed to the previously accepted social doctrine that it was the duty of democratically elected governments to provide for universal healthcare and equitable systems of education, amongst other social services, permitted them to relentlessly pursue a policy of direct income tax reduction. This fact, combined with the ruthless and unambiguous support for supposedly wealth-engendering private healthcare, ensured that the Irish State emerged from the boom period of the Celtic Tiger with an education system which was patently the prerogative of a social elite and a public healthcare system which was failing to provide universal access to even the most rudimentary standards of care.

For damning evidence of this, we need look no further than the words of health minister Mary Harney herself. In a speech in 2000, in which she infamously remarked that Ireland was closer to Boston than Berlin, she arrogantly lectured those who had questioned the principles of the laissez-faire free-market ideology which she had propagated. Undoubtedly buoyed by the apparent transformation of the Irish economy from basket-case to beacon of free capitalism under her supervision, her hubris knew no bounds. Her words, though, serve now as a salutary reminder to all those who would complacently give free-reign to the innermost thoughts of an unrestrained and irrational ego:

"What really makes Ireland so attractive to corporate America is the kind of economy we have created here. When Americans come here, they find a country that believes in the incentive power of low taxation. They find a country that believes in essential regulation, but not over-regulation. On looking further a-field in Europe, they find also that not every European country believes in these things. Look at what we have done over the past ten years. [...] We have cut taxes on capital. We have cut taxes on corporate profits. We have cut taxes on personal incomes. The result has been an explosion in economic activity, and Ireland is now the fastest growing country in the developing world. And did we have to pay some very high price for pursuing this policy option? The answer is no, we didn't."

Time would, unfortunately, tell a rather different story.

In one crucial respect, however, Mary Harney was undoubtedly correct. Ireland, more than any other country, I would suggest, had indeed moved closer to the American model of unregulated free-market capitalism and had probably implemented it in an even more aggressive manner than our neighbours across the Atlantic. In Ireland the Enron, or American, model was welcomed with open arms even after it had been revealed as a fraud from the beginning. Our political and economic masters adopted the unregulated free-market ideology passionately. The prospect of creating personal wealth never before dreamt of, or considered possible, clouded all judgement and dictated all policy. The Irish people would be carried on a roller-coaster ride of wealth creation, for which they would pay "not a penny," as Mary Harney so haughtily declared. The share price of choice, or stake, in this "no lose" poker game would be property, and consequently every man, woman and child in the State would be present at the table, whether they liked it or not. But, as Enron had so manifestly illustrated, this was nothing but a grandiose pyramid scheme. However, the country that conceived Enron, and subsequently declined to learn anything from the lesson it provided, was on the verge of shattering not just the fragile and fraudulently fractured financial system in Ireland but, indeed, throughout the world. The "very high price" that Mary Harney had precociously pronounced would not have to be paid, was now looming ominously on the horizon.

Chapter 6

The walls come tumbling down

The fact that, following Enron's downfall, no government saw fit to tighten the regulatory authorities' control over business practices struck me as alarming. Indeed, it was becoming ever more evident that the model adopted by Enron was being repeated on a gargantuan scale. During the course of a discussion with a senior class of leaving cert pupils in 2002, I recall suggesting for the first time that this morally corrupt business culture contained within it the elements which would ultimately result in the collapse of the world's financial system. As a result of a student's remark that we could not be certain that such fraudulent methods as were employed in Enron were not similarly employed in other huge corporations, the discussion turned to the consequences which would unfold if such a scenario proved to be true.

Enron had, after all, ranked only the tenth biggest corporation on Wall Street. We imagined the suspicions which would arise if seven drug cheats in an Olympic sprint final were trumped by an athlete who professed to be clean. It seemed likely that all was not as it appeared to be in the race to top in the business world's annual version of the

Olympic Games, the stock market valuation based on the companys' annual profits growth announcements. It was also clear that the practice of parking huge debt, which Enron's executives had indulged in, whilst simultaneously sucking the real capital out of the company for their own personal benefit, was being repeated on a grandiose scale worldwide. Share valuations were evidently being artificially and fraudulently inflated and then parked, primarily in pension fund schemes, which were ideally suited to the purpose, as there was little danger that they would be drawn down fast enough to cause the scam's collapse. The real capital, meanwhile, was being sucked out of the system as the masterminds of the fraud sold these worthless shares to innocent investors who were attempting only to provide for their financial futures.

This fraudulent manipulation became increasingly evident when the machinations of hedgefunds, and the effects which their operations would have on the system, were better understood and appreciated: the fact that vast amounts of real capital were being sucked out of the financial system, leaving the world's real economy precariously dependant on illusory stock market finance which could disappear into thin air at any point. The fact that the real capital that was sucked out of the system was subsequently used by the masterminds of these frauds, through the manipulation of the hedgefund system, to further embellish their obscene wealth was, in truth, nauseating. Those involved in hedgefunds could choose from a variety of products available in their deregulated ultra-casino, such as short-selling or CDF's, in order, in effect, to bet that those self-same companies which they had created, and which they manifestly understood were unstable, would proceed to fail. That the very same people who created the fraudulent share valuations were now using the capital they acquired from the initial scam to further increase their wealth by betting that those same share valuations would now fall was surely the final ignominy for the capitalist system itself. This practice was guaranteed to ensure that there could be only one outcome to proceedings: the complete and utter collapse of the world's financial system.

My pupils were being asked to consider the likelihood that the world's financial structure was fundamentally unstable and that it would inevitably fail. They were being challenged to accept that the ideas which underpinned the economic structure of the entire planet were fundamentally flawed and that the comfortable life which the majority of them had known since birth was in danger of disappearing before their very eyes. When one considers the difficulty more experienced and supposedly far more intelligent experts had in accepting this notion at the very height of the crisis, it is easy to understand young people's reluctance to embrace such earth-shattering suggestions from their teacher back in 2002. All the more so when one considers the consensus of opinion which existed which complacently proclaimed that they had never had it so good and that the unbounded prosperity which they were enjoying was guaranteed into their futures now that the geniuses of free-market liberalism had been given full reign.

This cosy, complacent consensus was, as we have seen, all-prevailing in the political arena, with all parties adopting a right-of-centre approach to economic thinking, with little or no regard for the effects such an approach would have on society. This philosophy would be, almost unanimously, adopted by the media, which was privately owned and functioned as a mouthpiece for the vested interests of the property industry, in particular, a sector of the business world from which the media itself benefited greatly. There were, of course, honourable exceptions in both the political and media worlds, who remained committed to the pursuit of the truth and the discharge of their duties in the interest of the public. The Socialist Party's Joe Higgins, and George Lee, RTÉ's chief economic correspondent, deserve particular mention in this regard. However, a coordinated campaign to educate the public with regard to the devastating effects which complacent acquiescence to free-market liberalism would have on society and, indeed, on the very economy it professed to serve, was sadly missing. The absence of such a debate in the political and media worlds ensured that the public, in general, were left largely ignorant about the dangers which were looming.

In such a void it would have been natural to look to other areas of society for leadership and guidance. One would have thought, that a religious institution worthy of the name, which was desperately searching for a role in a modern society which increasingly viewed organised religion as an outdated irrelevance, would have eagerly grasped the opportunity afforded them to put forward their thoughts on equality, fairness and respect for others which, if adopted, might have ensured that the worst effects of the economic crisis could have been averted. However, the Catholic Church's position in society had been so undermined, by the self-same corruption of moral behaviour that infected the business world, that it was in no position to give guidance.

It was the manner in which the establishment within the Catholic Church dealt with the victims of child sexual abuse by the clergy which ultimately destroyed the trust which the people of Ireland had previously placed in them to uphold, respect and defend the moral principles and responsibilities of the country. The cowardly and morally bankrupt manner in which perpetrators of the most heinous crimes imaginable were secreted away and afforded the opportunity to repeat those crimes is unforgivable. The effort to save the establishment from the embarrassment and shame which would accompany such revelations dealt a deserved deathblow to its standing within the community. In truth, for generations its relevance to the social and economic affairs of the people had been insignificant. That it was, and remains, an important element of the privileged sector of society which constitutes the Golden Circle is an undoubted fact. This was demonstrated when the issue of compensation for victims of child sexual abuse by the clergy became a very public concern in the late nineties. It became apparent at that time that the Catholic Church was increasingly vulnerable to litigation as a result of the years of physical, emotional and sexual abuse which members of its clergy had perpetrated on men, women and children in various church-run institutions over a long period.

Though it was difficult to place a precise amount on it, it was generally accepted that the final figure in compensation which would be owed by the Church would approach €500 million at least. This left many religious orders facing potential bankruptcy. The Minister for Education, Michael Woods, caused consternation in 2002 when he agreed, on behalf of the government, to cap the Church's liability at €128 million and committed the government – though in reality the taxpayer – to accept responsibility for the remaining €380 million. This, from a government, a Fine Gael led incarnation of which, shamefully fought innocent victims of the hepatitis C blood transfusions all the way to their death-beds in an effort to avoid admitting liability.

We were now being asked to believe that 'a road to Damascus' change in collective conscience had occurred at the very heart of our government and that, despite all the evidence to the contrary, they were now accepting responsibility for their actions. Of course, the real devil lay, as it tends to do, in the details of the agreement which reflected the 'special position' which the Catholic Church has enjoyed in Ireland since the foundation of the State. Though Michael Woods would have had us believe otherwise, it was common knowledge in legal circles at the time that the extent of the liabilities facing the church far outstripped anything witnessed previously in the State. The current estimate is that compensation claims are likely to top €1.1 billion, of which the taxpayer will now be liable to pay 90 %. Though the terms of the deal remain clouded in secrecy, it is known that the Church had committed itself to paying the bulk of the €128 million that they owed through the transfer of land assets which have been in their possession since time immemorial.

Although precise information is exceedingly difficult to come by, it is known that only twenty-one of the sixty-four properties promised to the State in lieu of compensation have actually been transferred. Of the properties transferred, many were in prime locations in the country and eventually found their way into the hands of property magnates who acquired the relevant planning permission and amassed huge profits from their subsequent development. Meanwhile, the Church, unburdened of the threat of compensation claims by the largesse of the government with taxpayers' money, proceeded to amass immense fortunes for itself by selling off further large tracts of land in its property portfolio. A fourteen-acre site on the Merrion Road in Dublin, a coveted location for development, was sold by the Sisters of Mercy, in the same year as the agreement was signed, to the private sector for €45 million. The manner in which the privileged sections of Irish society – in this case the government, the church and the property industry – collaborated to ensure they extracted the maximum financial benefit for themselves from a human crisis which was unrivalled in this State in the preceding century marks a particular low point in this odious story.

Meanwhile, as this unedifying spectacle continued apace within the elite of the economic community, the ordinary citizens struggled in vain to cope with the effects of their unscrupulous behaviour on society at large. As house prices rocketed, the commuter towns which sprang up on the green field sites within an hour or even a two-hour drive of the capital became ever more frequently the only realistic option for first-time buyers. That this would entail regular three-to-four-hour daily commutes to their places of work so that they could afford the luxury of acquiring their own home was deemed unimportant by the ministers who sanctioned such economic and social policy. That they were encumbered with extraordinary levels of mortgage debt over ever-extending periods of time was also considered irrelevant. That they, furthermore, had to send their children to crèches which had benefited from tax incentive schemes which the government had set up to encourage married women to return or remain in the workforce was also considered immaterial. These crèches were the only, though certainly not the preferred, choice of many couples, as they valiantly struggled to cope with the financial and social demands which the Celtic Tiger economy placed upon their shoulders. That financial burden was immeasurably increased when the €1,000 per child average monthly crèche fees were taken into consideration. This sum, the equivalent of another mortgage in most cases, significantly increased the financial pressures which our young generation, in particular, were faced with.

That the fruits of their labour were to amount to a house which was hours away from their place of work, and that their salaries went primarily to cover the crippling costs of that house and the childcare which made it possible for them to work, paints only a fraction of the depressing picture of the lifestyle of a growing percentage of people in Ireland at the time. That this was marketed as a lifestyle option that only the very fortunate could conceivably enjoy was surely the final indignity. Although a small, but influential, minority were reaping the rewards of this unrestrained free-market liberalism, the vast majority of people were living with ever-increasing personal debt levels which were dangerously acquired and supported by using a precariously valued asset as its collateral.

As a result of the government's decision to place all our economic eggs in the property sector basket, everything in the country – every asset, every product, every service – had its valuation inextricably linked to the exorbitantly priced property market. Rents in the commercial property sector escalated alarmingly, with the consequential negative effects for inflation. The cost of living rose alarmingly as prices for commodities kept pace with the new gold-standard: house prices. Salaries in all sectors of the economy rose startlingly, but they also reflected the disproportionate inequality which was to become such a feature of Celtic Tiger Ireland. Anyone directly associated with the world of city and business finance, which in Ireland primarily revolved around the property sector and the movement of capital derived from such investments, benefited to an obscene extent from the property boom.

Be it the wages of sin of Chief Executives in banks, to the 1% fee charged by solicitors for conveyance, or the further 1% which auctioneers charged for their role in the sale of houses, all those directly involved in the property industry reaped grotesquely inflated rewards which were hardly commensurate with the services they provided. These wages became the benchmark for others in the economy who thought they were deserving of comparable salaries, a section which included politicians, leaders of the business and financial worlds and members of the media and their invited affluent circle of friends, which then proceeded to propagandise on behalf of the system they had created and which they, primarily and indeed almost exclusively, benefited from.

This exclusive arena of Celtic Tiger society, membership of which was predicated on access to exorbitant incomes, was obviously not the preserve of the ordinary citizen. Relative income poverty rates in Ireland were amongst the highest in the European Union and in fact increased during the boom years of the Celtic Tiger. Over 750,000 of the population lived below the poverty line. The situation for the middle ranks of income earners was only marginally better. Though wages had increased during the course of the boom, they had done so only within the narrow confines of the national pay agreements. These, the product of discussions between employers, the government and union representatives, served only to accentuate the pay disparity which existed between the golden circle and the ordinary workers in both the public and the private sectors. They prevented industrial relations turmoil but, more importantly, they enabled the ruling elite of the business world to grossly extend profit margins. Though salaries rose, they never kept pace with the phenomenal rise in property prices. As we have already seen, the average public sector salary would, in the year 2006, have required a mortgage loan of sixteen times its value in order to afford the type of house that could have been bought for a multiple of five times the same salary some twenty years previously.

The role which the public and private sector union leaders played in facilitating the exploitation of their members by the vested interests of the property industry should neither be underestimated nor forgotten. Wage increases, which were a natural by-product of the boom in the property sector, did not remotely keep pace with the mortgage repayments that were now being demanded. That this directly affected our competitiveness is undeniable, but by this point in the Celtic Tiger fantasy tale major economic considerations such as this mattered not a whit to the economic masterminds who were in charge of our destiny. The real economy had become a secondary and very much minor player in the 'all eggs in one basket' property-centred economy which the mercenaries of our fateful destiny, Fianna Fáil, had masterfully created for us.

This recurring theme of so-called economic experts ignoring the absolute fundamental tenets of economic theory and practice, when those considerations threatened to come between individuals and vast amounts of capital, is one which reoccurs repeatedly in the tale of financial institutions inevitably sliding into economic disaster. It was becoming increasingly evident to anyone who wished to acknowledge the facts that the government's espousal of the unrestrained free-market ideology was having not just a profoundly negative effect on Irish society but also, ironically, on the very economy it purported to be supporting.

This economic philosophy had, to all intents and purposes, become dangerously untenable a long time previous to its ultimate collapse in 2009. In fact, particularly if judged by the sound and well-worn tenets of traditional economic theory, it can be diagnosed as having reached a critical point in the years preceding the millennium. It was during that period, in particular when the dot-com bubble burst, in 2000, that stock-market valuations were first exposed as being unrealistic and untenable. However, instead of heeding the initial warnings of the patient's ill-health, which these major stock market tremors undoubtedly were for the capitalist system, the astonishing decision was taken to allow the market free-reign to gorge itself on a different commodity, through unbridled access to the unlimited amounts of wealth which were available through property. Though this was, most assuredly, the time when moderation was called for and, most certainly, the time for taking the harsh decisions relating to the curbing of excessive profits, both personal and institutional, which were at the root of social and economic problems worldwide, governments baulked at taking measures which would have meant outright confrontation with the vested interests which controlled, and ultimately benefited from, the manipulation of the stock markets.

These economic masters of the universe were increasingly, it appeared, the only section of the economy which governments considered when formulating policy. This resulted in governments worldwide refusing to acknowledge that the root cause of the collapse in the stock market system, which the dot-com bubble had heralded, was the unrestrained and unregulated pursuit of profit. The maximisation of stock market share valuation and, indeed, all the corrupt behaviour associated with it were fundamental elements of the economic ideology which resulted in the ultimate failure of the financial system itself.

In Ireland unrestrained support for a financial system, the ballooning value of which had incontrovertibly reached a ceiling in 2000, took the form of the government, and its collaborators in the fraud, removing any restraints which would inhibit these vested interests from financially gaining from the artificial inflation of the value of the most elementary and rudimentary share of all, the house deed. This was achieved through a combination of two primary methods. The first was the creation of a massive ball of debt which would facilitate the continued upward momentum of property prices. The second was the policy of continually 'opening valves' in the economy on every occasion when the effects of the illogical and futile economic policies threatened to clog the financial system itself and bring the ostentatious façade crashing to the ground. Both of these decisions would ultimately have disastrous long-term ramifications for the economic viability of the country itself but, also, appallingly dire consequences for the unwitting victims of this fraud, the citizens of the State.

Responsibility for the creation of the massive ball of debt which financed the massively overblown boom in property share prices lies primarily with the banks themselves. The manner in which traditional banking practices were dispensed with, as those individuals involved in the banking community enriched themselves, was crucial. The new bullish chief executives were light-years removed from their conservatively staid counterparts of years gone by. In the well-worn traditional methods practised by the bank managers of yore, both the bank's and indeed the customer's financial security were thoroughly risk-assessed when considering any loans which the customer might consider acquiring. This tried and tested safety mechanism, which lay at the very core of responsible banking, was dispensed with in the new dynamic era of super-charged banking, based exclusively on increasing lending whilst ignoring any duty of care towards securing the vast quantities of capital loaned. This was a complete derogation of duty by those concerned and placed the banks and, indeed, the customers at great financial peril.

The principles underpinning the security of loans were considered irrelevant and consigned to the dustbin. The requirement that the customer possessed a significant deposit was dispensed with. This, of course, opened up the market to untold numbers of mortgage seekers, but also unfortunately to the risks inherent in such reckless management. The expansion of the customer base was achieved in the increasingly deregulated mortgage lending section of the banking industry by mindlessly undercutting the percentage which was required to fund a loan: an unashamedly ruthless attempt to garner larger and larger shares of the lucrative mortgage market for their business portfolios. Banks started falling over themselves to foist unserviceable debt onto customers' shoulders. The era of 90% and 95% mortgages was hastily followed by the outrageous 100% and, indeed, the ultimately unconscionable 115% loans. These were business practises more commonly associated with loan-sharks, rather than responsible and credited banking institutions.

The fact that these loans were unserviceable was conveniently ignored. House prices had to continue to rise inexorably for the capitalist financial system, as then constituted, to continue. The inability of creditors to secure these loans, an obvious indication that the financial system had reached breaking point, was addressed by further 'valve opening' in order to reduce the imminent danger of collapse. The terms within which mortgage repayments had to be made were extended endlessly. From the traditional twenty-year term, itself generally considered a substantial burden, home owners were now being required to consider a future which would demand that both partners would continue to work permanently for thirty or forty years to service their mortgage debt. The likelihood that couples could conceivably be working into their seventies to service the debt on their primary residence, and the consequential negative impact this would have on their lifestyles and on society in general, should have given policy makers cause for concern.

Personal levels of indebtedness, of which mortgage debt was a significant part, were increasing at an alarming rate. Encouraged and, undoubtedly once more, incentivised by the practice which saw employees' remuneration in banking and investment institutions indelibly linked to their ability to create wealth, the country witnessed a dangerous boom in personal credit. Credit card debt was but one aspect. It was countenanced, primarily, as it was essentially the fuel which was driving the rampant consumerism which was effectively the sole engine of that economy. The constant flooding of the market with financial products which facilitated easy access to this boom in personal credit was, however, an indicator that the public was having great difficulty in servicing the loans which were fuelling the over inflated economy. Addressing this issue would have required the authors of the fraud admitting their own culpability in the proceedings and therefore was never liable to occur. Instead, the decision was taken to continue with the policy of postponing the inevitable day of reckoning, a decision which served only to multiply greatly the suffering and distress which the public would undoubtedly endure when the outcome became unavoidable.

When it became apparent that the property sector needed further purchasers to ensure the unabated rise in house prices that the scam required to continue, all conceivable assistance was given to the vested interests in achieving their collective aim. Interest-only repayments facilitated initial, and apparently pain-free, access to a rapidly spiralling market for prospective buyers. Young people, in particular, felt pressurised into accepting the overwhelming financial burden which these long-term, crippling mortgages imposed, as the consensus economic opinion at the time was that the housing boom was perfectly justifiable and that the fundamentals of the Irish economy were rock solid.

As late as 2007 Jim Power, chief economist with Friends' First, was confidently predicting that" the death of the Irish housing market is grossly exaggerated and that, while 2006 should represent the peak of the housing cycle, in terms of price inflation and completions, the market looks set to remain solidly based". "Beyond 2007", he confidently predicted, "house price inflation should settle down to levels broadly consistent with general inflation out to the end of the decade". He furthermore insisted that "the fundamental demand in the market place is still strong and is not about to disappear". Other leading analysts, such as Austin Hughes, chief economist with IIB, and Dan McLaughlin, of Bank of Ireland, contributed even more positive assessments. McLaughlin was quoted, as late as 2008, as "remaining optimistic" that "the fundamentals of the Irish economy are sound". He foresaw, at that late date, "a bottoming out of the US housing market which suggested the seeds of a stateside recovery were then being sewn," and that this would spill over into Europe and Ireland. Austin Hughes, to his eternal discredit, remained the super optimist amongst this particular band of disreputable brothers in arms. In his frequent comments on the state of the investment property market in Ireland, Hughes continually spun an overly positive assessment of affairs.

When it became apparent that prospective purchasers, particularly investors, were becoming increasingly reluctant to commit to the Irish property market, a concerted effort was made to manipulate a further opening of pressure valves. It was decided that a decrease in European interest rates would significantly encourage investors into the property market once more, and a campaign for such a decrease was initiated. Unfortunately, for those in the property industry in Ireland who would benefit from such further artificial market manipulation, the interest rates were the preserve of the European Central Bank. The governing council of the ECB, and its president, Jean Claude Trichet, presented a more difficult challenge than a national Government at home to influence. Furthermore, the self-inflicted difficulties of the Irish housing market economy were not the only concern for the European Central Bank at this point in time, as it was preoccupied just then with the battle to curb the ever increasing inflation rate which most member states, including Ireland, were suffering from. Now we were witnessing the signs on a European level that the financial system was heading for collapse.

Though a number of States, such as Ireland, were campaigning for a decrease in inflation rates to provide a kick-start to their failing property markets, the ECB recognised that such an interest decrease would adversely affect inflation rates, which were threatening to spiral out of control. Thus the European financial system found itself with contradictory measures being required simultaneously in order to address the conflicting problems with which it was faced. On the one hand the ECB was demanding that interest rates be forced higher in an attempt to curb a growing inflation rate problem in the Eurozone, while at the same time governments and economists in countries such as Ireland were calling for a decrease in those rates to stimulate a housing market that was in the midst of a major slump. The invidious position in which the ECB found itself in this regard, where it appeared to be damned if it did and damned if it didn't, was clear evidence of the dire situation of the financial system as a whole. Although Jean Claude Trichet and the governing body of the European Bank stood firm in their opinion that interest rates should, if anything, be increased, it was highly significant that the economic experts in the employ of the major banking and investment institutions and the major media corporations which benefited significantly from their property sector advertisements were steadfast in their demands for interest rate cuts. Trichet had cause at one juncture to publicly refute suggestions that interest rate cuts were being considered and that the ECB had not fuelled speculation, and was not responsible in any way for the heightened expectation that such a decrease was imminent.

Meanwhile indicators were emerging which confirmed that the Irish economy was fast approaching its own particular day of reckoning. Evidence that our economy had become a 'one trick pony', with an ever increasing over-reliance on the property sector and its related industries and services, was manifold. For example, between 1998 and 2000, a period that pre-dated the worst excesses of the property boom, permanent full-time employment in manufacturing in Ireland rose from 227,857 to 243,071. This represented a healthy 15,200 jobs created over the two-year period in an essential sector of the economy. It is significant that in the period that followed, between 2000 and 2007, full-time employment in manufacturing and internationally traded services fell by 10,300, this at a time when the total workforce expanded by a massive 605,000. This increase in employment was achieved in sectors such as construction, public services, distribution, retail and other services. When this increase is combined with the decrease in employment in manufacturing, it is clear that the government was slavishly adhering to a policy of ignoring many essential elements of the real economy in favour of the solitary egg in their economic policy basket, the construction industry and its related services.

Meanwhile, the burgeoning salary levels required to service the ever-increasing house and rental prices were adversely affecting our competitive ness internationally. It was becoming increasingly difficult, if not impossible, to entice new international investment to the country and, ever more regularly, multinational corporations were choosing to relocate to countries that could provide a cheaper workforce. Once again, the government, and those who were benefiting directly from the property boom, chose to disregard these indicators of doom and continued to pursue policies which would support the housing bubble while irrevocably damaging the fundamentals of the real economy. This policy, ironically, would eventually have a devastating effect on the housing market and ultimately be a significant factor in the inevitable collapse of the property industry, and indeed the Irish economy itself.

The initial steps leading to this disastrous outcome were taken by the government under the direction of the Minister for Finance, Charlie McCreevy, and the Minister for Justice and law Reform, Michael McDowell, in 2002. It was then that the Government chose to adopt a completely 'open-door' policy towards immigrant workers from the states of Eastern Europe which were applying for membership of the European Union. This policy was adopted far in advance of other European Union members, who judiciously decided to permit such a potentially massive inflow of workers only at a much later date and under far more controlled circumstances. The fact that Ireland had health, education and social services which were already crumbling under the excessive demands being placed on them, prior to the arrival of upwards of half a million more people at very little notice, caused not one iota of concern to the ministers who proposed this action.

In the years following 2002, in particular, companies involved in the Ireland Inc. sham were finding it increasingly difficult to demonstrate continued profit growth. The masters of the economy then turned to yet another dubious 'valve' with a view to flushing the system once more with further capital to provide further stimulus for apparent profit growth. That this would ultimately result in the complete collapse of the real economy was apparently of little or no significance to these economic gurus. With their capacity to increase profit margins any further diminished, having employed apparently all the ethical and unethical methods available to them, the masters of the Ireland Inc. scam decided to eliminate cost from the bottom of the system and thus increase profits. The manner in which they did this was to flush the labour market with cheaper foreign labour, which they could exploit to the benefit of their profit margins. That this would consequentially have a disastrous effect on the economic and social well-being of the established workforce, and would ultimately be a major contributory factor in the destruction of the entire economy, was immaterial to the short-sighted and greed-inspired masterminds.

In 2005 one private company, Irish Ferries, decided it would be the first to take advantage of the cheaper workforce that the government's open-door policy afforded them. Claiming 'increased global competition' and, more significantly, 'projected falling profits', Irish Ferries announced its intention to employ low-cost workers at the expense of the previous workforce. This was announced despite the fact that the company had a market valuation of €228 million and had made a profit of €28 million in 2004, the same year that Managing Director Eamonn Rothwell benefited to the tune of €687,000 – his personal remuneration from the operating profit. Though the company also announced that the projected profits for the following year, 2005, were in the region of €24 million, this was not deemed adequate. The company chose to proceed with its policy of increasing that operating profit by any available method. It had previously announced its intention of reregistering its vessels in Cyprus, a move which would legally enable it to avoid paying the Irish minimum wage and also to avoid adhering to Irish legislation governing working hours and holiday entitlements. Irish Ferries set about maximising profits regardless of the devastating effects this would undoubtedly have on the salaries and working conditions of the established workforce. The employers' trade union IBEC supported their stance unconditionally, and the Taoiseach, Bertie Ahern, blithely announced that, "nothing could be done".

Some of the main players in the Ireland Inc. scam had colluded once more in a 'valve opening' exercise which would come to the aid of the vested interests which needed to demonstrate continued share price growth for the sham to continue. A twenty five million euro profit for Irish Ferries in 2005, following on a €28 million profit in 2004, would not be sufficient to ensure directors' pay continuing to rise outrageously. The introduction of low-cost labour to the Irish economy would be the next irresponsible method the Irish government would employ to ensure that the financial stakes of the vested interests of their golden circle of friends would be protected and insured. The spin-offs which would accrue to other sectors of the services industry, in particular those which were closely aligned to the construction sector of the economy, were plain to see.

The hotel sector, which had boomed as a result of tax incentives, will suffice as just one example of an industry which would benefit tremendously from the arrival of a cheap foreign labour pool which it could exploit. That this would severely undermine the position of the established workforce, by threatening job security and severely undercutting salaries, thereby adding significantly to the growing difficulties this sector of the economy was already having in servicing its debts, was an irrelevance to those who were concerned only with their own self-interested motives. Ironically, though, the absence of any joined-up economic thinking in the implementation of the scam at the heart of Ireland Inc. resulted in these methods contributing greatly to its inevitable ignominious collapse. How those who had been enticed to purchase property at outrageously over-valued prices and at severely stretched income-to-debt ratios could now service those over-inflated mortgages, whilst watching their salaries decrease, was a conundrum that, it appears, never entered the minds of the chief executives of Ireland Inc.

Irish Ferries, in collusion with their allies in government and IBEC, pressed-on regardless in their pursuit of outrageous personal profit. In September 2005, IBEC supported management plans in Irish Ferries to replace 543 established workers on their vessels with low-paid agency crews, earning €3.50 an hour, imported from Eastern Europe. The following November, the crew of two Irish Ferries vessels were abruptly fired mid-voyage and attempts were made to have the replacement low-cost workers installed in their stead. One vessel, the *Isle of Inisfree*, while docked in Pembroke, was boarded by private security forces employed by the company, who attempted to gain control of the ship. These heavy-handed security personnel, dressed in the requisite baseball caps and flack jackets, attempted to install two bus loads of agency workers on the vessel, only to be met by fierce resistance by the established crew, who themselves commandeered the ship. Emboldened by growing public concern, which increasingly understood the dire ramifications which would ensue if low-cost workers such as these could be employed to undercut salary levels across the board, the public took to the streets. Over 100,000 people joined a nationwide protest called by the Irish Congress of Trades Unions, on one of the very few occasions it discharged its duty with regard to the protection and welfare of workers in the State. On this single solitary occasion the ICTU, and indeed the Labour Party, were embarrassed into forsaking their chosen position in 'partnership' with government and the vested business interests in the country by the scandalous details which emerged of the exploitation of foreign low-cost workers.

The worst such example of this naked exploitation of people, the case of Salvacion Orge, left these supposed campaigners for the working people of Ireland no option but to abandon their well-remunerated positions within the consensus of vested interests for the day and march with the rest of the population that was rightly appalled by the details that emerged. Salvacion Orge was a Filipina woman, who was employed as a beauty therapist on the aforementioned *Isle of Inisfree* and who, it emerged, was being paid €1 an hour whilst enduring twelve hour shifts, seven days a week. This revelation was enough to awaken much of the country's population to the extent to which society had been demeaned and diminished by our leaders' naked pursuit of the wealth of the Celtic Tiger economy. These were the depths to which our Celtic Tigers were plunging us all in an attempt to increase their personal fortunes, regardless of the effects it would have on society and, indeed, the economy.

The Government, led by Bertie Ahearn, disingenuously announced that there was "nothing they could do" to stop the importation and exploitation of low-cost workers. The employers' trade union IBEC, led by Turloch O'Sullivan, shamelessly and enthusiastically campaigned for it. Indeed, IBEC's forthright support for such a reprehensible policy of human exploitation and degradation was, ironically, one of the very few occasions in which they were deserving of praise. They, alone, amongst the cosy consensus of politicians and vested interests, refused to speak from both sides of their mouths and brazenly supported even this most nauseating element of the fraud which was being committed on the people of Ireland.

Alarmingly, according to figures provided by the International Monetary Fund and the Bank for International Settlements, in 2008, total gross indebtedness of Irish residents, including the State, the banks and the non-financial personal and corporate sector, stood at a staggering €1,671 billion. This was over eight times total gross national income at the time. Further cause for concern arose from the fact that the State was accountable for only €51 billion of this debt. The private sector, on the other hand, accounted for €1,549 billion of the debt, which had more than doubled in the preceding two years, when the worst excesses of the manically uncontrolled financial system in Ireland were practiced. This was leaving the Irish State and its citizens vulnerable internationally. Overall foreign claims on the Irish economy in 2008 stood at a staggering seven times our national income. Further 'enlightened' economic thinking would be required in order to postpone the inevitable and fast-approaching day of reckoning.

Chapter 7

Lehmans

The collapse of Enron Inc. undoubtedly caused shock waves to reverberate around the financial and political systems, in America and worldwide. A detailed investigation by Congress finally revealed the true extent of the market manipulation and fraud indulged in by the major participants, and Kenneth Lay and Jeff Skilling received long prison sentences for their particular roles. It remains a fact, however, that the USA decided not to learn any of the lessons that the case provided. Indeed, if anything, rather like the authors of the Enron scam, it appears as if the decision was taken by Government authorities that the financial ruse was so far down the line that the only option left was to continue with market manipulation and deceit.

The ludicrous point had been reached in the development of the financial system worldwide that any decrease in stock valuations signalled the end of a company as a viable concern, notwithstanding any valuable contribution that company might be making with regard to services or employment or, indeed, if it was generating a profit. As was witnessed with Enron, the pursuit of increase in stock valuation became the paramount factor in business method and practice. In the final years before its collapse, although it was difficult to provide examples of any valid business service which it actually provided, Enron's stock valuation stood at dizzying heights on the stock exchange. All this evidence was available to government and economic experts in America and around the world, and yet the decision was taken to leave things alone. In fact, and in particular when George Bush and the Republicans gained control of Congress and the Senate, the masters of free-market capitalism were to be given ever more freedom to continue the fraudulent manipulation of the stock exchange for their own personal gain.

Light, or indeed, non-regulation of business was to continue to be the order of the day. Further ingenious business methods and practices, or 'wheezes' as they were referred to in Enron, were to be allowed on the basis that they created, or at least appeared to create, incredible amounts of new money on the stock exchange. Sub-prime, Credit Default Swaps, Derivatives, Securitisation and Short-selling were but a few of the new business products and practises which were allowed by governments which disdainfully disregarded the dangers that products such as these contained. These products were, by and large, the instruments with which newly formed private investment funds with recourse to vast amounts of largely unregulated cash effectively bet on the stock markets, further artificially distorting, and ultimately, weakening it to such a degree that its ultimate collapse was inevitable.

A pattern, similar to that which was described earlier with regard to Enron, was beginning to emerge. Stock market valuations had reached their ceiling, yet the business psychology of the day required that valuations continued to rise. Innovative business products and practices were required to maintain the semblance of continued upward growth. Fortunately, for those tasked with discovering an escape from this apparent cul-de-sac, they would be given carte-blanche by government and regulatory authorities to come up with any policies which might have the desired effect. Unrestrained by government watchdogs, who had long-since abdicated their role as defenders of the public interest in favour of the wealth-creators, they were comfortably numb to the obvious dangers which lurked within these products that they so enthusiastically endorsed. Surely, even the most rudimentary examination of a concept such as Sub-prime by an intelligent person possessing even a modicum of business acumen would have alerted them to the fact that this was a practice which went against all standards of good practice and would inevitably result in catastrophe.

Instead, the business knowledge and experience acquired over generations were discarded by those who should have known better when they were presented with the possibility of further aggrandisement. The allure of wealth, once conceded to absolutely, will, it appears, leave the victim with an insatiable desire for more and incapable of even the most elementary degree of rational thinking. How else could one explain the acceptance of Sub-prime lending by, it appeared, everyone within the banking community? It is an insult to intelligence to suggest, as some would have us believe now, that it is only with the benefit of hindsight that it could have been foreseen that this outrageous indulgence in reckless and fraudulent money making contained within it the elements which would bring the world's financial system to its knees.

Subprime lending in the mortgage industry was the product which can be identified as one of the primary toxins to infect the financial system and eventually cause its demise. The brainchild of reckless, irresponsible and greedy entrepreneurs who were content to ignore the safeguards of traditional mortgage lending policy and logic in their undignified rush to enrich themselves through the high risk lending it entailed, it would, however, have had no disastrous effect on the system as a whole if it had been ignored by the traditional banking system.

However, the traditional mortgage lenders were seduced by the huge profits which the subprime lenders were making and eventually over-rode their own initial scepticism and plunged wholeheartedly into the same illogical and high-risk enterprise. The fact that banking institutions eventually ended up buying enormous packages of mortgage debt which they themselves would have recoiled from issuing in the first place is but one more example of the irrational, indeed idiotic, behaviour which ensued when the temptation of extraordinary wealth became too great to refuse.

Subprime mortgage lending was basically the practice by newly established mortgage lenders of lending to customers who would have failed to acquire a mortgage from the traditional lending institutions. Usually this would be on account of the applicants' inability to satisfy the safety requirements which were inbuilt into the traditional mortgage lending institutions' packages. These would include, in the nineties at least, the need for an applicant to possess a considerable deposit or down payment, the verification of a relatively dependable income and an independent valuation of the property being bought. All the above criteria would eventually be dispensed with as the numbers of newly established subprime lenders increased and they fought each other for their share of an ever-increasing market. Traditional lending houses initially questioned some of the business practices, such as the aggressive lending and doubtful accounting measures. However, as the numbers of lenders in the subprime market tripled from 70 to 210 between 1993 and

1997 and these companies saw an increase in originations from $523 billion to $5,125 billion in the same period, the traditional lending institutions' resolve began to waver.

When the subprime market was hit by its own crisis in 1998 for a variety of reasons, and six of the top ten subprime lenders went out of business, the traditional commercial banks had their judgements clouded by the apparently tasty rewards on offer, and they jumped at the opportunity to fill the vacuum that had arisen in the very market they had previously warned was unsound and unstable. Many of the leading Wall Street investment banks, such as JP Morgan Chase, Citibank and Bank of America, took the opportunity to acquire former subprime lenders or to enter the market themselves. The financial system itself was becoming ever more increasingly contaminated by toxic loans, which were issued without the safeguard of traditional banking good practice. The finance system of the world's leading capitalist country, the USA, was becoming ever more dependent on the ability of the least well-off in that country to continue to repay their debts. That these people had been granted their loans without having to satisfy the traditional requirements with regard to deposit and secure income, in particular, should have been a cause for great concern.

In fact, Wall Street firms and private investors enthusiastically endorsed the subprime product when they were given their first opportunity to do so. This endorsement occurred through the acquisition by banks, financial institutions and private investors of mortgage-backed securities, Collateralised Debt Obligations and Credit Default Swaps. These were all new products, 'securities or derivatives', which were heavily contaminated by toxic subprime mortgages. From the very beginning, in the 1990s, when debt from subprime lenders was packaged into Mortgage-backed securities and enthusiastically bought up by banks and other institutions, there appeared to be a keenness to legitimise this risky lending which also provided impetus for expansion of this product in the market.

The same endorsement is evident in the next product which the banks produced, Collateralised Debt Obligations, or CDOs, which incorporated the subprime loans they had acquired through mortgage-backed securities. The banks bundled together packages of 'high-yield' but 'high-risk' subprime debt and included some 'low-risk' debt from safer 'traditional mortgages'. This was apparently sufficient to earn these predominantly high-risk packages, or CDOs, a Double and indeed Triple A rating from the credit rating agencies. These CDOs were then sold on to other banks and institutions, many of them in Europe, where banks had access to cash deposits from a traditionally stronger deposit market than that which existed in America. This process further legitimised these toxic mortgage products and inculcated them ever more deeply at the very core of the financial system, where the damage they would cause, should there be defaults on a significant scale, would indeed be catastrophic.

This cataclysmic conclusion became ever more likely with the advent of a financial product which was produced to generate even more profit for the banks and financial institutions which wished, and indeed were required by stock market demands at the time, to demonstrate continued growth and upward annual movement in share price. The similarities with Enron become even more evident with the development of Credit Default Swaps as the latest financial product on the stock exchange which seemed, in the best traditions of Enron, to create enormous amounts of capital out of thin air.

Credit Default Swaps (CDSs) were conceived as a method of insuring the 'high-risk' mortgage-backed securities which the banks and financial institutions worldwide had bought up in enormous quantities in the previous years. The banks that had bought these securities generally used them as a means to increase their capital base, which in turn allowed them to borrow more money, which they would frequently use in order to repeat the process. Banks, however, were required by international banking regulations (Basel 11) to ensure that they maintain adequate capital in reserve to cover their loan book. The riskier the loans, the greater the amount of capital the banks are required to maintain in reserve. But the accepted financial wisdom in the bullish and unrestrained banking circles of the era was to leverage to the extreme in an attempt to increase profits.

Leveraging, in the case of the banks, was the practice of increasing the spread between the amount they paid for deposits and the amount they could earn from lending to its maximum. Banks wished to invest in the 'high-yield', though 'high-risk', profits that were available through the subprime-packed, mortgage-backed securities. This, though, would have a negative effect on their ratings by the credit rating agencies, as they would be perceived to be holding risky loans. Consequently, they would be required, by Basel 11 regulations, to maintain more cash in reserve as collateral than they would have wished. To overcome this, the banks decided to insure the risky loans they possessed in their portfolios. They could then receive high credit ratings and continue to leverage or over-extend their lending without any requirement to maintain adequate collateral in reserve. Credit Default Swaps were the instrument employed to insure these risky subprime mortgage-backed securities.

The giant insurance firm AIG was one of the predominant forces in the CDS market. It undertook to insure these high-risk subprime mortgages for possibly a five-year period at an annual cost of a small percentage of the total amount to be insured. This released the banks from their commitments under Basel 11, which were, of course, in place as a protection mechanism for the banking system itself, and allowed them continue their reckless over-leveraging. The insurance companies benefited from the huge fees they obtained from the premiums they received each year. Taking a leaf out of Enron's book again, they also used 'mark to market' accounting to book the complete profit from the five-year deal in the first year, thereby allowing them to announce startling profits at year end, which in turn resulted in huge bonus payments for directors and executives.

These startling results, for both investment and insurance institutions, were all predicated, however, on the stock market valuations continuing to rise and contained not one iota of consideration for the possibility of default. This was all the more alarming when one considers that the CDSs, though insurance policies at heart, were not liable or accountable to normal insurance regulations. These financial products (CDSs) were completely unregulated, and AIG and other giant insurance corporations were not, unbelievably, required to provide collateral for the massive insurance policies they were issuing. Again, financial institutions were allowed to behave recklessly, simply banking on a positive outcome to their bets when, in fact, these were ever more likely to end in disaster. All the more so when one considers that these countless new financial products – which were being endlessly re-packaged, re-branded and sold on in order to magically create apparently enormous new capital from thin air – were in fact dependant on the highly questionable ability of the poorest minority homeowners in the USA to continue to repay huge mortgages which had been lent to them.

It is important to stress that it is the irresponsible lending by the financial institutions which lies at the heart of this matter: it is they who bear the blame for what transpired later. The investment banks' lust for wealth simply knew no bounds. They had dispensed with traditional banking norms, such as stress testing, provision of adequate collateral and prudent lending, which would have provided safeguards against financial disaster on a catastrophic scale. It was to transpire, for example, that AIG did not have the capital to back up the insurance that it sold through the CDSs because it conveniently pronounced that they did not expect a default, a fact that illustrates perfectly the devil-may-care attitude which prevailed at the very top of the business community. Unfortunately this was but the beginning of the calamitous effect which Credit Default Swaps were to have on the financial system. Having initially been introduced as a means for institutions to insure or 'hedge' against the possibility of default of a bond or loan, or a downgrade in credit rating, it did not take the main investors in the stock market long to identify another more beneficial way to exploit these for their own financial gain.

This second method of deploying CDSs in the market was of an even more cynical nature and contained within it the capability of destroying the stock market itself. Private investment funds, or hedge funds as they are known, were quick to recognise the boundless possibilities which CDSs afforded to reap spectacular rewards when used in a different manner from that which was initially intended. CDSs afforded the opportunity to investors or speculators to take a position on a company's worth without having to buy the actual bonds or shares. This was the 'supercasino' which was referred to in an earlier chapter, in which the real capital which had been previously sucked out of the financial system was used to place bets on the credit quality or worthiness of a particular entity on the stock exchange. Investors who took a positive view of the credit position of companies or entities on the stock exchange could sell CDSs, or insurance protection, and collect the annual fees which accrued, instead of spending a lot of money buying shares in that company. More worryingly, for a very small annual fee, speculators who took a negative view of an entity's credit outlook could buy insurance protection, or CDSs, on a company in which they had no shares, and could then reap the huge rewards in the form of insurance payouts if that company failed.

There was now no real incentive to buy shares in the stock market. The real capital resided outside the stock market, in the supercasino which was the playground of the super-rich speculators in the hedge funds. The fact that the CDS market ballooned in the ten-year period up to 2007 to $45 trillion dollars – twice the size of the total value of the US Stock market at the time – serves to illustrate the point. The US stock market was, along with many of its worldwide counterparts, in fact stocked with worthless shares which were worth little more than the paper they were written on. This of course left easy pickings for those hedge fund managers who read the situation correctly and could bet, to their hearts' content, that many (if not most) of the companies on the stock market were liable to fail in the foreseeable future. This was like shooting fish in a barrel, save for the fact that they were dealing with real people's lives and livelihoods.

Hedge fund manager John Paulsen made a $3.7 billion dollar profit in 2007 when he correctly predicted the collapse of the US subprime market. At its peak hedge funds grabbed two trillion dollars to manage, illustrating clearly once again that the real capital had left the financial system and that all that remained was a paper trail of worthless shares. This was the feeding ground which the hedge funds could gorge themselves on, once the implications of the collapse of the subprime market worked itself through a financial system which had collaborated so wholeheartedly in introducing this toxic element into its own workings.

With the collapse of the US subprime market, and with many hedge funds relentlessly betting on the collapse of banking and other financial entities on the stock markets of the world, events quickly turned the subprime fiasco into a catastrophic crisis. The credit crunch occurred when banks began to hoard any available cash, as they were unsure as to the extent of the toxic loans that they themselves were holding in the mortgage-backed securities and other such products that they had bought in the preceding years. They were also reluctant to lend to other banks, as they were unsure of the extent of the bad loans these were holding. This led to a drying up of liquidity, which resulted in the first public indicator that there was a problem in the financial system when the European Central Bank injected €71 billion into continental money markets on 7 August 2007.

This was quickly followed by Northern Rock seeking emergency financial support from the Bank of England on 12 September of the same year. In October Citigroup in America announced $6.5billion of losses and write-downs on sub-prime related debt. In March 2008 the US Federal Reserve engineered a rescue takeover of the broker Bear Stearns by JP Morgan, the first such bail-out since the great depression of 1929. On 7 September 2008 the Federal Reserve Chairman, Henry Paulson, took the decision to nationalise the giant sub-prime mortgage companies Fanny Mae and Freddie Mack, as it was decided that to let them fail would have disastrous effect on the mortgage market. Then, on Black Monday September 15, Lehman Brothers became the biggest bankruptcy in US history, Merrill Lynch succumbed to a rescue takeover by Bank of America, and the giant insurance company AIG scrambled for capital to ensure its survival. Global stock markets took a pummelling and, only three weeks later, the Government of Ireland resolved to guarantee all deposits, bonds and debts in the six main banks, a decision that amounted to the most monumental mistake in the history of this State.

Chapter 8

It's the economy, stupid!

The shockwaves that followed the collapse of Lehmans Banks were not confined to stock exchanges alone. This colossal collapse in the business world was of such magnitude that it lifted the fast-developing financial disaster from the business sections of the media to mainstream headline news, for probably the first time. The possible disastrous effects on economies and societies worldwide, and the calamitous consequences that could unfold if this really did signify a meltdown in the financial system, suddenly became more apparent to politicians, economic commentators and the public in general. The print media, in particular, in England, sections of which had been forecasting for some time, that a significant 'negative event' was about to occur within the international financial system, were well placed to inform and educate their readership as to the importance of what was happening. Having long-since despaired and dispensed with the media in Ireland as a reliable and unbiased source of information, I discovered that sections of the media in Britain provided a far more comprehensive and instructive coverage of the financial world.

Robert Peston, the BBC business editor, who was widely credited with breaking the Northern Rock bankruptcy story, deserves tremendous credit and praise for the manner in which he kept the public informed, through his television reports and, more particularly, his impressive blogs, on the dire situation confronting the world. Thanks largely to the sterling efforts of journalists such as Peston on the BBC and Will Hutton, writing in the *Guardian* and *Observer* newspapers, the average man in the street who wished to be kept informed as to events in the financial world could have access to the same information as those in the know in the business world. As a person who had some years previously become convinced that the financial system was fatally flawed and was careering irrationally towards inevitable collapse, the information which responsible journalists, such as Hutton and his colleagues on the *Observer*, provided, helped convince me that the disaster which I had imagined previously was, indeed, on the verge of occurring. These journalists' professionalism served the British public well and afforded the most perceptive and receptive amongst them the opportunity to prepare to some extent for the impending disaster which was about to unfold. The contrast with Ireland, and the complete and utter unawareness of politicians, economic commentators, the media and therefore the public in general as to what was occurring, could not have been starker or more shocking.

As has been outlined earlier, the natural 'ceiling' in share valuations on the Irish Stock exchange was reached as early as 2001. The 'share price' of housing and property, on which, realistically, all shares were dependant and through which they had previously boomed, had stalled. From then on, the outlandish rises in those self-same shares were achieved by means of artificial methods or 'valve opening', as I call them, which flushed new capital into an already precariously unstable financial system with seemingly no thought for the disastrous consequences this would have for the economy or, more importantly still, for society itself. That those decisions were taken with such complete disregard for the welfare of people should come as no surprise. This was a basic tenet of the economic and political doctrine of the period. There was no such thing as 'society', with its implicit demands for fairness, respect and inclusion, according to these disciples of Margaret Thatcher. Wealth was created by individuals, who should be allowed to keep that wealth. This was the period when the most respected and valued members of 'high society' were those who could make, or at least appear to make, money from money. Money, and those who appeared to have the ability to create it, was the subject of glorification on a scale that resembled idolatry. The corollary of worshipping at the high altar of the fat cats of capitalism was, of course, a barely concealed contempt for those unfortunate enough to find themselves on the wrong side of that capital divide.

This was the prevailing philosophy. It permeated every element of society, eventually becoming a mantra which all were required to adopt. It had been enthusiastically welcomed by the 'golden circle', zealously endorsed by politicians, economic commentators and leaders of the business world who appreciated the untold opportunities it awarded them to amass previously unimaginable wealth. It dictated thinking in politics to such an extent that every policy decision was taken in terms only of what the 'economy' required. The decision to base government policy exclusively on the requirements of the economy and to ignore totally any possible effects on society, was to lead to levels of inequality that threatened its very fabric.

Inequality, as the former PD leader Michael McDowell so infamously remarked, was the welcome result of the freedom of individuals to create and retain wealth. If inequality did not exist it would, he argued, have to be created for the sake of a properly functioning economy. His former party colleague Mary Harney, when asked to comment on the rising levels of inequality, arrogantly remarked that "not all of us could play in the Premiership". Both of these ex-Tánaistí apparently felt comfortable in publicly revealing the extent of their contempt for those less well-off in society. Moreover, both McDowell and Harney understood that, by the time they made those remarks, political debate regarding matters such as equality and fairness in Ireland had all but ceased. The PD agenda had been adopted wholeheartedly by Fianna Fáil, who recognised immediately the opportunities it afforded them to enrich their friends in the 'golden circle'. This exclusive club, which, as we have seen, had their fingers in the greasy till of every financial and tax evasion scandal in the history of the State, now had their operations sanctioned by PD philosophy. No need to concern yourself about illegal tax avoidance and tax evasion when the prevailing political philosophy encouraged the creation of extraordinary personal wealth and facilitated, by legal means, tax avoidance and evasion.

Fine Gael provided no opposition, as it saw its natural soul mates in the PDs implementing policies that it endorsed completely. The Labour Party, however, stands indicted for the appalling manner in which it abdicated totally its responsibility to instigate debate and offer the public the opportunity to appreciate the contrary options available. In many respects, its role in facilitating those who committed this financial deceit is deserving of most opprobrium. One could hardly have expected the right wing ideologists within The PDs, or Fine Gael, or the supporters of the 'Golden circle' in Fianna Fáil, to lead the debate against the tide of free-market capitalism that was benefiting them so generously. But surely it was incumbent upon members of the Labour Party, as proponents of the concept of fairness and justice for all, to represent those who believed that these elements were fundamental to any civilised society. This, the Labour Party lamentably failed to do. One cannot but believe that the majority of its members wearied of the battle to get their message across, in the face of the unyielding opposition amongst political opponents, economic commentators and a hostile media. Others within the Labour Party, frankly, seemed to accept the unassailable position of rampant capitalism and appeared to be seduced by the comforts it undoubtedly bestowed on them too.

The voice in the wilderness of real and meaningful debate during this period, that of the only socialist member of the Dáil, Joe Higgins, was the one solitary exception. Higgins, an excellent Dáil performer, was, to all intents and purposes, the opposition during his period in the Dáil, constantly highlighting the inequity and the inherent dangers that lurked within government policy. His commitment to his ideals, which he patently held with deep conviction, served him well in his lonely battle with his opponents who occupied the majority of the Dáil chamber. His dogged determination, his intelligent arguments, whether you agreed with all of them or not, and his quick wit and eloquence, made him the bane of the Taoiseach, Bertie Ahearn. On one occasion, in a memorable rant by the Taoiseach, Higgins was accused of being a "failed politician" and a supporter of a "failed and discredited ideology," words which will surely serve as an adequate political epitaph for the ex-Taoiseach himself.

Higgins's reward for his sterling work as leader of the opposition for five years in the Dáil was to lose his seat in the general election in 2007. That the public were to turn against the very TD who would ultimately prove to have provided the correct analysis at the very time when the economic fraud that was committed on them was beginning to unravel, and instead return the very parties that had instigated the scam, was ironic indeed. It also demonstrates how the public were still completely unaware of what was going on.

This ignorance and unawareness on the part of the public was an essential and distinguishing component in the success of the entire deceit. Its origins lay in the vacuum that occurred within political debate as the overwhelming majority of Dáil members became disciples of the doctrine of free-market capitalism, supported by economic commentators, the new religion's high-priests. These gurus – such as Jim Power, of Friends First, Austin Hughes at IIB Bank and Dan McLaughlin, of the Bank of Ireland – drank from the same ideological well as Mary Harney and Charlie McCreevy and brashly lectured the public about what was best for the country. In common with the politicians, their respect was reserved for those who had the ability to create money, and their only concern was to propose policy that would facilitate those wealth creators. They contemptuously dismissed any possibility of discussion on these matters and stifled debate, fortified by an intellectual arrogance on matters economic that knew no bounds. Their unrestrained egos were to scale ever increasing heights as the value of the stock market rose to unbelievable levels, supporting, they appeared to believe, their view of themselves as economic commentators beyond reproach. This hubris was illustrated time and again during this period and was accompanied by the same contempt as the PDs had for those in society who did not possess the wherewithal to create wealth.

After all, if you could not create wealth in the conditions that they and their political masters had created, you were obviously incompetent, unintelligent or lazy. Those who believed in fairness, equality of opportunity and justice, or in the concept of service to the State were, in their view of the world, seen as parasites whose only means of survival was to leach the riches of the super wealthy they were so painfully envious of. It was nauseating in the extreme to hear Power, in particular, as a regular commentator on public radio, gleefully revealing his contempt for the thousands of nurses, teachers, firemen and other public servants who, he proclaimed, "contributed nothing to the economy." Nurses, in particular, found to their cost what the general acceptance of the free-market capitalists' ideology meant in reality. Although it appeared to be generally accepted that their pay claim was entirely justified, it was to be refused because it would result in similar claims by those in other areas of the public service and would therefore be a threat to the sacred benchmarking system. All the major players – politicians, economists and media commentators – therefore rallied the forces, as was their wont on occasions such as these, to wage a concerted campaign to defeat the nurses, who were seen as a threat to the privileged positions they had carved out for themselves in Ireland's new economic model.

Nurses might be hard-working, compassionate, caring professionals who deserved respect and gratitude for the work they did in difficult and stressful circumstances, but they did not, after all, contribute anything to the economy. They did not create wealth. In fact, they were a burden on the exchequer, and therefore they could not expect to share in the spoils that had been created by the architects of the Celtic Tiger. The ferocity of the campaign that was waged against sections of society which had the temerity to seek to introduce an element of fairness into the distribution of the wealth created by the Celtic Tiger economy shows how our value system had been twisted to perversion. A new value system was in place which relegated nurses to the third division and substituted them with those who made a financially identifiable contribution to the economy. Entrepreneurs, economists, developers, bankers, barristers and builders were the darlings of this new and exciting Ireland. This overthrow of the old values and issuing-in of the new was heralded by the PR gurus through the media.

The nurses' demand for fairness in pay scales provides an insight into this phenomenon which threatened to undermine our entire democratic system. When originally made, their pay claim struck a chord with the public in general, who intuitively understood and respected the contribution they made to society. This support was, however, to dissipate in the face of the concerted campaign waged by the all-powerful elements in the Celtic Tiger coalition. The threat that the health carers' pay claim posed to the national pay agreements and benchmarking processes was deemed too great.

This pay mechanism had been assiduously put in place to control any possibility of a redistribution of the enormous wealth which those who orchestrated it had amassed. The politicians and economic gurus, in particular, heaped opprobrium on this impertinent section of the workforce which dared threaten the mechanisms which served their interests so well. It was the economy, stupid, and nothing – not even one of the most essential elements of a correctly functioning society, in this case an effective and equitable health service – would be allowed to stand in the way. Unfortunately, so effective had the propagandists for Celtic Tiger Ireland been in selling their particular brand of 'society', that it was no great surprise that the majority of the public chose to support 'the economy'. In mitigation for this betrayal of values for which the people of Ireland are traditionally renowned, it must be acknowledged that they were now indelibly wedded to the Celtic Tiger project. By dint of the fact that everybody was linked to property in some manner or form, and that property was the basis for all wealth, or at least perceived wealth, it was in everybody's' interest that nothing be allowed to disturb the smooth progress of this particular gravy train. Another mitigating factor was that the public were being manipulated towards supporting this particular model of economic philosophy by a force that was at least as powerful as the original authors, namely the media.

If a balanced and independent legislature, representing the totality of diverse opinions and ideologies and encouraging passionate yet reasoned discussion and debate in the interests of the greater good is a basic requirement in an effectively functioning democracy, then a truthful and truly independent media is not only desirable, but essential, in ensuring that that legislature is held to account and that the interests of all the people are served. The members of the 'Third Estate' were historically charged with ensuring that the legislature behaved responsibly and in accordance with the honourable principles at the heart of democratic governance. It will be to the eternal shame of the media in Ireland that the principles that lay at the core of this profession were jettisoned and that the public it was charged to inform and protect was so wantonly abandoned to the whims of fate.

A primary factor in this betrayal was, of course, that the giant news corporations no longer saw themselves as existing to protect the public. They were now global media enterprises which existed, as any other business enterprise does, to accumulate wealth for its executives and shareholders through the stock exchange. This crucial change resulted in the media not just facilitating the spread of free-market doctrine, but eventually collaborating completely in the indoctrination of the public at large. This phenomenon was illustrated on the world stage by the influence wielded by giant news corporations, such as those belonging to Rupert Murdoch and Ted Turner. They gained such a monopolistic control that they could inculcate the public with their free-market philosophy unopposed. In Italy, Silvio Berlusconi's control of private media was such that he could orchestrate his own election as Prime Minister, an event that left him subsequently in control of 98% of all media in the State, private and public. Ireland, of course, would not be spared the curse of agenda-dictated media.

Tony O'Reilly's Independent News and Media Corporation was a massive enterprise, with media assets worldwide, including the prestigious *Independent* title in Britain amongst its banner possessions. In Ireland O'Reilly controlled five major print titles, including the influential *Irish* and *Sunday Independent*, which had the biggest readership during this period. These newspapers, along with the others in the INM group, were the flag bearers for the Celtic Tiger phenomenon, and their carefully selected commentators ensured that the free-market agenda was relentlessly sold to the public. The contemptuous tone adopted by the feature writers in the *Sunday Independent*, in particular, to dismiss any perceived threat to the conventional wisdom of their particular agenda, and their arrogance in nauseatingly celebrating its excesses, perfectly represented the value system of Celtic Tiger Ireland. Although Tony O'Reilly would claim that he always respected the independence of editorial control at his media titles, it would be wise to remember the remarks of Andrew Neil, the former editor of the *Sunday Times*, on this matter. Writing on the subject of editorial independence, in his case from the Australian media mogul Rupert Murdoch, Neil wrote that it would be crazy to think that an editor would take a newspaper in any policy direction other than the one he indicated he would when he was hired.

Another entrepreneur who built a vast empire in the media arena was Denis O'Brien. With the benefit of the massive fortune he accrued from the sale of a national asset, ESAT, the first mobile phone licence, he set about establishing a foothold in the radio and television worlds which would eventually see him rival O'Reilly as the predominant mover in this field in Ireland and making full use of his power to propagate his economic philosophy through his media outlets' primetime news and talk shows. The presenters chosen to host them invariably preached free-market capitalism, ensuring that that agenda was predominant on Newstalk and Today FM, two of the jewels in the crown of the O'Brien media empire. O'Brien appeared to hold the view that the creation of wealth should be the exclusive aspiration for mankind. Those who possessed the ability to create vast wealth were entrepreneurial geniuses, entitled to hold a predominant position over other mere mortals. This was illustrated perfectly in the contemptuous manner in which he publicly refused to accept that he held a moral, if not legal responsibility, to pay tax on the vast personal profit he made from the sale of the ESAT Digifone licence. This was his money created through his entrepreneurial prowess, and he was entitled to keep it. Contributing to a tax system which funded a universal health and education system was far beneath his exalted status, and conveniently the tax legislation introduced by the Fianna Fáil/PD government supported this stance. The continual interplay between the members of this cosy coalition, a relationship that ensured that the system would continue to function to their mutual advantage, was clearly evident again.

Further evidence, if required, that these forces were at play and were continuously distorting the picture which the public was being presented with comes from *The Irish Times*. Formerly a highly respected newspaper with a reputation for fairness and propriety, it was to become embroiled in the conspiracy of complacency and silence as a result of a number of factors. That a former Progressive Democrat TD, Geraldine Kennedy, was editor unfortunately ensured that every major commercial title now had that party's philosophy represented at its core. That the newspaper itself, like its major competitor, *The Irish Independent*, became almost entirely dependant on the property market through the enormous advertising revenues generated by their property sections, completely compromised its independence. Its dependence was exacerbated further when *The Irish Times* acquired the Property website MyHome.ie for a staggering €50 million in 2006. The acquisition of this property advertising website at the very peak of market prices, when signs were clear that the bubble was beginning to deflate provides damning evidence that the controlling forces at the newspaper were as incapable as others to resist the lure of the riches which seemed to accrue from the property market.

The same year that *The Irish Times* acquired their financial millstone, MyHome.ie, Allied Irish Bank sold property they possessed in the prime location in Ballsbridge for €377 million, having sold a similar site a year previously for a similar amount. At a time when the main architects of the property bubble were recognising that the peak had been reached and had begun to dispose of assets for princely sums, a national newspaper which should have been in a position to inform and advise the general public of the significance this held for the property market was, instead, itself clambering with unseemly haste onto the runaway train laden with lucre from the property bubble. That the huge debt incurred in buying MyHome.ie subsequently distorted the coverage that *The Irish Times* gave to events in the property and, by extent, the political world which propagated the myth, is beyond question. Constantly ignoring the signs, which were appearing daily, that the bubble was deflating, the newspaper chose to consistently 'talk up' events and mislead their readership in the process.

One example of the manipulation which all newspapers indulged in comes from the manner in which the fall in share prices on the Dublin Stock market was reported. From the 2006 high of 10,000 points, there had followed alarming falls which suggested that a massive negative event was occurring not just in Ireland, but worldwide. The ever increasing downward spiral was punctuated by massive jolts, which saw the markets lose enormous value in daily trading sessions. On one such occasion, Black Monday, 19 March 2007, 4%, or €4 billion, was wiped off the value of Irish share values; and on Thursday 22 November 2007 the value of Irish shares dropped an unbelievable €8 billion in one day's trading. The significance of this was evident to anyone with even a passing interest in economic affairs, but to someone who had been forecasting a massive implosion in the financial system itself it was alarming evidence that that eventuality was fast approaching. Significantly, the following day *The Irish Times* did not lead with this truly shocking story, with its disastrous implications for the public at large. Indeed, it did not even make the front page, nor was it discussed in the editorial. Instead, it was relegated to the business section of the newspaper, far from the eyes of the general readership.

This failure by the media to properly report the collapse of the property-based financial system in Ireland, due to the compromised position they occupied within it themselves, would leave the public unaware of the dire situation which faced them, stifled debate and discussion which could have enhanced the decision-taking process when the disaster occurred, and leaves the media in the dock, accused of a shameful dereliction of its duty to the people.

The situation with the national broadcaster RTÉ one would have expected to be rather different. As a public corporation, with a remit to serve the public interest and the citizen in an independent manner, one would have expected RTÉ to remain loyal to its remit of defending the interests of the people and to preserve its independence from government interference. However, many of the fundamental principles of public service broadcasting worldwide had been undermined in the preceding quarter of a century. This change in the ethos of public-service broadcasting occurred over a period of time, but its origins can be traced back to the 1970s and stemmed from tensions that arose between the government of Margaret Thatcher and the state-sponsored public service broadcaster in Britain, the BBC.

In the years before and after the 1979 general election in Britain, Margaret Thatcher became increasingly fixated with what she perceived as being a left-wing inspired anti-government agenda within the BBC. She was particularly agitated by what she claimed was anti-government bias in the coverage of the Falklands War and the troubles in Northern Ireland. The BBC, however, claimed that they were acting as the 'trustees of the public interest', as they were constitutionally required to do, by reporting truthfully, objectively and impartially, a reputation for which they deservedly enjoyed worldwide. Thatcher, though, took grave exception, in particular, to a BBC report that highlighted the fact that an Argentinian battleship, the *Belgrano*, had been sunk, resulting in the deaths of 350 people, as it was leaving the exclusion zone that had been imposed around the Falklands. This was the last straw for Thatcher, who viewed it as treasonable, rather than the truthful reporting it undeniably was. With the aid of her trusted lieutenant, Norman Tebbit, she set in motion a series of events that would eventually have a profound effect on public service broadcasting not only in Britain, but around the globe.

To achieve her aim of curbing the BBC, she turned to Rupert Murdoch, the Australian media mogul who was in the process of acquiring a huge portfolio of print titles in Britain at the time. These, which included the tabloids *The Sun* and *The News of the World*, as well as the broadsheet *Daily Telegraph*, were used by Murdoch to cement his relationship with Thatcher, a relationship that was beneficial to both of them. Murdoch's titles waged a ferociously vindictive campaign against the Labour Party and constantly endorsed the policies of Thatcher and the Conservatives. The fact that an estimated three quarters of all unemployed people in Britain voted for Thatcher's Conservative party in the 1979 general election, in the process helping to ensure her victory, is generally attributed to the campaign waged through the pages of Murdoch's tabloid titles. It is indicative also of the power the media exerts, which is precisely the reason that there were strict regulations restricting monopoly in the area. Immediately after that election victory in 1979, however, Murdoch was permitted, despite concerns about his growing monopoly of the print media, to acquire the influential *Times* and *Sunday Times* titles.

When the licence for British Satellite broadcasting was subsequently awarded to Murdoch by a Thatcher-led cabinet which bypassed government policy regarding monopolisation at the time, two of the Prime Minister's aims had been achieved. With one of her staunchest supporters in control of five national newspapers, she could be assured that her political agenda was positively reinforced amongst their huge readerships, and simultaneously she had dealt a blow to the BBC. The loss of the satellite contract was a severe setback to an organisation which was already under pressure from the private terrestrial stations, such as London Weekend Television. Thatcher's next move was to challenge the licence fee, which was the very life blood of the public broadcaster. The continuation of the licence fee was made dependant on the BBC becoming, like their commercial competitors, entertainment centred, rather than concentrating on their previous commitment to educate, entertain and inform.

When John Birt was lured from London Weekend Television in 1987 to become head of programming at the BBC, this shift towards entertainment continued and another significant change occurred. Though delighted to be occupying one of the most prestigious positions in television broadcasting, Birt was forgoing a salary at the commercial LWT which was based on lucrative share schemes which could make millionaires of his former colleagues there. He decided, in his wisdom, to introduce new management and contractual pay agreements which greatly increased the remuneration which employees at the BBC enjoyed. This dilution of the principles of public service broadcasting by the commercial culture of private television stations was to have a profound effect on Public Service Broadcasting not only in Britain, but also in Ireland, where a similar confrontation between the leader of the government and the national broadcaster was to end with the citizens of the State very much the losers.

Ireland's version of this struggle between Government and the national broadcaster, whose independence it is constitutionally obliged to respect, dates back to a confrontation before the 1981 general election between the then Taoiseach, Charlie Haughey, and the governing body of RTÉ. Displeased with what he considered biased and negative coverage of his Government's performance from the State broadcaster, Haughey vowed, should he be successful in the election, to restrict RTÉ's influence. Shortly after claiming victory, Haughey and his Minister for Communications, Ray Burke, issued the licence for the first commercial national radio station to Century Radio and a raft of local radio licences including, incidentally, one to Denis O'Brien at 98FM. That decision remains to this day mired in controversy as an example of political cronyism at its worst. Although it undoubtedly heralded the welcome beginning of diversity within broadcasting, it, as well as many other licences subsequently issued, could never quite escape the cloud of suspected cronyism which hung over it.

Burke continued his campaign to undermine the National broadcaster when he placed a cap on advertisement revenue and also ordered the station to provide a costly transmission service to its newly licensed competitor, Century Radio. Despite Burke's apparent best efforts, Century Radio had difficulty in generating the audience and revenues which could challenge RTÉ on a national level. In desperation they attempted to lure the top presenters from the national broadcaster by offering lucrative contracts, far in excess of what they were previously earning. Though RTÉ managed to retain the services of their top stars, they were now in a much more difficult negotiating position than previously when entering into contract talks. A culture began to emerge which saw the top stars demand salaries commensurate with their perceived value to the station. Salaries rose at an alarming rate, and by 2004 the top ten presenters shared a total of €3.3 million between them. The top earner, Pat Kenny, took home a staggering €899,000, Gerry Ryan €350,000, and Marian Finucane €439,265. A spokesperson for RTÉ defended the salaries on the basis that they represented "the market rate".

When it is recalled that the RTÉ governing board, appointed by the government, had also presided over dramatic changes in staffing levels at the station in 1992, a picture emerges of an organisation fast adopting the culture and practises of the private commercial world, leaving it exposed to the inherent dangers which this represented. That presenters' impartiality, in particular regarding the debate concerning free-market capitalism, was subsequently compromised through the adoption of this commercial culture is beyond doubt. As a result of its implementation they had witnessed their salaries rise massively. Subconsciously, or otherwise, presenters on RTÉ have propagated the free-market mythology, allowing it to impinge on their impartiality and seriously damaging the station's reputation for fairness and balance as a result. When challenged to defend the huge salaries they earn, RTÉ's top-earners habitually adopt the same line. They brashly claim that they "are worth it" and that they earn millions for the corporation. When asked to defend his €350,000 salary in 2004 – a salary that rose to over €600,000 in 2008 – Gerry Ryan said the following:

"The only reason I'm paid is that RTÉ makes a huge amount of money through radio sales on the programme I present. That's the only reason anyone should be paid a large amount of money. It's a simple argument; you only get what you're worth and that's the way it is across the board. They can look, I make millions more for them than they pay me."

The government could indeed rest easy. Neither Mary Harney nor Charlie McCreevy could have said it better. The performance-related bonus payment ethos was now at the core of public service broadcasting, a fact that was to impinge greatly on its ability to inform the public in an impartial manner, as it was constitutionally required to do. The fact that employees of the station, particularly the 'star performers', were reaping massive financial rewards from liberal capitalism impaired their judgement and rendered them incapable of balanced debate on the issues that arose for society as a result of its adoption. A further contributory factor to the dearth of debate was the complacency which undoubtedly festers in the vacuum that is created by the absence of discourse.

This alarming complacency, which originated in the arrogance of the architects of the free-market model and was fed by the enormous wealth they were wallowing in, appeared to spread, unchecked, through all sectors of society, rendering them seemingly incapable of rational thought or behaviour. Irrational exuberance abounded. The false god of the property market, which had supposedly brought wealth and prosperity beyond our dreams, was beyond reproach or contradiction. That schools were being closed so that their sites could be sold to property developers who proceeded to build tiny apartments to house families whose children would have no local school to attend did not, it appears, raise alarm as to the effects of this policy on society. That pubs that only a few years previously had been seen as having a licence to print money were being shut in order to reap far greater rewards through the property market did not alert the public to the huge bubble being inflated in the economy. That, at a time when oil prices were going through the ceiling and heading for $150 dollars a barrel, petrol stations in Ireland were being closed to facilitate the building of houses and apartments did not instil a whit of disquiet was, quite frankly, outrageous. Arrogance, hubris, complacency and greed had brought us to the edge of the precipice. All that was required now was an unexpected jolt to send us over the edge.

Chapter 9

Shooting Fish in a Barrel!

Having come to the opinion many years ago that unfettered liberated capitalism was fundamentally flawed and manifestly unstable, my interest in matters financial and economic intensified as one alarming revelations after another reinforced my conviction that the system would end in meltdown. The Thatcherite principle of trickle down economics – which held that releasing wealth creators from any obligation to act like responsible members of society would result in beneficial returns to society – seemed to me an obvious contradiction in terms and indeed, as far as economic theory was concerned, a blatant falsehood. The notion that a rising tide of unrestrained economic wealth raised all boats appeared to be patently untrue, and in fact served only to exacerbate the two-tier society. The introduction of further inequality into the health, education and legal systems – fundamental elements in any properly functioning society – served only to highlight the fallacy even more blatantly. Inequality and unfairness had been introduced and legitimised by this model of liberated capitalism. This distasteful creed, which exclusively propagated the notion of self-advancement, eschewing any regard for morality or responsibility to society, lay at the core of the business and economic world from the early 1980s onwards. The last constraints on its worst excesses disappeared with the fall of the Soviet Union in 1989: "Greed was good," as Gordon Gekko, the main character in Oliver Stone's 1987 Film *Wall Street*, so memorably proclaimed.

It was greed, though, that was at the very heart of the financial disaster. To suggest that one side could extract outrageous profit from a transaction without this having a detrimental effect on the other party concerned was obviously utter nonsense. Paying €1,792 million of public money to acquire the M50, which cost only €38 million to build, was just one example. There was no reasonable correlation between an economic service, or good, provided and the price being demanded and paid for it. The market decided the value, and if this resulted in someone paying 1,000% multiples of profit, so be it. Far from discouraging excessive profit making in the financial system, the practice of lucratively rewarding employees and executives through bonus and incentive schemes actively encouraged it, and would eventually result in this model of finance cannibalising itself. Excessive profit making, we were lectured by the gurus of the economic and political worlds, would have no detrimental economic or social effect and in fact was to be celebrated because it rewarded entrepreneurial skills and was beneficial to all.

Convinced that this was sheer and utter nonsense, I began to question its viability, concluding that the only sensible answer to this economic lunacy was a cap on profits which would limit the most reckless excesses of a system which was ever more evidently spiralling out of control. Of this eventual calamitous outcome I was by 2003 becoming more and more certain. However, Irish proponents of Enron-style fraud became so accustomed to its seemingly guaranteed fantastic returns that an irrational confidence was cultivated which contained within it the seeds of inevitable destruction.

The fact that our competitiveness was being eroded by wages that were spiralling out of control as they pursued ridiculously inflated property prices is but one example. The arrogance and imperiousness of the masters of Celtic Tiger Ireland knew no bounds. They contemptuously dismissed the need for a rational appreciation and re-evaluation of the direction the economy was taking. The dramatic drop in the value of the ISEQ index of shares from its high of 10,000 in 2006 was ignored. Corporate collapses, such as that of the Dublin based International Securities Trading Corporation, which had been founded in 2005 by high profile investors such as Denis O'Brien, Sean Quinn, Dermot Desmond and Gary McGann, and was forced to suspend trading in November 2007, writing off over €70 million in the process, did not seem to register alarm.

The flight of capital from world stock markets to oil and gold was not considered relevant. Both these commodities rose to unprecedented levels during this period, with oil fast approaching $150 a barrel, and gold $1,000 an ounce, as jittery investors deserted the paper shares in which they were now losing confidence. Unemployment was on the rise, with the rate in Ireland jumping from 4.6% in 2007 to 6.6% in September 2008. The European Central Bank were intent on adhering to their stated policy of raising interest rates in an attempt to counteract inflation, which was on the rise and perceived as a threat to the European economy, but it was forced to reduce them, instead, in an attempt to stimulate the economy, which was beginning to slow down. The 'dammed if you do, dammed if you don't' situation which the ECB found itself in was a clear indicator that the system itself was failing. The fact that the European Central Bank was implementing economic policies which ran counter to their own perceived wisdom ought to have been worrying. In fact, all these indicators were symptoms of a much greater malaise which was lurking beneath the world's financial system, a malaise that could and should have been diagnosed.

In Ireland, as elsewhere, these warning signs were ignored. Arrogant confidence in the system that had seen them amass outrageous fortunes led our masters of wealth creation to believe that it was only a matter of time before circumstances would change and their vast stockpiles of share-based capital would return. Like the gambler in the casino who refuses to accept that the 'system' he has created that has brought him prosperity beyond his wildest dreams has simply failed him, they recklessly persevered in the belief that the wheel of fortune was bound to turn in their favour once more. But across the globe events were now conspiring against this eventuality. The hedge funds in the super-casino were busy ensuring that the last dollars and euros were being hovered up from the unfortunate suckers in the stock market. The real capital bets were being placed on the, by then, absolute certainty that these vast corporations and financial institutions were in fact piled high with toxic debt.

The activities of the hedge funds were the final throws of the dice by those who had corrupted the financial system to breaking point. The most astute of the hedge fund managers recognised that, through their own activities in particular, the stock market was polluted with financial institutions holding nothing but toxic debt. Believing that the creation of wealth and capital took precedence over all other considerations, they proceeded to 'take positions', or bet, on these companies failing. This was the economic equivalent of 'shooting fish in a barrel', save for the disconcerting fact that the fish being shot were, in fact, the millions of people employed in those corporations which were now, through the hedge funds' activities, doomed to failure.

When Lehmans Bank was allowed to collapse it set in motion a chain of events that shook up the world. The realisation that the world's stock exchanges were dealing in shares that had little or no real value saw share prices crumble to virtually nothing. The credit crunch took hold and, as fear gripped the markets and financial institutions, banks refused to lend to each other for fear of the crippling debt they could be holding. In the USA, panic the likes of which had not been witnessed since the Great Depression in the 1930' spread like wildfire. A massive emergency bail-out of the banks and financial institutions, worth a staggering $700 billion dollars, was announced. This decision caused outrage and ignited a fierce debate about the morality of bailing out the banks and investors of Wall Street who had gambled the economy to the very edge of the precipice while no help was forthcoming for the ordinary man and woman on Main Street who were losing their houses and jobs in ever increasing numbers.

Surprisingly, though, opposition to the bail-out plan came not just from the Democrats, but also from their supposed ideological opponents within the Republican Party. In truth, as had occurred in most western democracies in the eighties, there had been a monumental shift to the right by centre-left political parties. It could not, in all honesty, be claimed that the old traditional parties of the right, the Conservatives in Britain or the Republicans in America, were solely responsible for the economic chaos that spread through the financial world. Tony Blair in Britain and Bill Clinton in the USA endorsed fully the free-market ideology of their traditional foes and rendered real discourse and debate within politics almost redundant. However, remnants of the left did state their commitment to equity and fairness on the occasion of the bail-out.

The outrageous injustice at the heart of the bail-out proposal was so blatantly obvious that it reignited political debate along the old ideological divide for the first time in a generation. With both sides of that divide having spent the previous thirty years of one mind as regards the free-market ideology, and having cited the amazing wealth it created as evidence of the effectiveness of keeping government out of the affairs of business and the market, it was now suggested that, now that that ball of wealth had turned into a ball of debt, that debt be turned over to the government – or, in reality, the taxpayer. This proposal was, thankfully, a step too far for some Democrats, who rediscovered their commitment to equality, justice and their natural supporters and by many Republicans who saw it as an unfair and unwarranted interference in a correctly functioning system of capitalism. Amazingly and ironically, they were joined in their opposition to the bail-out by the staunchest of free-market capitalists within the Republican Party, whose hatred for government interference in the market was so great that they would have seen that market collapse rather than let the government take shares in their prized free-market financial institutions. Their better senses were appealed to by the Chairman of the Federal Reserve, the ultra right-wing Hank Paulsen, who declared that it also made him "sick to his stomach" to sanction government intervention of this sort, but that the situation was so dire that, in the President George Bush's own words, "if money wasn't loosened up, this sucker (the financial system) could go down."

Astoundingly, the right-wing zealots among the Republicans walked away from the deal, and world stock markets plunged once again. Hank Paulson was required to interrupt a meeting of top Democrats who were discussing the bail-out and go on bended knee before their Speaker, Nancy Pelosi, begging her not to "blow up" the deal. When the Democrats angrily turned on Paulsen, blaming the Republicans for the mess they were in, Paulson replied: "I know, I know." A deal was struck and, by 3 October, the $700 billion buy-out of toxic debt was sanctioned by the House of Representatives.

Here in Ireland the dramatic events which had culminated in the collapse of Lehmans had a prolonged adverse effect on our already precariously positioned financial system. The startling fall in the ISEQ index of top one hundred shares continued at an ever more alarming pace. During August 2008, the share prices of our leading corporations would leave no-one in any doubt as to the frightening pace at which the economic meltdown was occurring. Page upon page of red figures on the Irish Stock Exchange made extremely uncomfortable viewing. On many occasions Irish financial institutions fell 20% and 30% in value in the course of one day's trading. Many of the leading quoted companies had lost an astounding 90% of their market value from their peaks of one and two years previously. The property market had slowed to a standstill, but economists and property market experts were still reporting the fall in property prices as being of the order of 20% from market peak. The strange anomaly of a stock exchange which was almost exclusively based on the property industry having fallen 90% in valuation while the property market itself, we were being asked to believe, had only fallen 20% to 30%, and was approaching a floor, was confusing indeed.

The financial institutions which had supported the property boom were certainly not benefiting from the idea that the property sector was on the verge of collapse. Their shares nose-dived to all-time lows as hedge funds around the globe merrily placed massive sums on the sure-fire certainty that the Irish banks would collapse. At one point €8 billion euro would have acquired all the Irish banks. Rumours of bank-runs were rife, and the government had moved to assuage the public's concern by guaranteeing deposits up to the value of €70,000. Similar measures had been put in place in Britain and in most European countries. Britain, in particular, had been forced to guarantee all deposits in the Northern Rock bank in September 2007, due to its exposure to the sub prime market in America. In Germany several of the largest banks were in difficulty and required massive bail-outs. In September 2008, Dublin-based Hypo Real Estate, located in the Irish Financial Services Centre which had been infamously dubbed the Wild West of the finance world in 2006 by the *New York Times,* due to its lax regulation and perceived corrupt business culture, had to be rescued by a consortium of other German banks. Hypo Real Estate was but one of a number of European banks and international corporations that had chosen to relocate a small portion of their total business to Dublin in order to avail of the generous corporation tax rate of 12.5% that prevails in Ireland. This extremely low tax rate effectively resulted in Ireland being a tax-haven within the European Union that countless member states' corporations availed of, thereby vastly increasing their own profits and conversely cheating their indigenous country's population of their legitimate and deserved tax-takes.

Ireland's reputation worldwide was by then besmirched beyond the point of rescue as observers, who previously had been seduced by the beguiling allure of copious wealth, suddenly awoke to the appalling reality of our property bubble. The massive wholesale borrowing by Ireland's banks on the international credit markets, especially in Germany, which had financed the credit bubble, had resulted in the Irish economy having a debt mountain greater than Japan's. According to figures supplied by the IMF, the total gross indebtedness of the private sector was a staggering €1,594 billion, which was nearly eight times national income and almost double the €876 billion it had stood at in 2002, coincidently the year that the worst excesses of the Ireland Inc. scam were initiated.

This damming judgement on Ireland's economy was reflected in the decline in Irish share prices, which continued apace. For example, shares in Irish Banks which were trading at nearly €24 per share in 2006 were now floundering closer to 24 cent. After the 35% crash in the value of Ireland's bank shares in 2007, followed by a further 45% in 2008, the rating agency JP Morgan downgraded the credit ratings on all Irish banks. Hedge funds took negative positions on Irish banks, Anglo Irish Bank being a particular favourite of the short-sellers who could make fortunes betting that the price of certain shares would fall. The evidence was there for all to see; the market had decided. Irish banks' shares were not worth the paper they were written on. The fallacy of Ireland Inc. had been ruthlessly exposed. Like Enron before it, Ireland's property scam, whose proponents claimed to possess the Midas touch, proved to be no more than a two-bit pyramid scheme which had collapsed in an unedifying mess leaving a mountain of debt where an illusionary edifice of unimaginable riches had once stood.

Fears concerning the financial stability of the banks in Ireland gained currency. Rumours that one of the major banks was on the verge of collapse were sweeping the country. The RTE phone-in programme, Liveline, reflected those growing worries when it devoted an entire edition to the topic, only to have the Department of Finance contact the station warning them, ironically, of the importance of responsible broadcasting and the danger of starting a run on the banks. Once again ironically, though typically, unbeknown to the public in general, the run on the banks had long since commenced amongst the massive investors, who benefited from their insider knowledge and would be granted first call on the limited capital that remained in the system. Ireland's banks were on the verge of collapse. An unseemly money-grab was about to commence. And then, the credit crunch!

Chapter 10

Don't worry! Everything's okay!

The realisation that the entire financial system was on the verge of collapse had come to some rather sooner than others. As we have seen, the canniest of the hedge fund managers had realised that that eventuality was the logical outcome of their own activities and had hastened its demise by adopting a series of positions, through derivatives and short-selling in particular, which bet on this negative outcome and consequently ensured that they would profit handsomely from the disaster. That this would result in massive unemployment, as giant corporations tumbled ignominiously, causing hardship not witnessed since the Great Depression, was apparently of no concern to them.

Free-market capitalism had built a tower of wealth which witnessed not the much vaunted trickle-down capital, but a propelling of real capital to the top floor. The penthouse suite at the very top of the tower was home to the super-rich, the hedge fund managers and investment bankers, in particular. Their activities contributed most to create the illusionary citadel of capital which the world's economy had become, leaving the remainder of the de-facto economic system starved of true capital and dependent on a fragile paper-based foundation of economic shares and 'notionally' valued money. As the notional value of all derivatives reached $863 trillion, approaching three times the value of all economic activity in the world, the point of no return had been reached. Stocks and shares, which at the peak of the boom were valued at an astounding $51 trillion, were now being exposed as nothing more than worthless pieces of paper. Banks' share values, which contributed greatly to the $51 trillion, had been exposed as a toxic property bubble.

That bubble had been at the very core of the increased borrowing which financed nigh-on all subsequent economic activity and resulted in the USA, for example, having a $13 trillion national debt, which it primarily owed to China. That this money was subsequently used to buy goods produced by the Chinese illustrates perfectly how illogical the world's finance system had become. China's economy was booming, through the dubious measure of lending capital to their biggest and best customers, the American public, allowing them, the Americans, to continue to live beyond their means by acquiring imports from China! This had the further effect of hastening the decline of the service and manufacturing industry in the United States, industries whose intrinsic value and importance had been wantonly neglected in the wake of the property gold-rush that consumed the nation. Crucially though, unlike the original American gold-rush, the gold which they were mining as a result of the property bubble was of the fool's variety.

The very fact that central banks had stopped securing the value of currencies to the value of this precious metal had a considerable role to play in the eventual disastrous outcome of events. Since there was no longer a 'gold standard' to act as a guarantee for currencies, money itself became increasingly more 'notional' in value. That this paper money – like its counterpart, the share certificate, before it – developed an irrationally high valuation during the boom can be illustrated by the fact that, although there was $3.9 trillion of nominal cash in circulation, gold reserves in central bank faults stood at only $845 billion.

With the flight from paper shares and currencies, the dollar in particular, investors took refuge in the traditionally safe commodities, oil and gold. That was why oil prices headed for $150 a barrel and gold an astounding $1,000 an ounce. Smaller depositors invested in safes, sales of which took off significantly, and withdrew their cash from banks they considered in danger of bankruptcy. Large flights of capital began from one bank to another and one jurisdiction to another as larger depositors became anxious about the financial health of particular saving institutions and their susceptibility to toxic debt. These larger depositors were faced with possibly greater challenges than smaller ones, as the space under the mattress, increasingly the safest-looking option, limited the scope for savers with large deposits.

Instability and chaos became the hallmarks of the financial system from early 2007 onwards. Fear of impending doom was heightened as banks and financial institutions across the globe began to publicly admit their exposure to toxic debt and embarked on massive write-downs of their liabilities. This process can be dated to 23 June 2007, when Bear Stearns announced that it had to pledge $3.2 billion dollars to one of its hedge funds which was on the verge of collapsing as a result of bad bets it had placed on the sub prime market. In August 2007 the German bank WestLB and the French BNP Paribas declared huge liabilities. In January 2008 the Swiss bank UBS confirmed sub prime losses of $18 billion. The following April the same bank wrote down a further

$19 billion in losses. When Deutsche Bank followed, announcing a $4 billion write-down, the worldwide nature of the phenomenon became ever more apparent. These were but a tiny sample of the harsh realities of a financial system that was fast approaching total collapse and were the primary reason why the international credit system ultimately froze. No financial institution could be sure of the extent to which another was exposed to toxic debt. Suspicion and mistrust gripped the money markets. No-one was willing to lend to anyone else, even overnight. The financial system had simply stopped lending. The credit crunch had begun in earnest.

As reality dawned on the free-market capitalists that their mountains of wealth were in fact pillars of debt, their reaction to the enormous difficulties their own actions had created for them was astounding. Their previous imperious insistence that their precious market be kept free from government interference and intervention – the most fundamental tenet of their ideology, the very bedrock on which their exorbitant wealth had been fraudulently created – was to be cast aside in the face of the threat which now existed to their personal capital. 'Small government', a theory which they supported that held that all business, enterprise and services should be privatised, thereby creating the opportunities for wealth-creators to aggrandise themselves to obscene degrees, to the expense of the government, and therefore the general public, had been at the core of their self-serving ideology. Revealingly, however, now that their own financial situation was threatened, they immediately betrayed that core principle and demanded that 'big government' – i.e. the general public – ride to their rescue.

The massive government bail-outs were nothing more than massive tax increases which the tax-paying public, and their children, would be burdened with for decades.

This betrayal of another basic element of their ideology, their championing of low-tax economies, was of course of little regard to the wealth-creators who, in general, through deliberate government policy, were required to pay little or no tax on any account. So it was that the public, who had been the victims of the property fraud in the first place, and on whose backs the offensive wealth of the boom years was made, would now be told to shoulder the burden once again and carry the incalculable cost of the debt which the irresponsible behaviour of the drivers of the boom had created.

The downright immorality of this situation reflected perfectly the cultural values of the period. That the neo-conservative, right-wing President of the United States of America, George Bush, whose policies had supercharged the engine of free-capitalism, could then propose the most fundamentally socialist measure to ward off its impending disastrous date with destiny, was astounding. That his complete betrayal of his philosophy was to be performed in an attempt to preserve the culture and ideology that had brought us to the precipice was absurd. That no preconditions were imposed that would ensure that the morally corrupt business culture which had brought us to this precarious position would be changed was utterly alarming. That this 'bail-out' of the debased, debauched and devalued banking system was to be introduced with hardly any debate and with cross-party support revealed the desperately demoralising condition which democracy found itself in.

In Ireland, for example, none of the issues concerning the gross immorality and inherent unfairness which underpinned the decision of the American Congress and Senate to support the massive $700 billion bail-out were discussed or debated. The only commentary made regarding the issues amounted to the fervently expressed hope that the US would pass the legislation as quickly as possible so as to facilitate some improvement in the Irish economy, which was experiencing difficulties of its own due, we were repeatedly told by Government ministers, to the crisis sparked off by the sub prime market collapsing in America. The Taoiseach, Brian Cowen, and the Minister for Finance, Brian Lenihan, in particular, consistently perpetuated the notion that the difficulties Ireland was experiencing were nothing to do with problems in our own economy, but were entirely the result of the worldwide credit crisis. Their understanding of the situation appeared to be that, if the money markets could be loosened up and credit flow freely again between banks and financial institutions, then our economic gravy train could resume the merry journey it was on before it was so rudely interrupted by the inconvenient sub prime obstruction.

This fundamentally naïve and guileless understanding of the dire economic situation in which Ireland found itself, by those charged with guiding the country through the unprecedented financial turmoil which it soon would be faced with, was indeed disturbing. But then what else could one expect from the arrogant architects of what *Observer* journalist Ruth Sunderland called the "Great Disillusion", a twenty-five year period when most of people's 'wealth' was really nothing more than an illusion. Sunderland observed that, "on a grand scale, policymakers, financiers and economists ignored the huge risks inherent in asset bubbles, with an over-confidence born of a belief in efficient markets." The unconcerned dismissal, by Brian Cowen and Brian Lenihan, of our economic woes at the time, as being brought about by the international credit crunch, illustrates perfectly the Government's complacency and conceit. Our political masters were still incontrovertibly wedded to the free-market culture. Even in the face of the irrefutable evidence that this culture had brought not just the Irish economy, but the world's financial system as a whole to the edge of the abyss, our leaders stood fast in their loyalty to its principles and, even more importantly, to the members of the Golden Circle who stood now to lose all of the illusory wealth they had spent the previous twenty-five years amassing.

This was not a time for prevarication or faltering nerve. The stakes were much too high. The greatest social and economic revolution in the history of the Irish State was on the cusp of occurring. Due, ironically, to their own insatiable greed, the Golden Circle had been enticed to wager all their ill-gotten capital gains from the proceeding twenty-five years on a dud horse, named 'the property market', and now stood transfixed as, their greatest fear in life, the prospect of the most revolutionary redistribution of wealth in history, appeared likely. The fact that the more extreme free-market capitalists were, through their own belligerently immoral behaviour, in clear danger of having engineered the socialist revolution which they so despised was indicative of the extent to which economy and society had been thoroughly perverted. The supporters of free-market capitalism need not have been concerned, though. A hundred years, or more, of time, energy and money had not been spent in creating the purest example of democratic autocracy, where institutionalised cronyism was rampant, to let this unthinkable fate befall them. Our – or should that be their? – political leaders would, along with all the other influential elements of our corrupted society, come to their aid in this their most perilous moment of need.

Chapter 11

It's a Dunne deal!

The speed with which free-market capitalists ditched their most fundamental tenets and embraced the most radical and abhorrent elements of the previously reviled socialist ideology would be laughable, were it not for the consequences that that shameless volte-face entailed for the majority of decent hard-working citizens of the country. Having witnessed their vast stockpiles of personal wealth suddenly turn into a massive mountain of debt, they now brazenly proposed to transfer that colossal debt to the State, and thereby to the people on whose backs it had been created in the first place. This was a crucial moment in the economic and social history of the State. The Golden Circle of the affluent and powerful had over-leveraged their wealth on the property market and were now realising that it was turning into a colossal millstone. Their answer was to switch that massive ball of debt from private to public ownership, enabling them to retain their privileged positions on the highest echelons of Irish society when the worst effects of this economic calamity had passed.

The Irish banks and property developers were, to all intents and purposes, the representatives incarnate of the Golden Circle. They, more than any other institutions, best reflected the opulence and over-indulgence of the Celtic Tiger period. The irrationally euphoric manner in which they conducted business was legendary and is best illustrated by taking a brief look at the proposed development of the Ballsbridge area of South Dublin. This area was regarded by the developers and the banks as the prime location in the country. When the Doyle family decided that they would put their Jury's Hotel in Ballsbridge on the market, it ignited intense interest amongst prospective developers. Having originally thought that they might realise somewhere in the region of €200 million for this prime location, the Doyles were pleasantly surprised, no doubt, when the frenzied competition amongst eager developers drove the valuation way above that amount. Thirteen developers finally expressed interest in the venture, and a final date was provided for the submission of sealed bids.

The Carlow-born developer Sean Dunne was, it is said, particularly keen on the Jury's site, which he saw as an ideal location to rival London's Knightsbridge. Apparently, as the deadline approached for purchasing bids, Sean Dunne fretted over the amount he should bid. While staying in the luxury Hyatt Hotel in Thailand, the story goes, he deliberated between bids varying between €253 and €275 million. Unsure of what value he should place on the table to secure the pot, he turned to his wife, *Sunday Independent* social columnist Gayle Killilea, and asked her to pick a figure. Killilea, having been born in 1975 and therefore considering 75 a lucky number, chose €275 million, and Sean Dunne proceeded to instruct his solicitor to make a bid for that amount. Dunne's bid was successful, though it is worth noting that this colossal sum, decided upon in the most flippantly nonchalant manner, was only €300,000 higher than the next highest, that of former Fianna Fáil councillor Bernard McNamara.

In fact, although Sean Dunne is regularly name-checked as being the worst example of reckless and irresponsible behaviour in the property market, it is worth recalling that thirteen others placed offers in excess of €200 million, with four bidders coming within €2 million of trumping Dunne's bid. Dunne was eventually to buy property in the area for a combined total of €510 million, which left the price of land in the Dublin 4 area at a staggering €53.7 million per acre. This outrageous valuation did not apparently ring alarm bells in the financial institutions funding such purchasing. As Sean Dunne himself explained to Marian Finucane on her Saturday morning radio show, the €250 million he required was granted to him over the phone from Thailand by Ulster Bank, the bank which was generally credited with being the first to offer 100% mortgages in Ireland.

Dunne's largess while acquiring land was by no means an isolated case of property developer madness. Having failed to acquire the coveted Jury's site himself, developer Ray Grehan proceeded to purchase a site on Shelbourne Road for what amounted to €84 million an acre. In 2006, developers Jerry O'Reilly and David McCourtney bought a third-of-an-acre site from the Office of Public Works for €36 million, the equivalent of €95 million an acre. By the time David Daly, of Albany Homes, had bought Franklin House for €25 million the price of land had reached a frankly mind-boggling €133 million per acre! By this time, land to the value of over €1 billion had been bought in the Ballsbridge, Dublin 4, area, financed by bankers who were tripping over themselves as they rushed to provide the funds for this property feeding frenzy. The irresponsibly nonchalant manner in which vast loans such as these were being made demonstrated perfectly the complacency at the heart of the Irish banking system, which was by then rotten to its very core. When Sean Dunne subsequently ran into difficulties with An Bord Pleanála, the planning authority, for the proposed 'Knightsbridge' development in Ballsbridge, at a time when property prices were in the process of tumbling, the direness of the situation began to become apparent to all concerned.

With the ISEQ index of top one hundred shares heading for an 80% decrease in valuation, and most banks losing 90% of their valuation, it was not unreasonable to speculate that the Irish property market, on which the booming economy had almost exclusively been built, would inevitably fall by similar amounts. The value of property in Ireland had indeed begun to fall but, officially at least, much less than the other officially recognised shares on the Irish Stock Exchange. This was due to the fact that property was, in fact, not selling at all. Fortunately, people in general were afforded a period of grace before having to sell by a series of interest rate decreases by the ECB which greatly reduced their mortgage repayments and warded off the dreaded day of foreclosure, forced sale or repossession. However, with unemployment increasing, as it was steadily doing, it was but a matter of time before greater numbers of householders would be faced with increasing difficulties in servicing their massive mortgage debt and left with no option but to sell. Similarly, increased unemployment rates would result in a reversal of the immigrant trail, which had been a vital component in inflating the property bubble, and this would result in a huge loss of custom in the rental market which would increase pressure on property prices in general.

The commercial property market, the bedrock of the Anglo Irish Bank multi-billion pound expansion which saw its loan book grow to a staggering €73 billion, was facing decimation with the onset of a worldwide recession. Anglo

Irish Bank and, indeed, all Irish banks were sitting un-prettily on top of a time-bomb of toxic property debt that was primed to explode with devastating consequences. Alarmingly, as late as February 2008, despite a very pronounced slowdown in the commercial and residential property markets, it was reported that several financial institutions, headed once more by Ulster Bank, had agreed to lend Sean Dunne a further €500 million to finance the next phase of his Ballsbridge development. No wonder then that, when the international credit markets unexpectedly dried up completely in August of that year in the wake of the Lehmans collapse, these over-leveraged and over-extended banks, stuffed with toxic assets and with massive loans to property developers who were technically insolvent, were starved of the credit inflows which would enable them to keep the giant 'ponzi' schemes functioning. In fact, so suddenly had those credit markets dried up that the chief architects of the scheme were themselves, unusually, caught off-guard and faced the unedifying and unpalatable prospect of having their spoils swiped from under their noses.

The Irish banks were on the verge of bankruptcy, the reserves that were being plundered by those in the know had been exhausted. No credit facilities were available from international money markets to recapitalise the banks' coffers. The date was Sunday 28 September, and the chief executives of the six major banks were staring into an abyss of their own creation. There remained but one avenue open to them. It was time for them to make the short walk from their headquarters on St Stephen's Green to Government Buildings in Leinster House, to the offices of the Taoiseach and the Minister for Finance, their erstwhile collaborators in the property ruse from the very beginning. There was to be one further reckless throw of the dice. They had one more proposal for the

Taoiseach and the Minister for Finance that would see them open one more valve and flush further reserves of capital into a financial system which, on the passing of every day and with the opening of every valve, resembled more and more the ill-fated *Titanic* as it undertook its ill-fated journey to its date with destiny.

Unfortunately, like the designers of that vain-glorious symbol of man's supposed superiority over nature herself, the executors of the Ireland Inc. scandal contemptuously dismissed any notion that their creation could conceivably sink. The banks and their government supporters disdainfully rejected suggestions made by a small group of informed commentators – including RTE chief economic reporter George Lee, UCD economics lecturer Morgan Kelly and the economist David McWilliams – that the property bubble was on the verge of bursting, with calamitous effect on the Irish economy as a whole. The Taoiseach, Brian Cowen, and Minister for Finance, Brian Lenihan, in particular, blithely championed the cause of our financial institutions and rounded on any commentators who dared to suggest that all was not well. Adopting the tone of the previous Taoiseach, Bertie Ahearn, who had scolded economic commentators who had ventured to suggest that ominous signs were beginning to emerge and had advised them "to go off and commit suicide," Lenihan and Cowen castigated those who questioned the health of the financial system.

George Lee, whose informative and incisive commentary on radio and television news broadcasts had a wide listenership, was a particular target for the Government's bile. We were repeatedly told, by the usual suspects in the property industry deceit, government, mainstream economic commentators and the media, that everything was fine and dandy and that it was only a matter of time before the international credit-crunch, which in their opinion was the sole cause of our current difficulties, resolved itself, and insisted that the Celtic Tiger miracle-vessel would escape the choppy waters and continue on its merry money-making way once more. Unfortunately for all concerned, guilty and innocent alike, the vessel had been holed beneath the waterline and was destined to produce far more wide-ranging repercussions than the previously mentioned Irish-built liner. When the Government announced, on Sunday 27 September, that they had acceded to a request from the chief executives of the six largest Irish financial institutions for a meeting in Government buildings the following day, it looked very much as if the next move in this Irish version of Russian roulette, with the financial futures of Irish citizens on the table as collateral, would be fateful.

Chapter 12

This sucker is going down!

The following day, 28 September, the whole world was teetering on the very edge of economic chaos. In the preceding weeks, oil prices had tumbled from their previous historic highs, as investors realised that the global recession that was fast approaching would lead to a huge decrease in demand. In Russia, turmoil in the credit markets lead to several banks being rescued by the government. As the Russian energy boom ground to a halt, huge stock market falls forced the authorities to suspend trading on the Russian stock exchange. In China the Shanghai stock market was reeling, having witnessed a 60% drop in value in the preceding twelve-month period. Foreign investors had withdrawn their capital as the global recession loomed, and fear spread that the USA, China's largest customer for exports and indeed loans, would be unable to continue to meet either debt or repayment obligations.

On 28 September the British government were forced to nationalise the Bradford and Bingley Bank, and their prime minister moved to reassure extremely nervous money markets by announcing that Lloyd's takeover of the

HBOS would proceed. On September 29 pandemonium spread throughout the world financial system like wildfire. When the US House of Representatives threw out the big Government bail-out plan, world stock markets plunged. In Iceland the government was forced to nationalise the country's third largest bank, Glitnir, after a run on deposits by nervous customers. The governments of Belgium, Holland and Luxemburg had to nationalise the giant Fortis bank. Employing 85,000 people, it was deemed to be too big to fail. Greece was teetering on the brink as a massive run on their financial institutions gathered momentum. Many of Germany's, Austria's and Switzerland's biggest financial institutions were in what looked like meltdown. In Australia the national Australia Bank shocked markets there by announcing a 90% write-down on its £550 million holdings of US mortgage debt.

The global nature of this financial crisis, the likes of which had never been witnessed before, had become apparent to all. The excesses of the previous twenty years had finally come home to roost. The great delusion of wealth 'beyond our wildest dreams' had been scattered to the winds. Panic set in. The imperious veneer of 'irrational euphoria', the hallmark of rampant free-market capitalism, had been shattered. The autocratic poise of previously imperious wealth-creators gave way to a contemptible grab for whatever cash remained in the system from their previously obscene stockpiles. This was the disturbing economic reality which the world was faced with on the morning of 29 September 2008.

"This sucker was going down," as US President George Bush so succinctly put it. All that remained for those 'in the know' was to hold their nerves, assure everybody that everything was fine and simultaneously siphon off any capital reserves that remained in the system. There was, however, one major problem in Ireland which stood in the way of this handy little ruse. There was little or no cash left in Ireland's banks at the end of September 2008. The international markets had realised that the emperors of Celtic Tiger Ireland were wearing no clothes. Investors had withdrawn their deposits on an alarming scale. End of year records would reveal that €45 billion of deposits were transferred out of the country during this period. Hedge funds were making a killing, betting on the inevitable collapse of Irish financial institutions, in particular. There appeared to be no room for manoeuvre for the architects of the Ireland Inc. scandal.

Home owners were facing massive negative equity, a huge increase in repossessions and further weakening property prices. Unemployment would crash through the half-million barrier as a consequence of over-reliance on the construction industry and neglect of the manufacturing sector. This half a million addition to the dole queues would have a knock-on effect on mortgage repayments, not to mention the strain it would place on the exchequer, which had to service the enormously increased welfare debt on decimated income from taxes. The level of welfare payments, along with public service salaries, had of course been allowed to increase enormously in an attempt to keep pace with rising house prices. Our low tax model economy would be exposed as the ineffective sham that it was. The government's attempt to sustain an economy almost entirely on secondary taxes, such as capital gains, stamp duty and VAT, would be revealed as the patent nonsense it had always been. All the disastrous decisions taken by the proponents of free-market capitalism were now coming home to roost.

That this calamitous conclusion to the scandalous excesses of the Celtic Tiger period would come to pass was not in doubt. The only question remaining to be answered from the meeting of the our governmental representatives and the chief executives of the banks was whether the huge debt would remain in the hands of the private individuals who created it or the architects of the scheme would conspire once more to transfer it to the tax-payers. It was patently obvious that all the banks would be manifestly over-exposed to the worst effects of the tsunami which was overwhelming the world's financial system. Since property prices collapsed, and would continue to do so until they reached their floor, somewhere around 80% below peak prices in 2006, the Irish banks were undoubtedly technically insolvent at this point. As terror gripped the money markets worldwide, no international credit provider in its right mind would come to the aid of the Irish 'basket case'. However, one thing which could never be underestimated was the ingenuity of the wealth-creators when it came to discovering valves that could be opened to replenish their personal coffers. The financial institutions demanded of the Government, and were granted, a rescue package for their self-serving affairs which was shocking in its total disregard for the consequences.

I awoke on the morning of Monday 29 September 2008 to discover that the government had taken a decision which far exceeded anything I had imagined possible. They had summoned RTE reporter David Murphy to government buildings in the early hours of the morning to announce that they had acceded to a request from the six main Irish banks to commit themselves to a two-year period during which "it would offer an unlimited guarantee covering all retail, commercial and inter-bank deposits, bonds and debts of those six designated financial institutions." Unbelievably, the Taoiseach, Brian Cowen and the Minister for Finance, Brian Lenihan, had committed generations of Irish citizens to guaranteeing a €460 billion sum, which was manifestly un-guarantee able! It was perfectly clear what the rationale behind this decision was: not to protect the deposits of ordinary citizens, but to flush huge sums of new cash into the Irish system from abroad.

Those major depositors all around Europe who were desperately searching for a safe haven for their massive deposits in a terrifyingly turbulent financial system would jump at the opportunity to guarantee their assets on the backs of generations of Irish tax-payers whom the government had just placed at their mercy. That these colossal new funds were to be placed in the hands of the very same chief executives who had brought us to the brink of economic collapse, and who themselves were involved in the unedifying rush to grab their perceived share of what remained in the world's corrupted financial kitty, was shocking. Ireland had indulged in an outrageous 'beggar thy neighbour' policy which would result in fresh capital injections into our institutions which could then be used to replenish the personal coffers of those in the Golden Circle who had been caught unexpectedly off-guard by the credit crunch. This outrageous decision also bore the potential of bringing Europe's financial system to its knees and reflected the manner in which the financial chaos in Europe had exposed the underlying weakness of the European model.

Ironically, at a time when Brian Cowen and his government were publicly scolding the Irish population for having had the temerity to harm the European model by voting against the Lisbon Treaty, he had just sanctioned a state-sponsored national bank guarantee which brought many of our European partners to the very edge of the financial abyss. Worst of all, though, the guarantee was in the name of the Irish people and was unquestionably going to be called in. €460 thousand million of debt had been transferred from insolvent banks to ordinary Irish citizens in a clandestine meeting of like minds in our Government buildings on the night of 28 September 2008. The bankers had been cleared to resume operations, bolstered by their newly replenished cash stockpiles acquired once more on the back of the tax-payer. Not one caveat was introduced as a means to admonish past reckless behaviour or to highlight future increased diligence on the part of the regulatory authorities. The obscene performance-related bonus system was to be allowed to remain unchanged.

It was as if a hopelessly incurable gambler had come to the Taoiseach in complete and utter desperation, having wagered himself to the hilt of indebtedness, and the Taoiseach had sent him happily back to the casino with a government endorsement ringing in his ears and a blank chequebook stuffed into his pocket. The government would conspire with their gambling partners to ensure that the gains they had made from the original property bubble would not be lost to them and that their lofty position at the uppermost level of Irish society would remain unchallenged. The *Titanic* was heading directly for the ocean bed, while the Minister for Finance was nonchalantly loading the innocent men, women and children of Ireland onto the back of the doomed vessel. As unlimited guarantors of all retail, commercial and inter-bank deposits, bonds and debts, current and future, the government had placed the State at the mercy of the financial institutions. Furthermore, the banks could at any point threaten to close their doors, thereby invoking the nightmare scenario of the State having to service a €460 thousand million guarantee!

Never in my life had I experienced such a feeling of incandescent rage as I experienced on the morning of 29 September. My rage increased as the day wore on and the magnitude of the scandalous subterfuge sank in. When the opportunity arose, I checked the ISEQ index of leading Irish shares and watched in horror as the Irish bank share valuations rose inexorably as the markets reacted to the announcement. The fresh capital from abroad would undoubtedly make its way into the hands of the greedy architects and executives of the Irish property-market sham who would scavenge the last vestiges of what remained of the financial system. As I made my way home from work, I had already decided to join the protest which I assumed would take place outside Dáil Éireann that evening, as the emergency debate to pass the legislation began.

When I arrived home my anger and frustration grew ever greater on realising that the announcement of the government guarantee had exacted almost unanimous support amongst newspapers editorials and commentators on radio and television. One notable exception was the ever-honourable RTE chief economic correspondent, George Lee, who once again flagged up the dangers that lurked within government economic policy decisions. However, more representative of the media in general was the commentary provided by two tax experts on the Mary Wilson Drive Time programme on RTE radio one, which lauded the prompt action taken by the Minister for Finance and roundly welcomed the decision.

After cycling to the nearest Luas station in Windy Arbour, I waited for the tram which would bring me to St Stephen's Green, from where I would proceed to Leinster House, where the debate was scheduled to begin at approximately five o clock. While sitting on the Luas tram, I became aware for the first time of the apparent total lack of awareness of my fellow passengers of the frightening situation which the country, and indeed they, found themselves in. There was an air of calm normality amongst my fellow travellers which contrasted sharply with the complete and utter sense of impotent outrage which I found myself consumed by. Suddenly, though almost imperceptibly, I became cognizant of the disturbing possibility that the years of ineffective and politically biased journalism had been so effective that it had succeeded in inducing a dream-like complacency amongst the population. This feeling was only exacerbated when I disembarked the Luas in St Stephen's Green, to be confronted with shoppers, on Grafton Street, merrily making their way through the commercial and retail outlets which sported the highest rental valuations in the world. My apprehension grew apace as I made my way towards the Dáil, aware that nothing seemed askew with the world for revellers on Dublin's streets.

Listening intently to peoples' conversations as they passed, I strained to hear even the most cursory mention of the guarantee, but heard none. As I approached Molesworth Street, which faced the Dáil, I hoped against hope to hear the strained voices of the protestors gathered there that would ensure that I would be spared the embarrassment of being the only middle-aged demonstrator amongst the massed youthful agitators of the socialist left. As I turned the corner from Dawson Street onto Molesworth Street, the scene that awaited me stopped me dead in my tracks for what seemed like an age. There was no-one there. Not one person. The most disastrous policy decision by a government in the history of the Irish State was on the verge of being debated in an emergency sitting of the Dáil, and nobody, it appeared, knew.

Standing alone outside Leinster House, it struck me how mind-numbingly effective the control of the public's ability for cognitive reasoning had been in the proceeding years. Though momentarily prompted to consider returning home, instead I decided to try to get into the Dáil and possibly instigate a protest within the chamber, should the opportunity arise. Although I had never been to Leinster House, I was aware that I would need an entry pass, which could be obtained from a local constituency representative. With no means to acquire one at that late juncture, I decided to chance a conversation with the two gardaí who were on duty at the gates. When I explained to them that I would be very interested in attending what was surely to be an historic session in Dáil Éireann that evening, they told me I would need to obtain a pass from a TD, so I crossed the road and made my way into Buswell's Hotel, more in hope than expectation that I would meet someone who could facilitate my entry.

When I entered the bar I noticed the independent TD from Kerry, Jackie Healy Rae, seated at the bar enjoying a bowl of soup as he presumably waited for the debate to begin. Beside him the huge flat-screen TV was broadcasting Sky News, which was covering the fallout from the financial crisis in Britain. It struck me as ironic that the Irish parliament was on the point of discussing the most crucial piece of legislation in the State's history and yet RTE television seemed unaware of this fact. As Healy Rae supped his soup contently, behind his head, obscured from his view, Gordon Brown and David Cameron intensely debated the growing crisis threatening the world's financial system. Once again, in the bar, I was struck by the complete lack of awareness amongst the public as to the seriousness of the situation which faced the country. The only occasion in the entire day that I heard any mention of the crisis occurred when two men at the bar commented on George Lee's appearance on radio that morning, when he had apparently expressed serious reservations regarding the guarantee.

Time was ticking by relentlessly, and by the time the debate was supposed to start, five o clock, I was still no nearer to gaining entry to Leinster House. I walked to the door of Buswells and stared across at the Dáil, where I knew affairs would be commencing fairly sharply. I noticed the veteran political correspondent Stephen Collins, of the *Irish Times*, nonchalantly making his way up Molesworth Street, and I thought how privileged he was to be in a position to cover such historic events. As the rain started falling, I began to accept the fact that I would not be so lucky. A few minutes after he had entered Leinster House, however, there was a flurry of activity around the entrance of the Dáil and people began to leave in large numbers. As I stood in the doorway of the bar, casually watching those who were exiting the Dáil, my attention was suddenly drawn to a TD whom I recognised immediately and vaguely knew. Without a moment's hesitation, I ran from the doorway and caught up with him as he proceeded down Kildare Street. I caught his attention, but in the heat of the moment couldn't remember his Christian name. I introduced myself as being from Dundrum and reminded him that, as kids, some thirty years ago, I had met him on a few occasions when he had come to the street where I lived to visit his aunt. After some small talk I mentioned to him that I would be extremely interested in attending what was sure to be a historic Dáil session later that evening, and he generously offered to sign me in for the debate which he said, the Dáil ushers had informed him, could go on all night.

His curious reference to the length, rather than the substance, of the debate left me slightly puzzled. When he then proceeded to tell me that there had been an adjournment called and that he intended to take the opportunity to go to the gym for an hour, my suspicion grew that this particular TD did not fully comprehend the import of the business which he would later be required to consider. However, he took my mobile phone number and assured me that he would meet me at the gates of the

Dáil at seven o clock, a half hour before the debate was scheduled to resume. Concerned that he might forget, or indeed have second thoughts, about securing admission for someone he hardly knew, I asked him for his number, so that I could contact him. I then went back to Buswells Hotel, where I spent the following hour appreciating my good fortune in meeting such an accommodating member of parliament. At seven o'clock, however, I found myself apprehensively pacing the footpath outside the Dáil in the dark waiting for him. As the rain began to fall ever more heavily and five minutes more past with no sign of him, I decided to contact him to remind him of our arrangement. Having begun to think that he was already in the chamber, I was relieved to discover that he was still in the gym and followed his instructions to proceed to the admission hut at the Dáil gates and to wait for him there. The welcome relief from the rain was minor in comparison to the relief I felt that he was not about to renege on his invitation.

Approximately ten minutes later, he duly arrived and we proceeded to the Garda security desk in the lobby off Leinster House where the necessary formalities were completed, including the issuing of a Dáil pass to me. Having presumed that this would be where he would take his leave to pursue his own particular business on this busy night for Dáil members, I was rather surprised by his invitation to join him in the bar for a drink. Sitting at the bar over minerals and peanuts, we indulged in some small talk regarding the bill which was before the house. I decided to try to assess his comprehension of the situation and adopted the demeanour of an interested, though innocent, observer of the affairs of parliament. As the Government guarantee had only been announced overnight and had come as a bolt from the blue to most commentators, there had been little or no debate amongst political commentators, as far as I was aware. I asked him if he thought the legislation would have any difficulty in passing all stages, and he replied in the negative. As the government was a coalition with the Green Party, I then wondered aloud if he was confident of their support, to which he replied: "Once bought, you stay bought."

His confidence and his patent disregard for any danger inherent in the guarantee was revealed even more succinctly by the conversation that subsequently followed. The barman innocently enquired of him how the announcement of the guarantee had been received, and he replied that it had been warmly welcomed and that the Minister for Finance had been praised for his prompt action – "except," he added, his voice becoming increasingly animated, "for that little pr*** George Lee." He went on to castigate the RTE finance correspondent who, he claimed, never had a good word to say about anything and was "just pissed off because we took David Murphy in to break the news of the guarantee." This reference to Lee was indeed ironic, as he had generally been completely correct in his analysis of the economic situation and had been warning for some time of the downturn that was imminent. I myself had been suspicious when David Murphy had been summoned by the government, as his was definitely a more reserved and non-committal style of journalism than the more experienced and combative Lee.

This brief conversation rapidly convinced me that the inexperienced TD I was chatting to had no idea of the significance of the legislation he was being asked to pass in this emergency all-night debate. Our conversation was abruptly cut short by the ringing of the division bell, which summoned members to the chamber for the restart of the debate. I thanked him for his generosity and remained at the counter for a few moments, convinced that my initial assessment of the young TD was indeed correct.

The fact that he had chosen to go to the gym during the unexpected adjournment, instead of remaining with colleagues to discuss this historic legislation confirmed my suspicions that he had little or no appreciation of the measures he was about to vote on.

As I ruminated on this matter my attention was drawn to a group of what appeared to be college students who had gathered in the oval-shaped section at the back of the members' bar. Earlier, while I had been waiting in the entrance lobby for the TD to return from the gym, I had noticed a young student who had received permission to enter on introducing himself as the son of a former leader of Fine Gael. I assumed that he was one of this group of about ten students who were comfortably ensconced in this exclusive and restricted area of Irish society, and it struck me that they were very much at home in the environs of the members' lounge in Dail Éireann. I could not help but think that I was watching the next generation of our political leaders in the making, acquainting themselves with the trappings of the lifestyle which would be bequeathed to them in due course. The inexperienced member of parliament who had earlier brought me into the Dáil, and had demonstrated his total naivety as to the matters of immense national importance which he was being required to appraise was himself the son of a former Fianna Fáil TD who had spent most of his life inhabiting the same environment.

The only other people in the members' bar were three men I judged to be journalists, who were seated at the counter enjoying a drink. Having finished my own Seven-Up, I proceeded to join the rush of TDs as they left their offices in the corridors, and made my way up the stairs to the entrance of the Dáil chamber itself. As I approached the doors through which the members would enter, a Dáil usher directed me towards the public viewing balcony, off to the right. Suddenly, I remembered that, while I had a pen, I had no paper to write on, and the usher was kind enough to provide me with the only writing material available to him – a copy of the order paper for the Dáil Business for Tuesday, 30 September, 2008. I continued to the viewing balcony and took my place at the farthest point from the entrance in a seat which afforded a perfect view of proceedings, and of the government benches in particular.

First I watched familiar faces take their places and noted the absence of certain political heavyweights, such as Bertie Ahern and Mary Harney. Suddenly, though, my attention turned to the fact that the attendance in the public gallery was paltry. In all, I counted sixteen people, most of whom I presumed to be public servants and possibly ministers' assistants. When Brian Lenihan rose to speak, he announced that they would be seeking a further adjournment until nine o clock, as the government were still in the process of finalising the bill and hoped the opposition would understand. He had no cause for concern, as Fine Gael, the main opposition party, was supporting the bill and dutifully acquiesced. Everybody trundled out of the chamber and I considered what I should do during the adjournment.

As I made my way back to the entrance lobby, the general air of indifference and joviality which dominated the atmosphere in the corridors of the Dáil began to confuse me. I had come to the parliament on the assumption that I would witness the greatest conspiratorial deceit committed on the Irish people in the history of the State by a government who were not about to betray their circle of golden friends in their most desperate hour of need. I had, however, assumed that they would be concerned as to the disastrous effects their actions could have, seeing as they were undertaking to guarantee a virtually un-guarantee-able €460 billion of debt. However, there appeared to be little or no apprehension amongst members. Generally, TDs of both the government and opposition parties were going about their business in a calm and collected manner, which mirrored the scenes I had witnessed earlier on Grafton Street amongst shoppers. There were no frenzied scenes, as I would have imagined, of ministers and members deeply engaged in conversation as they debated their concerns about this momentous bill. That was it! That was what was perplexing me. Nobody seemed in the slightest bit concerned! Though I remained convinced that this was the greatest conspiracy in history against the citizens of the State, a further, possibly even more worrying, spectre was raising its ugly head: our public representatives were totally unaware of the dreadful repercussions which would follow from their actions. They didn't know what was happening around the globe, they didn't understand the implications of their actions and, worst still, they didn't seem to care!

I decided to leave the Dáil, pass secure in my pocket, and to head back in the direction of Grafton Street, where I bought a note book so that I could keep account of the evening's events. I paid a visit to Kehoes bar on South Anne Street to put in some time and also to gauge the public mood. It was apparent that no one was in the slightest bit aware of the monumental decision that was being taken in their name only a few hundred yards up the street. While standing at the door of Kehoes, I noticed the Casino in the lane-way opposite and could not help but think of the outrageous 'sting' that was being put into operation in government buildings, a sting that would be executed at a tremendous cost to the citizens of the State.

On my return to the members' bar in the Dáil, I found that the three men I had presumed to be journalists had now been joined by other groups, amongst them a handful of TDs, who were benefiting from the adjournment to enjoy some refreshment. I sat up at the bar and began to jot down some thoughts about events up to that point. After a few moments I sensed a presence behind me and turned around to discover one of the three men I had imagined to be journalists looking over my shoulder to see what I was writing. As I folded over the notes and put them in my jacket pocket, I turned to engage my over-inquisitive companion in conversation. He asked if I was a journalist, and when I answered in the negative he introduced himself as a news correspondent for Newstalk, Today FM and 98 FM, the three radio stations owned by Denis O'Brien. I informed him that I was just an ordinary member of the public who was interested in witnessing the historic proceedings in the Dáil that night. I asked him what he thought of the proposed legislation, and he replied that he thought the government had no option and were doing the right thing in "supporting the banking system and protecting the man in the street." When I asked him how he thought this proposal would protect the man in the street, he replied: "You know, the ordinary guy with three houses."

As it turned out, my intrepid reporter friend had, as he informed me, three houses himself and had a particular interest in ensuring that the property market bubble be kept inflated by the introduction of the guarantee. His intrepidness did not, however, extend to bothering himself much with the content of the debate. On this important night in the history of the State, as far as I am aware, our intrepid reporter with a duty to inform and educate his listenership about issues of monumental concern, such as a €460 billion guarantee, remained in the Dáil bar and never once ventured out to acquaint himself with the details of the debate. But then he, as he had blithely admitted earlier, was totally compromised by the fact that his own personal circumstances required that this latest and most dangerous valve be opened in an attempt to ensure the continuation of the inflation of the property bubble. Soon after he had rejoined his companions at the other end of the bar, the division bell sounded once more to announce the start of proceedings in the chamber. I left the bar and made my way to the public gallery once more, where the attendance had dwindled to a miserly eight other interested spectators.

When it was announced that the government was seeking yet another adjournment, the opposition began to get agitated. The delay in presenting the bill drew the wrath of the opposition, whose leader, Enda Kenny, described it as "high farce." The fact that Fine Gael were more discommoded by the delay in presenting the bill than by its outrageous content was indeed farce of the highest order. However, having made their annoyance known and having received an apology from the Taoiseach himself, Fine Gael dutifully accepted the further delay until nine o'clock. The Labour Party also expressed annoyance at the delay – in fact, it had expressed reservations about supporting the legislation – but at that moment it looked as though every single member of the house was intent on backing it. When I looked about the chamber I was convinced that the vast majority of TD's present were completely unaware of the significance of the legislation they were being asked to consider. Some bore the expressions of callow college students attending their first-ever lecture, giddily excited by the prospect of a once-in-a-lifetime all-night debate. Others, more experienced, personified world-weary boredom as they begrudgingly acquiesced to this latest delay in delivering the bill to the house, a decision which would inevitably keep them from obviously more pressing business elsewhere.

I retired to the members' bar once more, my anger and frustration growing with every second and with every new instance of political ineptitude. The bar was becoming ever busier with each adjournment, and the jovial demeanour of TDs from both sides of the house reaffirmed my conviction that they had not the remotest sense of the seriousness of the situation. It crossed my mind that I had not overheard a single conversation regarding the guarantee itself since I had entered the Dáil, three hours previously. In the TD's defence, if it is a defence, it was predominantly backbenchers who were enjoying affairs in the Members' Bar up to that point, but surely, I thought, if others had been aware, then their alarm would have spread to all and sundry in the house.

At nine o'clock yet another adjournment was announced, which threatened to test the patience of the opposition to breaking point. However, once again, when the complexities of the bill and its vital importance in ensuring a flush of foreign funds into Irish banks were explained, the opposition agreed to a further half-hour delay to enable the Minister for Finance, Brian Lenihan, to finalise the bill. Imagine my surprise, then, when I had just resumed my seat in the members' bar, when Brian Lenihan walked into the lounge and proceeded to occupy a seat no more than a couple of yards from me. Watching him casually wander around the bar engaging in idle chit-chat with various other TDs, I contrasted this bizarre reality with the image I had imagined of the Minister holed up in his office, surrounded by the highest officials, as they agonised over the details of the most dauntingly challenging piece of legislation that had ever come before the Dáil.

As he made his way back to his seat, I noticed RTE's Chief Political Correspondent, David Davenport, approaching the minister and I eagerly awaited the opportunity to hear, possibly first-hand, the minister's thoughts on the guarantee. In the event, the reporter took the opportunity which presented itself at this historic moment in Ireland's history to ask the Minister about a mutual friend they appeared to have in Tipperary! Not one word passed between them regarding the bill which would result in Irish citizens being the guarantors for a banking system which was on the verge of collapse. The timorous manner in which the Chief Political Correspondent approached the Minister, and the disdainful and almost contemptuous manner in which he was treated by him, made me wonder about the effectiveness of the Dáil reporting system.

As Davenport assumed a seat at the bar next to the *Irish Independent*'s Dáil reporter Lise Hand, the former *Hot Press* and *Sunday Tribune* social columnist, my attention was drawn to the conversation the Minister for Finance was having with his two companions, whom I took to be personal assistants. As he sipped his tea, just a short few minutes before introducing a bill which was the most perilous ever brought before the house, he was calmness personified. At one point he took up his mobile phone and placed a call to someone whom he instructed to "prepare a statement and get this news out to the markets." The outcome of the debate, he assured the person on the phone, was a foregone conclusion: the bill, he flippantly remarked, had already been signed by the President. When he finished the call, he recounted the conversation to his companions and laughed heartily as he repeated: "And I told them the bill had already been signed by the President." His arrogance and self-satisfaction were repellent when one considered the magnitude of the historic error he was in the process of committing. I felt even more revulsion when he received a text message, which he proceeded to read out to his companions, informing him and them that he was "playing a blinder."

Those words stuck in my craw. The language of the casino pathetically reflected the reality of the situation.

The Minister for Finance was indeed "playing" with the futures of the Irish people. Unfortunately, our representative at the casino table was an ignorant bluffer who was about to be revealed as such. But it was also clear from the Minister's actions that he possessed no respect for his democratic mandate. He was not there to serve the people, it appeared, but to serve the markets, which were to be informed, even before the house of parliament itself, that the deal to end all deals had been passed and that they were welcome to carry on making money.

Having been aware, like many others undoubtedly, that our democratic principles had long since been betrayed and that government pandered almost exclusively to the concerns of the golden circle of big business, it was nevertheless nauseating to see it function in this manner before my very eyes. The democratic deficit which resulted was all the greater when one considers that two of the public's supposed defenders in the third estate, journalists David Davenport and Lise Hand, were seated no more than a couple of feet from the minister while all this was going on, chatting happily together, seemingly indifferent to the events which were befalling our nation on the night in question. It appeared that everything I suspected regarding the nature of Irish society as a result of the free-market agenda was true. The overwhelming feeling which this revelation invoked was disgust at the dishonourable manner in which public representatives had behaved and the utter futility of the democratic system as I witnessed it in action that evening.

Here were the supposed brightest and best that the country could offer blithely, and in blissful ignorance, marching the five million Irish citizens they represented over a cliff and into an abyss of financial chaos, the likes of which the world had never seen. I took one more look around the room in the vain attempt to spot one face, just one face, that would reflect cognizance of the staggering decision they were about to take. The laughter and conviviality which had been apparent earlier were still the dominant tone of the conversations. Only this time it was not confined to backbenchers and opposition party TD's. Now they had been joined by the Minister for Finance, the most important member of the government, whose complacent confidence and haughty arrogance were essential components in the decision that was about to be made.

I left my seat in the members' bar once more and made my way, disheartened, to the public gallery. Only the merest of formalities, it appeared, had to be fulfilled before the final nail would be put in our collective coffin. When the Minister for Finance eventually stood to address the house, at 9.45 that fateful Tuesday, the manner in which he read the bill was highly revealing. Convinced as he was that he was "playing a blinder," and no doubt imperviously ignorant of the catastrophic consequences of the bill he was presenting, he raced through the reading, his voice betraying an almost total lack of interest, and his demeanour a complacent conceitedness as he nonchalantly rearranged his hair. Looking around the chamber, my despair for the democratic system grew greater by the minute, as I gauged the reaction of the members, both government and opposition, to a bill which they had been so concerned to receive a copy of earlier.

The behaviour on the Government benches, in particular, was shameful. Many of those present paid no more than a cursory interest to the proceedings, their inattentiveness blazoned across their faces like a badge of honour. Some were on the verge of torpor, as the initial childish excitement at the prospect of an all-night sitting wore off. Beverly Cooper Flynn shifted restlessly in her seat and continuously fiddled with her mobile phone. The TD who had earlier signed me in to the Dáil sparked into life when he happened to notice me in the public gallery and acknowledged my presence with a verve and vigour sadly lacking in him or his colleagues for the order of business of the day. As the lateness of the evening prevailed over the importance of the matters in hand, one TD desperately attempted to ward off the waves of sleepiness that overcame her. Not far from her, another TD struck the proverbial 'gombeen' pose as he stuck a pen in his ear and proceeded to clear it. Clearly, the majority of these members of parliament were out of their depth.

As I witnessed member after member nodding in support of the bill, I despaired for the democratic system. What was the point in having 166 elected members of parliament if not one of them, not even one, appeared to recognise the folly of the decision that was being taken? This feeling was re-enforced when Enda Kenny, the Fine Gael leader of the opposition, rose to offer his support for the government, effectively ending any possibility of serious debate and reflecting the parity of economic outlook which existed in our dysfunctional democracy. Further evidence, if required, that the Dáil was nothing more then a dispassionate debating theatre came when Kenny resumed his seat. The unseemly haste with which members jumped from their seats to exit the chamber brought to mind school kids exiting a classroom after a period of detention. It was obvious that they felt they had much more important business to attend to elsewhere. When Joan Burton stood to raise some valid concerns regarding the complete lack of reform of the performance-related bonus system within the banking culture, she was barely audible above the chattering amongst other TDs. When John Gormley, leader of the Green Party, Fianna Fáil's coalition partners, declared his pride in the Green

Party's input into the bill, I knew I could stand no more of it, so I retired to the members' bar so as to observe one last time the members of parliament in their more natural habitat.

The atmosphere there again showed members completely at ease with themselves and the work they had just completed. Instead of the anxiety that one might have expected, I found the exuberant ambiance of a local pub on a Saturday night. I removed myself from the main bar and took a seat in the now deserted oval area at the far end of the lounge, where the young future generation of TD's had previously been ensconced. From this privileged position I marvelled at the aptitude for ignorance and incompetence which our public representatives were in the process of exhibiting. It struck me that the Dáil bar's layout and décor lent themselves to favourable comparison with the *Titanic*'s. The air of complacent celebration lent itself to a rather more unfavourable comparison to the guests of that vessel who indulged themselves in the pleasures that the liner offered even after the first signs of the impending calamity had begun to appear. Nero was definitely fiddling while Rome burned in the members' bar that night.

When I decided to join the main body of partying TDs again, I noticed the Labour party spokesperson for Finance in conversation with three others, presumably members of the Labour Party. Having refrained from engaging in conversation previously, for fear of being removed from the house and denied this opportunity of a lifetime to bear witness to the crass behaviour of imperviously insolent decision-makers, I was nevertheless keen to leave a calling card as proof of my attendance on this historic night. Marvelling at the gormless expressions on the faces of most, if not all, of those present, including our unfortunate Tánaiste, Mary Coughlan, I decided, as midnight approached, and very much on the spur of the moment, to approach Joan Burton and her companions. I noticed that one of the young men in the group was nervously chewing his fingernails, and I used this as an excuse to interrupt their conversation. Pointing out that I had noticed that he appeared to be nervous, I suggested somewhat sarcastically that I was glad to see that at least one person might have appreciated the seriousness of the matter in hand in the parliament that night. When the Labour TD then challenged me as to who I was, I replied that that was of no concern but that I was an ordinary member of the public who had made his way to the Dáil that night to see for himself what was going on and what our public representatives were up to. She began to condescendingly congratulate me on being there, and once more it was immediately apparent that she had not got an inkling as to the severity of the situation. I informed her and her company that I had known for years that this eventuality was inevitable and that the Labour Party's opposition had been lamentable. Her reply to this was that "at least we're not Sinn Féin." I exaggerated a look over my shoulder to see if Gerry Adams had mystically appeared at my side, and then enquired what the hell Sinn Féin had to do with it, at which she assured me that she had not said those words to me and had presumed that I had left the conversation. This downright rudeness was just too much. I told her that Sinn Féin hadn't got a clue about economics and assured her that this whole thing – meaning the entire financial system – was going down, and that she and the rest of the Dáil were engaged in enacting legislation that would result in my wages, my wife's wages and, worst still, my young child's wages, being tied to it for our lifetimes.

Having questioned her intelligence in a not too polite manner, I left the Dáil bar, headed back onto the rain-sodden streets of Dublin and made my way rather disconsolately towards the Luas station at the top of Grafton Street. I joined the late-night revellers on the Luas tram and, as I once again lamented the dysfunctional democracy which had left the general public completely unaware of the massive deceit that had been committed on them, my thoughts returned to a conversation I had overheard in the Dáil entrance room as I waited for the TD to return from the gym, earlier on that eventful evening. While sitting opposite the front desk, I had heard the security personnel, during the course of a discussion they were already well engaged in, declare that "There were a lot of vulnerable people out there." Assuming that this was the first occasion on which I had heard people discussing the calamitous situation facing us, I had remarked to myself that it was an irony indeed that the ushers and security personnel seemed more aware of the facts than those inside the house. However, it transpired that they were talking about a woman who had rung the Joe Duffy radio phone-in programme Liveline and recounted her sad story of being €20,000 in debt on her credit card and unable to make ends meet. There had been, it appeared, huge interest in the poor woman's plight, and subsequently a generous listener had taken pity on her predicament and paid off her debts. It was later to emerge that the woman had been lying and that the vulnerable people the ushers were referring to were the unfortunate gullible people who were suckers for a sob story and easy pickings for determined and experienced fraudsters. As I looked around the tram carriage that night and remembered the people I had seen and heard that day, I could not help feeling that a similar con had just been committed on the whole population of Ireland by the bankers and their partners in crime, the politicians.

Chapter 13

Staring into the abyss

In attempting to describe the feelings I experienced while attending the Dáil session that night, my thoughts returned to the classic Frank Capra movie *It's a Wonderful Life*. In this morality tale the plot revolves around the conflict between the two main characters, played by James Stewart and Lionel Barrymore. Stewart's character, Harry Bailey, is the loyal and decent director of the Bailey's Building and Loan Association in Bedford Falls, which provides home loans for the working poor of the town, while Potter, played by Barrymore, is the heartless chairman of a larger financial institution which intends taking control of Bailey's enterprise and monopolising the lending market to the detriment of the poorest of the town's inhabitants. Potter is particularly offended by the Affordable Housing Project which Bailey sets up, whereby the poorest of the town's population are saved from paying huge rents to Potter to live in slum conditions by the affordable loans provided by Bailey's bank to buy their own houses. Potter attempts, through mainly foul means, to rid himself of the opposition which is preventing him from dominating the market. Having attempted all manner of despicable methods to put his competitor out of business, Potter is finally reduced to offering Stewart a huge contract to betray his loyalty to the townspeople, an offer he stoically refuses. However, by dint of an unfortunate blunder by Bailey's uncle, Potter mischievously spreads rumours that Bailey's loan association is strapped for cash and so starts a run on Bailey's bank. Bailey is left facing the prospect of bankruptcy. In abject misery at the thoughts of the hardship and distress this would cause his loyal friends and customers and cursing the fact that he had ever been born, he considers suicide. It is at this moment that his guardian angel arrives and presents him with the opportunity to witness what Bedford Falls would have been like, had he not played his part in its development. In a series of flashbacks, Bailey is presented with the opportunity to witness the dreadful lives his friends and acquaintances would have been condemned to had he never existed. Witnessing this hardship and strife in this surreal manner Bailey's character is revitalised and, hope rekindled, returns to his home to find friends, family and supporters gathered to offer financial support to his vitally important community based bank.

As I sat in the Members' Bar of Dáil Éireann on the night of September 30 2008 my thoughts returned to this wonderful film. I considered my situation that night eerily similar to that of Stewart's character in the movie. Though present in the scenes that recounted the tragic lives of hardship and suffering his friends would have been condemned to had he not been part of their community, Bailey was powerless to intervene. I too, was powerless to intervene as I watched in utter disbelief the peoples' representatives take a catastrophic decision that I knew full well would lead to untold hardship and suffering for the citizens of this State. The sense of being present and bearing witness as our political rulers took such a disastrous decision was surreal in the extreme. Being, it seems, the only person present who realised that the Irish banks, which were in the course of being underwritten to the tune of €460 billion by the taxpayers, were already bankrupt lent an air of total unreality to the proceedings. The total absence of alarm, or even apprehension, amongst the members of the Dáil defied understanding and was, quite frankly, nauseating. Indeed, what was abundantly evident that evening in Leinster House was the irrational euphoria which had distinguished the Celtic Tiger years of obscene wealth creation. To witness how public representatives basked in the self-reflected glory of their own perceived infallibility, not knowing that they had just taken the most disastrous decision in the history of the State, was the most uncanny feeling one could imagine. This fortuitous opportunity with which I had been presented served only to deepen my mistrust of our democratic process.

When I discovered next morning that the editorials in our daily newspapers were unanimous in their praise for the prompt and decisive action which our Minister for Finance had taken, I realised how deep the ignorance of our dire economic situation ran. Ireland's most listened to morning news radio programme, Morning Ireland, featured a report by the Political Correspondent, David McCullough, which was embarrassing in the extreme in its failure to appreciate the significance of the events which had taken place the previous night. After reporting the progress of the legislation towards its successful conclusion, McCullough was sympathised with for having had to endure such a long night in the Dáil. His colleagues in the studio mirthfully suggested that he must be hoping that not too many more debates of that duration would occur on his watch. Much like our politicians, who viewed the whole process as an inconvenient burden, McCullough replied that, if there were any more sessions like that, he for one wouldn't be there to cover it, a comment that inspired general mirth in the studio.

The message, repeated over and over again, was that the problems being experienced by the financial sector in our country were the result of the crash in world stock markets which followed the collapse of Lehmans in America. Our banks were more than adequately capitalised and were simply the victims of the crunch which had frozen the credit supply lines. This was the mantra which the Taoiseach, the Minister for Finance, the Financial Regulator and the banks themselves repeated ad nauseam. On 15 September, the Minister for Finance, Brian Lenihan, had assured citizens that "Our banks, uniquely, have weathered this storm," and, even more incompetently, that "We are in a zone of financial stability in a very troubled financial world." The guarantee which he was forced to issue to those self-same banks less than two weeks later was, he self-righteously announced, "the cheapest bail-out in the world so far." The guarantee, the government proclaimed, had addressed the issue, and the public could be assured that everything was under control and that credit would begin to flow once more into the coffers of the financial institutions, and from there to the public.

The corollary of this, though, was that credit flowed out of the other financial institutions across Europe as nervous depositors frantically searched for a safe haven for their cash deposits in a world financial system which was on the verge of collapse. The decision of the Irish government to supply the Irish people as underwriters to the greatest guarantee ever granted, flushed Irish banks with credit, while in the process bringing the financial system in Europe to the brink of the abyss. The terror which the Irish government's decision instilled in people across Europe was palpable. The German Prime Minister, Angela Merkel, was the epitome of fear as she realised the consequences the Irish decision could have on already destabilized German Banks, and was left with no option but to jump to the measure of last resort herself and issue a similar, though not as disastrously all-encompassing, guarantee. Other countries followed suit, as Ireland's 'beggar thy neighbour' policy threatened to starve them of capital by losing deposits to Ireland's safe haven accounts. Anger over Ireland's self-serving guarantee was tangible, but public expression of this anger was tempered by the fact that a second Lisbon Treaty vote was imminent, and European leaders, though incensed by the blatantly anti-European nature of the guarantee, reserved outright public condemnation for fear of antagonising the Irish public and running the risk of a 'No' victory on a second occasion.

In fact, Brian Cowen and Fianna Fáil could thank their lucky stars that there had been a 'No' vote on the first referendum, as the importance to European leaders of securing a 'Yes' result to the Lisbon Treaty left them unable to antagonise public opinion in Ireland. In private, though, the Taoiseach, Brian Cowen, was left in no doubt as to the extent of the resentment that existed amongst European leaders at the way he had damaged his European partners, and he emerged from subsequent European summit meetings a discouraged and dispirited man. Somewhat surprisingly, this monumental act of European treachery was not seized upon by opponents of the Lisbon Treaty as an example of the utmost irony, coming as it did from a Taoiseach who had chastised the Irish people for being 'bad Europeans' for voting 'No' in the first referendum. Cowen, as it happens, had reason to thank his stars that this had indeed been the result, as, otherwise, the Irish 'beggar thy neighbour' policy would have attracted a much harsher reaction.

None of this concern was apparent in Ireland, though. Politicians continued to bask in the self-deluding belief that they had achieved the most ingenious coup in the history of the State. Naively, they believed that our banks were sufficiently well-capitalised, and blithely dismissed any notions to the contrary. Our problems were not homemade, but were, supposedly, the result of the collapse of the sub prime market, and subsequently of Lehmans Bank. This self-righteous arrogance, which had been a fundamental factor in the creation of the financial crisis in the first instance, was now a major factor in exacerbating an already dire situation. The government, through its decision to provide a guarantee which was inevitably going to be called in and which it obviously could not afford to pay, was now in the invidious position of being over a barrel, entirely at the mercy of the banks. Should the banks require further support, the government was now obliged to provide it, as the consequence of insolvency of any of the financial institutions was too calamitous an eventuality to remotely consider, now that the public were underwriting the debt. But in any event the government, the banks and the financial regulator continued to brazenly pronounce that the banks' financial affairs were in exemplary condition and that they were well capitalised.

The markets, however, took a different view, and the share price of the Irish banks continued to crumble, following a positive period immediately following the granting of the guarantee. During this period it was abundantly clear that the markets were being manipulated by vested interests in the Irish banks themselves. Before the announcement of the guarantee, for example, certain privileged members of Ireland's golden elite benefited from the prior knowledge they had of forthcoming government support, buying shares at rock bottom prices which they subsequently sold at a huge profit when prices initially rocketed after 29 September. The government chose to ignore this blatant exploitation of the Irish taxpayer and idly stood by and watched as the Irish citizens' largesse was exploited to the full by stock market scavengers. In one particularly galling interview on the Marian Finucane radio show, Seanie Fitzpatrick, chairman of Anglo Irish Bank, disdainfully refused to apologise for bringing the financial system to the brink, but condescendingly thanked the Irish people for providing the guarantee which allowed the banks to benefit from the ensuing inflow of credit. He admitted in the same interview that executives in the bank had bought shares to the value of millions of euro in Anglo Irish in the week preceding the guarantee but, he claimed, this had been done as a demonstration of faith in the company and not in any way to benefit from the prior knowledge they possessed regarding the government's intentions. The complete interview remains one of the most appalling examples of the unashamed effrontery of these disreputable architects of our doom. His mission, to buy time for the primary instigators of the sham to scoop up what remained of the available cash before the true extent of the banks' dire situation became clear, was made all the easier by the fact that the presenter, Marian Finucane, lacked the requisite appreciation of economic affairs and was incapable of taking on one of the leading players in the game. Fitzpatrick was able to peddle blatant falsehoods as he confidently explained why Anglo Irish Bank was perfectly secure and would remain unaffected by the worst affects of the crisis, as it had little or no exposure to the housing market.

The fact was that it was the commercial and retail market which was being worst affected by the crisis at that moment in time and that Anglo Irish Bank, which had enormous exposure in the commercial development area, had already been flagged-up in media circles in Britain as being particularly vulnerable. Yet the presenter, who herself benefited from Celtic Tiger largesse to the tune of €500,000 for approximately seventy days' broadcasting a year, simply let this outrageous assertion go unchallenged. To be fair, she was but one of many examples of exorbitantly paid radio and television stars who revealed themselves as undeserving of those salaries. Her show, though, was a favourite medium for bankers, property developers and complicit economic commentators to attempt, successfully in most cases, to manipulate public opinion to their own advantage. Fitzpatrick's performance on this occasion was a master class in public deception, put out by our supposed public service broadcaster. While being afforded the opportunity on the national airwaves to brazenly dismiss any suggestions of current or indeed possible future difficulties within Anglo Irish, at a time when the bank was technically already insolvent, Fitzpatrick was in fact engaged in the age-old practice of buying time while the rats desert the sinking ship, taking with them whatever remained of value.

It has subsequently emerged that directors at the bank had withdrawn millions in personal loans in the period up to 30 September, the day the guarantee was introduced, and that Fitzpatrick himself had loans amounting to over €100 million from his own bank. What will also be interesting to learn is how much capital was withdrawn in loans from the banks covered by the guarantee in the weeks after it was granted, and who were the beneficiaries of those loans. Ironically and shamefully, Seanie Fitzpatrick was allowed to facilitate this clandestine run on the bank's assets by the well-off depositors, but when members of the public attempted to use another radio programme, Joe Duffy's Liveline, to afford ordinary citizens the opportunity to discuss their concerns regarding the safety of their deposits within the Irish banking system, the Department of Finance contacted the station privately and angrily warned the national broadcaster to put a stop to public discussion on the matter. A run on the banks was, it appeared, like everything else in Irish economic life, a privilege reserved for the upper echelons of our society. The government, through their actions, were ensuring that the golden circle would have first call on the limited reserves that remained in Irish banks and that Joe Public would be keep completely in the dark until the surreptitious run on our financial institutions was complete.

The government's shameful complicity in this 'rip-off' of the public was equalled only by the shocking incompetence which they also exhibited. That they were completely unaware of the disastrous consequences that would ensue from the breakdown of the world's financial system was evident to anyone with even a modicum of common sense. Sadly, none of our journalists and very few of our economic commentators seemed even remotely cognizant of the events which were taking place across the globe. While newspapers in Britain in early October 2008 led with headlines such as 'Staring into the Abyss' (over a picture of Britain's Prime Minister, Gordon Brown, looking suitably traumatised as the appalling reality appeared to dawn on him that the world was on the edge of financial meltdown), our media was welcoming the completion of a national pay deal, agreed between the government, employers and unions, which would result in pay increases for employees in the following year!

This would be laughable if it were not so serious. What on earth are our public representatives paid to do? That they were so completely incompetent as to fail to recognise that the world's financial system was, in the words of the ex-chairman of the Federal Reserve, Paul

Volker, "completely broken" and that the world was on the verge of a depression the likes of which it had not witnessed since the 1930s, beggars belief. Did these people understand anything about what was occurring in the world of finance? Did they read a newspaper other than Irish ones, which were busy congratulating them on the successful completion of national pay deal talks or inflating their oversized egos by suggesting that the guarantee was an example of prompt and decisive action by government? These people stand condemned as ignorant, indolent fools, whose actions in inflating the property bubble would suffice to warrant such a description, but whose inactivity in the eye of the worst economic storm to hit the world was incredible.

It is easy to imagine the mirth and incredulity with which the Irish government's incompetence was greeted by their European counterparts. As Gordon Brown wrestled with the threat of devastating depression, the Taoiseach, Brian Cowen, himself a former Minister for Finance, regarded the decrease in the price of oil and the drop in the rate of inflation as indicators that it "was not all bad news on the economic front." Unfortunately, his incompetence was even more evident in the manner in which he proceeded to deal with the financial institutions under State guarantee. Although the international markets had clearly decided that the Irish banks were shockingly over-leveraged and under-capitalised, and hedge funds continued to, in effect, bet that they would inevitably collapse, the government continued to accept the bona fides of the banks that they were perfectly well capitalised.

On 24 October the Chief Executive of Allied Irish Banks, Eugene Sheehy, pompously declared that his bank was more than adequately capitalised and that he "would rather die than raise equity." Brian Lenihan and Brian Cowen continually rubbished suggestions that

Irish banks were dangerously under-capitalised, and in one particularly embarrassing development the Financial Regulator, Patrick Neary, went on the Prime Time current affairs television programme, on 2 October, to dismiss suggestions that there was a problem of funding within our banks. His particularly supercilious, though blatantly inept, performance was one of the lowlights of this whole charade and, for possibly the first time, caused real concern amongst the population as a whole. The Financial Regulator began by incredibly suggesting that "bad lending by Irish banks had nothing to do with the current international crisis which was all to do with liquidity." He then proceeded to confidently announce that "Irish banks had plenty of capital to absorb any losses on property loans," and that he "did not believe that overexposure to the property market was a weakness of the Irish banking sector."

If this was the man who had been mandated to be the watchdog over our financial services industry, there were clearly grounds for worry. Public concern was gathering apace, and Irish banks' shares continued to tumble alarmingly on the stock markets. The initial confidence provided by the guarantee had been dissipated as the enormity of the banks' difficulties became increasingly evident. The government, though adamantly asserting that there was no cause for alarm, commissioned the auditors Price, Waterhouse, Coopers to examine the banks' books and report their findings. Recalling the major part played by auditors and accounting firms in the Enron scandal, and finding it difficult to escape the feeling that a conflict of interests would preclude the auditors from revealing the true nature of the difficulties within the banks, it came as no surprise that PWC reported to the Minister for Finance that the banks were well capitalised and would not require recapitalisation. This was frankly ridiculous,

audit, for which they were doubtless very
.emunerated, was proven to be complete
.hin weeks.

 Irish Bank, which its Chairman, Seanie
.rick, had confidently claimed to be well set to ride
ou .ne turmoil in world markets, continued to witness its
share price plummet as international investors realised the
extent to which its €73 billion loan portfolio left it alarmingly
exposed to the downturn. Fitspatrick was forced to step
down in December 2008, following revelations that he had
moved personal loans totalling €87 million off the balance
sheet towards the end of the last eight financial years. A
few days after this announcement, the government made
a complete about turn, and though Brian Lenihan had in
early November asserted that "it is not the function of the
Government to fund or bail-out banks," they now went
ahead with a €1.5 billion recapitalisation of Anglo Irish
bank in return for a 75% stake in that insolvent basket-
case. Amazingly, the Minister for Finance admitted at the
time that he had failed to read the section of the PWC
report which showed that the former Chairman of Anglo
Irish Bank, Seanie Fitzpatrick, had been indulging in a
cosy arrangement with another financial institution, Irish
Life and Permanent, to cook the books at Anglo in the run-
up to the presentation of the bank's accounts. Instead, the
Minister, Brian Lenihan, and the government continued
to declare that Anglo Irish Bank, which had loaned
exclusively and recklessly to the commercial property
sector, was of systemic importance to Ireland's financial
system and could not be allowed to fail.

When Fitspatrick resigned, Donal O'Connor, formerly
of auditors, Price, Waterhouse, Coopers, who had served
as an external member of the interviewing panel that had
chosen David Drumm to succeed Fitzpatrick as CEO of
Anglo Irish Bank in 2004, was now himself appointed

chairman of the bank, and the recapitalisation was announced. Once again, this announcement triggered frantic dealings on the Irish Stock exchange, and the usual suspects were permitted to reap the rewards of the increase in Anglo's share price which inevitably resulted from the government's committal of taxpayers' money to the sinking ship that was Anglo Irish Bank. Shockingly, the turbulent conditions which existed on stock markets at the time, which were resulting in millions of people losing their jobs around the globe, provided ample opportunities for financial scavengers to reap vast personal rewards from the suffering of others, an opportunity they had no apparent qualms about accepting gleefully. Again, following an initial few days when the share price rose, on the announcement of the €1.5 billion government injection of taxpayers' money, the realisation struck that this was merely a token amount when set beside the €73 billion exposure Anglo had to the commercial property market, which was in freefall worldwide.

Astoundingly, both the government's own stress tests of the bad debt liabilities of all the banks, and those of PWC, seriously underestimated the level to which property valuations had fallen and therefore provided a deliberately flawed picture of the disastrous financial landscape which was panning out before us. When it was finally announced in January – after Anglo's share price had at one point fallen to 12 cents from its imperious high of €18.65 in February 2007 – that the bank was to be nationalised, the media finally appeared to awaken from its stupor and recognised that this decision was proof positive that Anglo Irish Bank was indeed Ireland's Enron. Finally, some three months after the rest of the world had recognised that there was a uniquely devastating 'event' occurring in the world's financial system, there appeared to be some acceptance of the fact within this country that we were indeed in a dire financial situation of our own making. On Sunday 28 December, as I waited in line to board an airplane to take me to Girona, in Catalonia, I shook my head in disbelief as I noticed a fellow passenger reading a copy of the *Sunday Tribune* which contained the headline: "Staring into the Abyss" over a picture of the Taoiseach, Brian Cowen, looking, at last, suitably traumatised.

This man, who as Minister for Finance had presided over some of the worst excesses of the boom, had finally and belatedly come to the realisation that the world's financial system had been shaken to its roots, admitting as much on the Gerry Ryan radio programme in late December when he obliquely referred to a "fatal fracture in the financial system." It is debatable how many people recognised the true import of this typically and deliberately circuitous attempt by the Taoiseach to address the appalling reality of the situation with which we the public were now faced as a result of his, and others, incompetence. One would have thought that possibly, on realising the extent of that incompetence, our public representatives might do the honourable thing and stand aside to allow others, more capable than themselves, to attempt to extricate us from the mess they had gotten us into. But no. The unfathomable reality of this particular democratic deficit, which masqueraded as an effective system, was that those who had incompetently led us to the edge of the abyss were to be charged with guiding us to safety while idiotically maintaining the same mindset which had brought us to the brink of disaster in the first place.

Nothing was to change, neither personnel nor policy. The same people, employing the evidently defunct and failed political philosophy which had created the fraudulent boom, were to be given the opportunity to raise the sunken ship, using the same methods once more. Bankers would retain their positions and would remain entitled to the outrageous salaries to which they had become accustomed, based on 'performance-related pay'. Shockingly, in America 10% of the $700 billion dollar bail-out provided to the banks was used to pay bonuses to staff in those financial institutions. $70 billion dollars was paid in bonuses to bank employees who had brought those very institutions to the verge of ruin. In Ireland Chairmen, Chief Executives and directors continued to reap lavish rewards for their incompetence. The announcement of Donal O'Connor as the new Chairman of Anglo Irish Bank, in place of Seanie Fitzpatrick, illustrated perfectly the fact that, though personnel might change, the philosophy would remain the same. O'Connor, it should be remembered, was a former Chief Executive of the auditors PWC, the very same auditors who had benefited generously for years from the contract to audit the accounts at Bank of Ireland without noticing any cause for concern. These were also the same auditors who had, as late as October 2008, conducted a massive audit of the main Irish banks and concluded that they had enough capital until 2011!

O'Connor and his new board at Anglo Irish Bank did not herald a new beginning. Dishearteningly, though not in the least surprisingly, the old guard on the boards had been replaced by a new guard comprised of same old tired faces. Although they were representatives of a discredited ideology, they were also, more importantly, card carrying members of the Golden Circle of power and privilege, an exclusive entity which had no intention of relinquishing the control they enjoyed over the citizens of the State. The king was dead. Long live the King!.

The very basis of the free-market capitalism ideology, that entrepreneurs or wealth-creators deserved their obscene financial rewards due to the fact that they had created those vast resources of capital in the first place, was exposed as the outrageous lie that it had always been. When the corollary of this ideology demanded that those incompetent oafs who had brought our banks, and therefore the country, to the verge of bankruptcy be dismissed, no appetite appeared to exist for this perfectly reasonable step. Executives continued to draw colossal salaries, even though their financial results were disastrous. When some were embarrassed into resigning, they just headed off into the sunset, shamelessly enriched by enormous golden handshakes, ostensibly, it appeared, to reward them for their gross incompetence over the preceding years. When they departed they were replaced by colleagues who had been their accomplices. Economic commentators slammed calls for these scandalous salaries to be reduced, claiming that they were necessary in order to entice the best financial minds to these important positions!

The question that begged to be asked was, where on earth were geniuses from the financial world to be found that could occupy these positions who had not been tarred with the same brush of incompetence, seeing as the world's financial system had been in thrall so utterly to the free-market capitalism doctrine for twenty to thirty years. Nothing had been learnt from this experience. So complete had the indoctrination of the previous generation been, it appeared that these brainwashed individuals were incapable of rational economic thinking. Unfortunately, for all the innocent observers of this pathetic excuse for economic intelligence, their subsequent contemptible actions, in an apparent effort to correct their own mistakes, were to ensure even more hardship and suffering for ordinary people.

Chapter 14

We Are Where We Are!

The appalling vista which finally appeared on the horizon for the Taoiseach Brian Cowen and his government colleagues at the end of December was more than likely exactly the one that had been uppermost in my own thoughts three months previously in Dáil Éireann. They had no idea of the scale of the calamitous dilemma which was now facing the State. They didn't realise that all Irish Banks were already irredeemably insolvent. The collapse of the commercial and private property markets, which was then in its initial stages, was an absolute inevitability, and the prospect of half a million people joining the dole queues almost a dead-certainty. Both events would occur concurrently and would magnify each other. The government would then have to finance those social welfare repayments on the dwindling tax-returns from Stamp-duty, Capital Gains and Income Taxes, which were all in freefall due to the collapse of the economy. This was all eminently predictable and foreseeable in September, a full three months before it finally dawned on our elected representatives.

Amazingly, when the government finally tumbled to the consequences brought about by the years of excess, self-aggrandisement and complete lack of financial regulation, they showed not one ounce of contrition. On the contrary, the politicians, executives and economic experts who had led Ireland and her citizens to the inflation of the property bubble for their own benefit, arrogantly proposed to employ the same methods which had caused the crisis in order to solve it. The Celtic Tiger years had indeed been a conspiracy of incompetents who, euphorically drunk on the spoils of their national scam, held that their method was the only method. It was generally accepted that wealth was the only barometer of worth in Irish society. The fact that such a moral deficit was permitted to occur was in no small measure due to the waning influence of the Catholic Church, which in its turn was mainly due to people's disgust at the Church's cover-up of its brutal treatment of some of the most vulnerable members of Irish society.

The public were to react with stunned fury in May 2009 when the Ryan report into allegations of abuse within Church-run institutions was published. Finally, those who had suffered in the most appalling ways imaginable at the hands of religious orders who professed to be their saviours, were given the opportunity to be heard. Having suffered the initial abuse of being physically tortured and economically exploited for no reason other than being poor, these courageous survivors of what has been described as Ireland's holocaust were forced to endure the further indignity of not being believed when they first highlighted their claims of mistreatment. The Ryan report conclusively and irrefutably demonstrated that the Church had abused its position of power and privilege and had presided over a system which treated children more like prison inmates than people with legal rights and human potential. The abuse that these unfortunate children suffered was "systemic, pervasive, chronic, excessive, arbitrary and endemic," to quote but some of the startling adjectives used in the report's findings.

The litany of allegations which were substantiated by the Ryan Report included "beatings, rapes, children being subjected to naked beatings in public, being forced into oral sex and even being subjected to naked beatings after failed rape attempts by Christian Brothers." This appalling story was spelt out in the most forthright and commendable manner, and entirely corroborated the claims by former 'inmates' as to the shocking conditions that existed within these supposedly Christian institutions. They had now been revealed to be nothing more than workhouse factories where less fortunate members of society were abused and exploited by the powerful and the privileged for economic gain. The impact that these revelations had on the collective conscience could not be overstated. The chord that these courageous survivors' harrowing tales struck with the public in general showed that the free-markets capitalists' agenda of creating an economic society bereft of any notion of empathy, decency and respect for one's fellow citizens had, thankfully, not been completely successful.

When public anger inevitably turned into outrage at the dishonest 'deal' that had been agreed between Church and State some years previously which limited Church liability to compensation to a mere 10%, the reaction of our public representatives and Church leaders was most revealing. That some survivors of the Church's exploitation and abuse would now, as tax-payers, be contributing 90% of their own compensation was seen as yet another form of abuse. The true nature of the Church-State axis was illustrated by the way in which both institutions rallied to support each other. The shameless manner in which the institution of the Church steadfastly refused to accept that they should pay more than 10% for its sins perfectly demonstrates that wealth, power and privilege, rather than peace, love and understanding, are its real core values.

Though notoriously cash rich, the corporation that is the Catholic Church had been revealed by this whole shameful episode to be, like their counterparts in the business world, morally bankrupt. That the government stood four-square beside their venerable partners, refusing to accept that the Church had even a 'moral' obligation to revisit the terms of the contract they had signed before the systemic abuse became public knowledge, showed quite clearly the corrupt nature of the relationship that existed between them. When these two supposed pillars of our Democratic and Christian society chose to defend the indefensible in the face of the outrage emanating from the general public, it perfectly illustrated the real divide which existed within Irish society. Despite valiant attempts by those at the very highest echelons of the free-market economy to suggest otherwise, the divisions that existed between the public and private sectors were not the most relevant. It had become abundantly clear that the truly relevant division was that between those who enjoyed positions of power and privilege and those who did not.

The contradictory message which was at the heart of the free-market capitalists' philosophy was perplexing in the extreme until one appreciated that there existed, as always, within its doctrine one rule of acceptable behaviour for the privileged and another for the victims of its exploitative agenda. Free-market capitalists required, for example, that workers in both public and private sectors be paid on the basis of productivity and introduced measures, such as benchmarking in the public sector and rationalisation in the private sector, to increase productivity and penalise those who failed to perform and conform. However, when it was revealed that the privileged and powerful in the public and the private sectors were incompetent or astoundingly wasteful, no corrective was sought or imposed. So we had the hypocritical situation where ministers such as Martin Cullen could extol the Progressive Democrat philosophy by demanding efficiency and cost effectiveness of the public and private workforces and yet be responsible for waste and inefficiency which amounted to hundreds of millions of euro. Similarly a blatant contradiction existed between the assertion made by the wealth-creators that they were entitled to their vast personal fortunes as rewards for their ingenuity and entrepreneurial skills and their subsequent unwillingness to forego any of their riches when it was revealed that they had in fact been unbelievably incompetent and thoroughly incapable throughout their tenure as the doyens of our economy.

The fact that the electorate, both here and in Britain, were faced with the dilemma of turning to an opposition party which was of equal, or possibly more extreme right-wing philosophical tendencies, in an attempt to rescue them from an economic chaos that had been created by that self-same doctrine revealed the desperate condition which the democratic system itself was in at this juncture. In Ireland Fine Gael, the main opposition party, who had supported the government guarantee of the banks, was the first out of the blocks to assign blame to the public sector for the collapse of the free-market economic model. Their clamour for public sector reform was a clear sign that the forces of political and economic power were set fair to absolve the privileged and powerful. The hypocritical suggestion that the people who had been exploited so appallingly in order to facilitate the amassing of immense wealth by the few were to blame for the downturn was born from the same mindset that had underpinned the rise of the Celtic Tiger economy in the first place. The creation of wealth was the only means by which one's value to society would be judged.

However, as the property boom turned to bust and the revenue from indirect taxes associated with the boom dried up, the deficiencies in the low-income-tax model of free-market capitalism became ever more apparent. The government now had to borrow increasing millions just to cover day to day expenses, and it chose to redirect public ire towards the usual victims of their bile in the public sector. The media in general, though the State broadcaster RTÉ in particular, rose to the challenge and mercilessly supported the parliamentarians. Day in, day out, the same tired faces that had led us to the brink of disaster were given the freedom of the airways to peddle their blatantly distorted views regarding who was responsible for the crisis. Listening to these bungling fools hectoring the public regarding the sacrifices they, the public, would have to make to save the situation, in the full knowledge that they themselves were solely responsible for causing the crisis, was one of the most unedifying aspects of the whole debacle.

One programme, in particular, broadcast on Saturday 8 March 2009 on RTÉ, Marian Finucane's weekend panel-based discussion programme, included the usual suspects in the free-market conspiracy sham as guests. The Friends First insurance company's economic expert, Jim Power, was allowed free reign to dispense his bilious contempt for the public services, which he audaciously blamed for all the wrongs in the economy, and became apoplectic as he fumed that his children faced the spectre of emigration, due in total to the inadequacies of the public sector. This appalling prospect, he reminded us, was reminiscent of the brain-drain that had occurred during the last major recession that Fianna Fáil – now a symbol of the public service in his warped understanding of events – had created in the late seventies and eighties. The public service, he proclaimed, had brought about a situation whereby his children could well be victims of this enforced 'brain-drain' emigration. It would, of course, have been interesting to hear Jim Power questioned about his competence to comment on any aspect of the collapse of free-market finance that he had dedicated his whole working life to promoting and sustaining.

Another guest who joined Power on the panel and was allowed the freedom of the airwaves that day to espouse her thoughts on our dire economic plight was Professor of Management at UCD's Smurfit Business School, Niamh Brennan. Seething with anger, she too launched a passionate attack on the inadequacies of the public services. Her particular ire was reserved for the inadequate politicians and their bungling advisers in the civil service who had presided over the banking fiasco. It was time, she fumed, that expertise from the private sector was introduced into the public service to ensure professional and competent administration of the country's affairs. Once again, one was tempted to ask if she had in mind the geniuses from the private sector who had been paid enormous sums for their incompetent and fraudulent management of those self-same banking institutions. Remarkably, or possibly not so remarkably, neither of these questions was asked of the UCD professor of management, author of over a hundred publications in the areas of financial reporting, corporate governance and forensic accounting. Nor was she asked whether she felt any qualms of conscience about the events that transpired in our economy – after all, she was a non-executive director at Ulster Bank, the bank which was first to offer 100% mortgages – nor how she evaluated the role of her husband, Michael McDowell, former leader of the Progressive Democrats, in the events that had led to the catastrophic conclusion she was now busy blaming the public service for. Instead, the well-remunerated presenter indulged her guest's outrageous and indefensible ranting.

Another of Finucane's contributors that day was business-man Ulick McEvaddy, thereby ensuring, as was habitually the case, that no-one earning less than one hundred thousand euro annually was present on the panel of this highly influential programme produced by the national broadcaster. The presence of McEvaddy ensured that it was, as on so many other occasions in the past, replete with the full complement of propagandists for the free-market ideology, thus guaranteeing that no worthwhile debate would occur or be countenanced and that RTÉ would be remiss, once more, in its duty of providing a fair and balanced service of information to the public. An aviation tycoon who had amassed a great personal fortune through his business endeavours, McEvaddy was a self-proclaimed staunch supporter of Fine Gael who 'obsessed' about the party. His avowed loyalty to Fine Gael had not, however, precluded him from making his villa in the south of France available to both the leader of the Progressive Democrats, Mary Harney, and her ideological blood brother in Fianna Fáil, Charlie McCreevy, later to serve as Minister for Finance for the State. The disclosure of this cosy relationship between pivotal figures in the world of big business and some of the State's most senior politicians was to cause disquiet when it was revealed to the public in 1999. McEvaddy's contribution to Marian Finucane's radio programme that day was to call, amongst other things, for the abolition of 'mark to market' accounting, the very accounting manoeuvre that had been exploited by Enron executives as an integral part of their fraud to falsely inflate profits.

Basically, random figures were plucked from the air which purported to demonstrate upward growth in profits, thereby ensuring that share price continued to increase in valuation and so guaranteed an enormous financial windfall for the company's directors and executives. McEvaddy was now calling for the outlawing of 'mark to market', not because of its pivotal role in the Ireland Inc. scam, but because prospective negative growth was having a disastrous effect on the future returns of corporations in Ireland, most particularly the banks.

As in so many other instances with the Ireland Inc. sham, theories that were used to instigate and enable the deception and, indeed, were hailed as basic tenets of the free-market capitalists' doctrine, were hastily dispensed with when they appeared to inhibit the capacity of its disciples to protect their own fortunes. Similarly, Jim Power and his colleagues would now rail against 'benchmarking', the system that the right-wing developed for 'ranking' public servants' salaries, in a manner commensurate with private sector modalities, as being responsible for irreparably damaging the country's competitiveness, conveniently forgetting that it was they and their partners in powerful and privileged trades union leaderships, who had foisted benchmarking on public service workers in the first place. That benchmarking had resulted in a significant diminution in the services provided to the public was of no great concern to its supporters. It had successfully achieved its primary objective of ensuring that the privileged elements of the public service were assured of generous remuneration commensurate with their obscenely rewarded counterparts in the private sector.

The private media, as one would expect, contributed in no small measure to the campaign being waged by those responsible for the crisis to absolve themselves of blame and to protect their standing within society. Once again, the battle to apportion blame was presented as one of the public versus the private sectors, with the privately-owned media, not surprisingly, choosing to berate those within the public services as being responsible. One of the most effective tactics they employed was to highlight the undoubted profligacy within the top echelons of the public services. This, they claimed, proved incontrovertibly that it was the public sector that had wasted the wealth that had been created by the Celtic Tiger. One of the prime examples, first highlighted by some fine reporting by *Irish Independent* journalists, was the scandal they uncovered at the Government agency FAS. The Irish National Training and Employment Authority were found to have spent upwards of €1 billion of tax-payers money at a time of nearly full employment. A significant portion of this money went in expenses accrued to support the lavish lifestyles of the directors at FAS. Obviously considering themselves entitled to similar luxurious lifestyles to their counterparts in the private sector, and indeed the government ministers who had appointed them to the board, the directors at FAS were revealed to have spent scandalous amounts of tax-payers money while enjoying the highlife of Celtic Tiger Ireland.

In a four-year period FAS director-general Rody Molloy spent €48,000 on business-class airfares. On many occasions he was joined by his wife, and their excesses, which included outlandish hotel and golfing expenses, caused uproar when revealed to an outraged public. The Chairman of the Authority at the time, Peter McLoone who was also President of the Irish Congress of Trade Unions, the largest trade union in the State, had joined Molloy on one such trip to America at a combined cost to the tax-payer of €14,000. These were but a few of the expenses which were revealed to the public at this time and interpreted as being bona fide evidence that the public sector was to blame for bringing the Celtic Tiger economy to its knees. The public sector, the rationale had it, had squandered the wealth and should therefore be punished by crippling wage deductions and massive reductions in staffing levels.

What this deliberately ignored was the fundamental fact that it was not the 'bust' that lay at the heart of our economic woes, but the 'boom'. It also deliberately attempted to set 'public' against 'private' in a diversionary tactic to avert people's attention from the real divide that had been at the core of the Ireland Inc. fraud, that of people who enjoyed power and privilege, whether in the public or the private sector, against those who did not. The members of these State boards were, after all, government appointees, primarily members of the Golden Circle or others who were deemed to have 'done some service' which benefited this exclusive club of wealth creators in some manner. Included in this latter group were the top echelons of the Trades Union movement, who had contributed in no small way to the Ireland Inc. fraud by ensuring, year upon year, national wage agreements which resulted in massive increases in profits for their partners in Ireland Inc. at the same time as they were condemning their own union members to inevitable future hardship.

The manner in which former trade union leaders benefited from the largesse of an appreciative ruling elite was a significant indicator of the vital role they played in the whole charade. When Peter McLoone finally bowed to media and public pressure to resign from the board of FAS, it was a momentous moment in many ways. His resignation, along with the other members of the board at FAS, including another ex union leader, Des Geraghty, for presiding over such alarming waste of tax-payers' money, was the first occasion in many a long year when someone in the service of the government had taken responsibility for their inept actions. At a subsequent press briefing, the Taoiseach, Brian Cowen, who had pointedly refused to ask the board to resign, congratulated them on having done 'the honourable thing' in resigning. It was truly pathetic to see that one of his ministers, who was busy nodding his head in earnest agreement with him, was none other than Martin Cullen, the self-same minister who had overseen the waste of more tax-payers' money than he dared to remember and yet was still in a position to continue his inept performance in government regardless.

The outright refusal to countenance resignation as an option, even in the face of the most damming evidence of incompetence or wrongdoing, was another defining tenet of the Celtic Tiger period. It was a bizarre feature of our democracy that opposition parties were reluctant to call for a minister's resignation. They also seemed very reluctant to highlight situations where ministers could be accused of corrupt or questionable behaviour. There seemed to exist a form of 'omerta' which precluded such 'punishments' amongst the political fraternity, an oath of secrecy which extended to large sections of the media too. How else could one explain the apparent reluctance of the opposition and the media to point to outrageous conflicts of interest which permitted the intricate network of close friends and family that existed in Ireland to financially benefit from our economy? The furore in FAS highlighted the fact that the former director-general, Rody Molloy, was a close friend of the Taoiseach. When he resigned, Molloy received a massive golden handshake, which was deemed by many to be simply a reward for incompetence.

Interestingly, none of the opposition parties were willing to push the Taoiseach, or indeed the Tánaiste, Mary Coughlan, who had handled the affair in a most cack-handed manner, to resign. Likewise, they failed to highlight a far more worrying example of political favouritism which arose from the FAS controversy. When Peter McLoone resigned as Chairman of the FAS board, his only plea in mitigation on his, and his board's, behalf was that they had only been in charge of overseeing affairs at the authority for the previous two years and that the worst excesses of overspending had been a legacy of the previous board's tenure in office. The Chairman of the previous board was Brian Geoghegan, a former chief director of economic policy at employers group IBEC. Geoghegan had been appointed to the board in 2000 by the Minister for Enterprise and Employment at the time, former Progressive Party leader, Mary Harney. One year later the two were to marry, and Harney and Geoghegan were later to enjoy some quality time together on FAS sponsored trips abroad. It was during Geoghegan's tenure as Chairman of the training and employment authority that the FAS budget doubled, at a time of almost full employment.

When he resigned from the organisation in 2005 Geoghegan, in his capacity as director of economic policy at IBEC, called for a firm hand to be installed as Minister for Health to oversee a more professional and efficient public health service, modelled on the private sector. He then took up a position with a private consultancy firm, MRPA Kinman. Within a short period his wife, Mary Harney, was appointed Minister for Health and set about reforming the public health service in a manner more suited to her free-market ideological beliefs. One step she took almost immediately was to set up the Health Information and Quality Authority (HIQA) with a mandate to effectively privatise vast parts of the health system. MRPA Kinman were employed as consultants, on a generous retainer from the tax-payer, to advise the HIQA how to best achieve this aim. Simultaneously, MRPA Kinman were also representing massive multi-national pharmaceuticals, such as the giant Wyeth corporation, that hoped to benefit from the generous grants that were on offer to set up shop in Ireland. It is worth noting that these massive pharmaceutical corporations were, and continue to be, amongst the worst exponents when it came to extracting excessive profits from the market and were one of the primary causes of the public health service budget spiralling out of control. When Minister for Health Mary Harney announced that the government were investing €2.75 billion in the biosciences sector, in an effort to entice more pharmaceuticals to establish their businesses here, MRPA Kinman were in a very advantageous position to benefit from that decision.

Interestingly, many of those associated with MRPA Kinman were former colleagues and acquaintances of the Minister for Health, with connections to the Progressive Democrats. The Managing Director at the agency was none other than the former press officer and spokesperson for the Party, Richard Gordon. Another even more interesting face on the board of directors at MRPA Kinman was a founder member of the Progressive Democrats, Stephen O'Byrnes. He, aside from being Assistant Government press secretary in the 1989–92 Fianna Fáil-led coalition with the PDs, had been a journalist with the *Irish Independent* and was appointed to the RTÉ authority in 2000, serving a five-year period with the national broadcaster. During his stint on the RTÉ authority he may well have come into contact with Harney's younger sister, Geraldine, who was also employed by RTÉ as a reporter on business affairs and who had had garnered just over 3% of the vote in the Dublin Central constituency when she stood for the Progressive Democrats in the 1989 general election. This network of close family and familiar contacts in positions of power is peculiar to Ireland, I believe, as a distinctive element in the form of free-market capitalism that was adopted across the world in the past twenty years.

Reflecting the relatively small population of five million people, and the even smaller section of influential people who dominated the highest echelons of the economy and society in the past eighty years, it has frequently averted the need for financial corruption. There was often no need in Ireland, as was the case in other countries, to illegally grease the palms of those from whom you required a delicate business favour, when the hand being extended was often that of a relative or a close acquaintance.

The worst example, by far, of the way in which power was the preserve of a privileged few was the democratic system itself. When one considers that the three most senior ministers in the Government at the time of the banking guarantee, those guiltiest of taking the most incompetent decision in the history of the State – the Taoiseach, Brian Cowen, the Tánaiste, Mary Coughlan, and the Minister for Finance, Brian Lenihan – were children of previous members of parliament, or niece in the case of Coughlan, the extent of political nepotism becomes shockingly evident. That their direct relatives were members of parliament for Fianna Fáil in the 1970s and 80s, when that party last brought the State to the brink of economic ruination, illustrates that rewarding incompetence was certainly not a new phenomenon in Ireland. It is, however, a very worrying concern for the democratic process that seats in parliament can be handed down from generation to generation of privileged political dynasties in a manner reminiscent of the 'rotten boroughs' of pre-industrial revolution times.

That the people of Ireland continue to elect individuals to our parliament, some of whom have been convicted of defrauding the very State they are supposed to honourably serve, is one of the most dismaying elements in this sorry saga. How those found guilty of tax evasion and tax avoidance could be expected to uphold the values of an equitable and just society is beyond comprehension, and yet that was exactly the state of affairs that pertained for the duration of the Celtic Tiger period. The political dynasties that ruled this country did so, not from any ideological predilection for equitably and honourably serving the people of the island, but primarily in order to profit from their positions of power within the political system. This was the motivation that had inspired the original decision to provide the State guarantee for the private banking system. The manner in which the government reacted to the alarming drop in exchequer returns by immediately turning on the middle and low income families to source new avenues of revenue was born of the same inequitable thinking. A substantial tax on the richest members of society would have meant the equitable extraction of what was retrospectively and rightfully due to the citizens of the State.

The same disregard for the basic elements of any properly functioning democracy was shamefully evident in another of the means which the government suggested be employed to boost the economy. Along with their propagandists, they insisted that recovering our competitiveness was an essential for economic recovery. While accepting that wages that had chased the hyper-inflationary property market needed to return to more sustainable levels in order to attract and retain employment, how they could have entertained doing so at the time beggared belief. With nearly half a million people unemployed, and the ever increasing pressure this inevitably brought to bear on mortgage repayments, the government now proposed drastically reducing wages. How they thought those who were fortunate to be in employment, who had already mortgaged themselves to the very limit, could continue to service those extortionate loans on decreasing incomes was once again beyond comprehension. That this would undoubtedly force tens of thousands more households to renege on their mortgage repayments thereby causing further catastrophic damage to the balance sheets of the very banks they were supposedly attempting to save never seemed to cross the minds of these supposed economic experts.

Once more, connivance with the powerful lobby in the business world was influencing policy decisions to an exorbitant extent. Had the government not been so duplicitously at the service of corporate business on the night that the financial institutions came calling for their fellow members of the Golden Circle to come to their aid with the public's guarantee, then most of the problems facing the State could have been dealt with rapidly. The financial institutions should have been told, in no uncertain terms, that the difficulties they were facing were of their own making, and that they were to be allowed to fail unless they went to those who held their bonds and negotiated a 50% decrease in primary mortgages. Having achieved this essential realignment in debt-to-income ratios, the opportunity would then have presented itself to regain competitiveness in a realistic and sustainable manner by reducing wages by up to 50%. Had they chosen the option of reducing the excessive mortgage repayments, which had been the basis for the property fraud in the first place, they would have been taking the first step in readjusting debt-to-income ratios which will inevitably be undertaken in all the economies of the world that succumbed to free-market capitalism.

The abolition of performance-related bonus payments, a repulsive element of the entire fraud, should have been accompanied by a capping of all salaries at a maximum in the region of €100,000 per annum. This, in effect a capping of personal profit, should then have been extended to a cap on corporate profit. Both could have been achieved by the introduction of extra taxes and should have centred on financial and insurance institutions, two areas of the free-market model that were particular guilty of extracting excessive amounts of wealth from the economy with little justifiable benefit in return. In fact, as we have seen, the grand effect of this over-profiteering was to starve the real economy of capital while simultaneously adding a tremendously heavy financial burden to the average person's and average business's daily costs. The reduction of this liability to cost and debt was one and the same concept, and it should have been uppermost in the minds of our public representatives on 29 September 2008. Instead, the government chose that night, and subsequently, to continue the policy of pandering to profit makers, or wealth creators, the self-same profiteers who had brought us to this catastrophic crisis in the first instance.

Favouring profit over people was of course a recurring theme in the economic doctrine of the wealth-creators and their supporters. This was the doctrine which formed the basis for the two budgets which the government introduced in a ham-fisted attempt to correct the problems which their policies had created. It heavily penalised the average earner in both the public and private sectors, while dismissing any notion that the obscenely wealthy in our society had any obligation to contribute to cleaning up the financial mess they had made. The Minister for Finance, Brian Lenihan, had the audacity to end his emergency budget speech in April 2008 with a rousing call for everyone to do their "patriotic duty" to save the economy. Unfortunately for Minister Lenihan his words, carefully chosen as they were, to provide a stirring finale to his speech, served only to remind some of the famous pronouncement of the poet and essayist Samuel Johnson who declared, quite prophetically, that patriotism was the last refuge of scoundrels.

The Minister for Finance set up a committee to investigate areas where savings could be made in the public sector. 'An Bord Snip', chaired by economist Colm McCarthy, was asked to investigate areas in public spending where cutbacks could be made. The philosophy of those who established the committee was patently evident from its mandate and composition.

Public services and payrolls would be slashed, as the right-wing economists took a vengeful cut at that sector of society for which they had always held particular opprobrium. That the decreases in public sector pay would impact particularly on the lower and average sections of the private sector caused no concern to the committee, as these were losers who had failed to benefit from the bountiful opportunities the Celtic Tiger years had provided.

The unwillingness of these free-market joy-riders to countenance any attack on the powerful and privileged was evident in the choice of Colm McCarthy as chairman of the board. A UCD economist, McCarthy was also a founding member and executive of the economic consultancy firm DKM Consultants. Consultancy firms such as this, much like the accountancy firms in the financial world, reaped massive rewards during the boom period from work contracted from both the public and private sectors. One particularly interesting report which Colm McCarthy and DKM consultants were commissioned to undertake concerned the West Link toll bridge on the M50 motorway. National Toll Roads (NTR), the company which owned and operated the bridge, commissioned DKM to prepare a report on this extremely profitable and highly controversial project. This was the bridge that had been constructed at an original cost of £38 million, but which had already taken in over a billion euro in profit from the tolls collected at the booths erected on the motorway.

The fact that these booths were now causing the same traffic congestion that the motorway had been built to alleviate, and that the contract still had a seven year period to run was a source of understandable consternation amongst the public and attracted particular negative publicity for National Toll Roads. They therefore commissioned DKM consultants, at considerable cost, to prepare a report on the running and cost-effectiveness of their concern. Colm McCarthy, who had always been a vociferous supporter of private over public in all areas, but in particular transport, was eminently suited to the task of furnishing them with a report which would be sweet music to their ears. His report found that, while NTR had accrued massive profits from operating the tolls on the M50, the government (and therefore presumably the State) were also benefiting from the arrangement. In criticising the initial contract agreed with the NTR, McCarthy endeavoured to pass the blame for any perceived flaws in the motorway project from big business to big government. In any event, the company had got what they had required from the report from the consultancy firm they themselves had employed to investigate the matter.

Interestingly, McCarthy predicted the value of the remaining seven years of the NTR contract at €616 million, a valuation which, coincidently or not, closely approximated the €600 million which the government finally paid the company in 2007 for the removal of the booths. Twelve years after it was built, and at a cost of nearly €2 billion euro to the citizens of the State, a wooden barrier was removed from across the motorway that cost less than €40 million to build, to allow it to function as designed. The profit, of some 2,000%, on a project which failed to deliver the service it was built to provide was deemed good value to the State by the man who had now been employed to oversee and identify areas where savings could be made in the public purse. An economist who had failed to recognise that free-market profiteering would inevitably, à la Enron, end in disaster, had been tasked with employing his economic talents to rescue the State from the crisis that an economic philosophy he staunchly supported had been responsible for creating. The omens were certainly not good.

The grotesque scenario whereby someone involved in the initial injustice was then afforded the opportunity to sit in judgement of the case and subject the public to further humiliation and punishment was to be repeated ad nauseam after the initial crash in September. That those responsible for the greatest injustice committed in living memory against the Irish people could not only avoid censure or punishment, but in fact be allowed to rewrite history and apportion blame on innocent others, sadly reflects the sorry state of democracy in Ireland. Politicians from all sides of the divide, supported by the other vested interests in the Ireland Inc. scam, selected the media to provide the revised history of the country's collapse and their blueprint for recovery. From their positions of privilege, they connived to focus attention on the weakest elements in society in order to ensure that they would take the greatest hit in the collapse that was about to take place. With unemployment, careering towards half a million, crippling the underprivileged in the private sector, they focused their attention almost entirely on the less well off in the public sector.

Emboldened by reports from supposedly independent economic opinion, such as the government funded ESRI, a body that has, from its very foundation, done nothing more than disseminate government free-market propaganda, the media accepted its challenge with gusto. Media outlets took particular care to highlight reports by the ESRI showing how salaries in the public services were an unbelievable 23% higher than those in the private sector. Reports such as these, which were subsequently proven to be as flagrantly incorrect as they initially appeared, served to prepare the ground for further cuts in public service pay. They were central also to the campaign waged by those who enjoyed positions of privilege to distract attention from their culpability in creating the crisis by instigating strife between workers in the public and the private sectors. The age-old adage of divide and rule was as relevant and effective as it had ever been.

As a result, the public, deprived of honest and independent sources of information, remained uninformed. Ironically, Tony O'Reilly's Independent News and Media Corporation, which controlled five newsprint titles, was one of the most spectacular failures on the Irish Stock Exchange as the unsustainable boom they had inanely championed ignominiously went bust. A bitter boardroom squabble ensued as that other champion of the free-market doctrine, Denis O'Brien, attempted to grab overall control of the group and add to his monopoly of the media. When news of this unedifying cockfight reached the streets, matters took a rather interesting turn. Childish accusations flew between the rival camps as the O'Reillys strived to stave off the pretender's audacious claim to their throne. When Gavin O'Reilly, Chairman of the INM group, accused O'Brien of making threatening remarks unbecoming of a corporate businessman, O'Brien retaliated with infantile allegations of his own. The undignified row escalated further, following an appearance by Denis O'Brien's spokesperson, the communications consultant James Morrissey, on Marian Finucane's radio programme. Morrissey used the opportunity to fling some more mud in this pathetic spat, accusing O'Reilly of having recorded private phone conversations between the two principal protagonists involved. Within minutes a spokesperson for Gavin O'Reilly had contacted the station to refute such claims, prompting Morrissey to change tack and launch a different offensive on behalf of his client. Once again, the national broadcaster, whose remit was to keep the citizens of the State informed of matters of national interest, had ceded the airwaves to the vested interests in wealth-creation.

James Morrissey, O'Brien's communications consultant, was, as it happened, a regular panellist on Finucane's programme, peddling his free-market views ad nauseam to an unsuspecting public, who may well have been unaware of his interesting history in Ireland's corporate affairs. One of the first occasions he came to public attention was in the early 1990s, when he was identified as being instrumental in a manoeuvre which, though legal, was generally accepted as being a disturbing example of the Golden Circle in opprobrious action. Apartments belonging to the State-owned Irish Life company and situated in a highly desirable location in Dublin's Leeson Street area were sold, over the heads of the sitting tenants, most of them elderly, well below market value to representatives of what could only be described as people with connections to privilege and power. Amongst those who benefited from the below-market price of these valuable former State assets were two daughters of the former Taoiseach, Albert Reynolds, the Comptroller and Auditor General, the Attorney General and the Radio presenter, Marian Finucane. Many of those acquiring the apartments also benefited from the largesse of the Irish Nationwide Bank, whose chief executive Michael Fingleton, also a buyer, provided 100% mortgages to those who wished to benefit from this excellent opportunity to increase their personal wealth at the expense of the tax-payer.

In all, 100% mortgages were provided by Fingleton's Irish Nationwide Bank to 51 customers to buy 93 apartments. Ironically, in 2008, when Irish Nationwide became insolvent following its similar overexposure to the commercial property sector as Anglo Irish Bank, its Chief Executive, Michael Fingleton, was called on to resign for his perceived culpability in presiding over a regime of over-generous lending to privileged members of the Golden Circle. However, he departed the scene, as many of those involved in that shameful period did, not in penury and disgrace, but with his pockets full. How he, as the Chief Executive of one of the six financial institutions which had been run into the ground, causing untold damage to the lives of millions of Irish citizens, could walk away with a reputed final pension payment worth €27.6 million, on top of a total pay package of €2.34 million for his final year's work in 2008, beggared belief. Only a communications consultant worth similar remuneration could then be expected to defend his audacity in claiming, and receiving, a one million pound bonus for his work. Fortunately for Michael Fingleton, he could direct, as he did, any questions surrounding the matter to his PR spokesperson, one James Morrissey.

On Marian Finucane's discussion programme that Saturday morning, however, the question that was generating most heated debate was the decision by the government to set up a 'bad bank' to deal with the massive number of impaired loans which, the Irish banks claimed, were restricting them from lending to the real economy. The government's suggested method of dealing with what they indicated was their primary concern, the re-establishment of a functioning banking system to supply a dependable credit line to the real economy, had the secondary function of transferring the massive debt that the members of the Golden Circle had amassed during the Celtic Tiger 'boom' to the already hard-pressed public sector. It is worth noting that the primary individual responsible for creating and managing the 'bad bank' or

National Assets Management Agency (NAMA) project, the ex-federal reserve economist Alan Ahearne, had publicly declared that all Government policy at this time, including the creation of NAMA, was concerned with ensuring that the State guarantee for banking institutions would not be called in.

Six months after its disastrous implementation, the awful truth regarding the catastrophic nature of the Government guarantee had finally dawned on those whom citizens could surely have expected to have known better. The National Assets Management Agency (NAMA) was the logical step which the privileged would take in a concerted effort to retain their positions of power through the worst period of the downturn, the worst effects of which had still not, unbelievably, been noticed by the general public. This was due in no small way to the deliberate policy of those in power to artificially support the commercial property market until such time as their zombie assets were transferred to public ownership. This dishonest manipulation of market conditions, which was being carried out with the primary aim of preventing the property sector from total collapse, was best illustrated by the manner in which the six main Irish banks supported one of the State's leading commercial property developers in his efforts to stave off bankruptcy.

Liam Carroll's Zoe Developments group, with liabilities in the commercial property sector amounting to billions of euros to Dutch bank Rabobank, were ensconced in a high court bid to ward off bankruptcy, which would have resulted in the collapse of prices to their actual market value. The placing of a 'floor' under true property valuations was, however painful it would undeniably be to the general public, an essential element for recovery. It was also the inevitable outcome of the fraudulently hyper-inflated property boom. Unfortunately, it was the reluctance of the public in general to accept this stark reality that clouded their judgement and facilitated the government in implementing policies which directly benefited their friends in the Golden Circle while simultaneously worsening the calamitous effects which would ultimately be felt by the citizens.

The Irish economy had been fraudulently over-inflated and, as a result, suffered a catastrophic crash. Accepting this fact was the first essential step in finding a route for recovery. This inconvenient truth had, ironically, been promptly recognised by those within the property sector who chose, for their own selfish interests, to hide this awful reality from the public in general. Instead, mischievously choosing to use the threat of economic doom, which would, they claimed, result from the failure of our banking institutions, they implemented policies which would leave them financially in the clear when the eventual total collapse finally occurred. This was the true motivation for NAMA. The suggestion that the 'bad bank' was founded in order to let our banks lend to the real economy was in fact a lie. It was simply a smokescreen which attempted to hide the true function of NAMA, which was to ensure the transfer of enormous private debt to the public sector before the inevitable collapse of the property valuations to a 'floor' somewhere in the region of 80% below the peak valuations of 2006. This was why Irish banks had refrained from indulging in massive repossessions, as that would have added further pressure to the downward spiral in property prices and would have negatively impacted on the price the government would eventually pay for the bad loans in our financial institutions.

The deal the government had committed tax-payers to would see them reward the banks with valuations only 30% below market value. €57 thousand million euro was being committed by the government to buy worthless property which would, eventually, be allowed to fall to its 'floor' valuation, leaving the privileged free of debt, which they had deftly passed on to present and future tax-payers. The Irish banks had chosen to support Liam Carroll's property empire, as it manipulated the justice system in its efforts to stave off bankruptcy and remain afloat long enough to enjoy the benefits which would accrue, once NAMA was up and running. That the banks, and one of the developers, who had brought unbearable suffering to citizens could then proceed to use the justice system as a delaying tactic, by being allowed to launch appeals to the highest courts in the land, was just one more unedifying element in this pitiful assault on democracy. None of this, though, appeared to bother Marian Finucane's guest, James Morrissey, that Saturday morning, who, when he was asked to provide his thoughts on the merits or otherwise of the NAMA concept, waxed lyrical in his support of the idea and championed it as the only game in town. That it most certainly wasn't the only option open to the government appeared to be all but irrelevant to those who supported the NAMA proposal. Interestingly, though, NAMA's defenders usually had very good reason to ignore concerns for the tax-paying citizen.

One good reason for James Morrissey to support NAMA was that he had, in partnership with the mega-property developer Bernard McNamara, bought a site for development for €52 million a short time previously. This fact had come to light as a result of the two developers suing Ronan McNamee for inducing them to buy a site for the above mentioned sum when in fact, they claimed, it was only then worth €33.6 million. It was a peculiarly revealing aspect of the whole NAMA debate that, initially, not one property developer or speculator genuinely protested against its implementation or took recourse to the legal option that was open to them to oppose it. They undoubtedly recognised that, when the complete collapse finally occurred, they would be in a position to re-enter the market at bottom-floor value and re-acquire property at more reasonable prices than the outrageous ones they had paid at the height of the boom. The general public, on the other hand, would be lumbered with the outrageous national debt that resulted from the NAMA deceit, combined with their massive personal mortgage burdens, which originated from the initial scam, for generations to come.

Once again, the compliant tax-paying citizen of the State, from both public and private sectors, would be forced to pay the price of the wealth-creators' indecent greed. The powerful members of Irish society who had been directly responsible for creating an economic crisis which should have fatally undermined their positions of privilege for ever and a day had somehow been allowed to remain in control and direct the social revolution in such a way that the mass of ordinary working people suffered the catastrophic consequences of their actions. The passive manner in which the public accepted this retribution as their inexorable fate indicates that generations of subordination to those in positions of power had left an indelible mark on the mass of ordinary citizens.

Some respected individuals within the economic community, from both left and right, had criticised NAMA's inherent unfairness, arguing that other, far more equitable and indeed economically effective, options were available. One such person was the Nobel Prize winner in economics, Professor Joeseph Stiglitz, who described the true function of NAMA as being "the kind of highway robbery which we see all over the world, with guns pointed at the heads of the political leaders and the bankers claiming the sky will fall down and the economy will be devastated unless they get the money." This former chief economist of the World Bank went on to say that the 'bank bailout', which NAMA undoubtedly was, "is a simple transfer from tax-payers to bondholders and it will saddle generations to come." It was, he commented, "the kind of thing we see happening in banana republics all over the world," and he suggested that there were plenty of other options available to the government, including letting the banks go. Professor Stiglitz, the former head of US President Clinton's Council of Economic Advisors, provided ample examples of countries which had allowed banks to go under and had suffered no disastrous consequences. "The important thing to remember about financial markets," he remarked, "is that they are forward looking, but what they do remember is the size of your national debt. If you spend money in bailing out banks without taking all the equity, you will end up having a huge national debt, a liability with no assets to show for it. Now that will scare off investors in the future."

Here was an eminent, internationally respected economic commentator supporting the line of argument taken by a majority of truely independent commentators in our country that NAMA was highway robbery. Yet NAMA was presented almost universally by the paragons of virtue and independent thought within the national media as "the only game in town." The phrase was repeated ad nauseam by political commentators, programme anchors and newsprint columnists in their attempts to stifle debate and, in so doing, ensure that their positions within the exclusive reserves of privilege and power remained unchallenged. An example which perfectly illustrates how the usual suspects from the Golden Circle's exclusive membership conspired to achieve their mutually beneficial aim centred on the national broadcaster's new current affairs discussion programme, Frontline, on RTÉ.

Presented by Pat Kenny, the highest paid 'star' in the National Broadcaster's stable, who earned almost a million euro per annum, the panels in the first three editions featured the same old faces of the Celtic Tiger sham. Political columnist for the *Irish Times*, Noel Whelan, previously a Fianna Fáil party activist, Tom Parlon, head of the Construction Industry Federation and former Progressive Democrat minister, Brian Lenihan, Minister for Finance, his aunt, 72-year-old member of Dáil Éireann Mary O'Rourke, and Fionnan Sheehan, chief political correspondent of the *Irish Independent*, whose wife had been a Fianna Fáil candidate in the previous general election, were all allowed access to the national airwaves to continue to propagandise on behalf of the free-market doctrine which had brought the country to the brink of economic oblivion. Not one guest panellist on this highly influential primetime current affairs programme proffered anything other than the discredited propaganda of the defunct free-market ideology.

One of the first editions of Frontline featured a debate on NAMA, which, despite the programme makers' best efforts in loading the panel with pro-NAMA lobbyists, the anti-NAMA side won decisively, thanks in no small measure to a sterling contribution by *Irish Times* journalist, Fintan O'Toole, one amongst the small coterie of journalists who had brought honour to their profession over the preceding years. O'Toole repeatedly urged the Minister for Finance to explain how the injection of over thirty billion euro of tax-payers money into an insolvent bank such as Anglo Irish, which had effectively ceased functioning and would never resume operations again, could be justified. This one question shattered all the myths which had sought to justify the NAMA project and directed viewers' attention to the Golden Circle who held enormous accounts with that bank. Yet this simple question had rarely, if ever, been put to those with vested interests who supported the venture. In conjunction with the evidence supplied by Stiglitz that over a hundred banks had been allowed to go under in the United States following the collapse of Lehmans, the entire myth of NAMA not being a bailout for bankers and builders was exposed as the repulsive lie that it was.

Further editions of the Frontline programme kept on attempting to effectively manage and influence the course that events were taking in the country to the benefit of the free-market ideology. A debate which focussed on whether the Green Party should continue in government, and support NAMA, a vote on which was imminent at a specially convened conference of the Green Party's members, concluded with all three panellists, again with highly questionable motives, strongly proclaiming that they should, and indeed were somehow morally obliged to. A third programme featured the venerable Colm McCarthy, of an Bord Snip and M50 tolls fame, as chief panellist in a debate over public sector cuts, which he had suggested in his Bord Snip report. The debate, chaired once more by Pat Kenny, was permitted to descend into a highly fraught public-versus-private sector slanging match, which perfectly suited the wealth-creators 'divide and conquer' agenda. When the intensity of the debate threatened to boil over, as McCarthy, in particular, revealed his contempt for the mere labourers who had the audacity to challenge his right to insist that the public pay for the sins of the Golden Circle's incompetence, the handsomely remunerated Pat Kenny jumped to his defence. As a member of the audience asked why he was being asked to forego a huge percentage of his pay packet so that the bankers and builders who had got us into the mess could be bailed out, McCarthy chided him for allowing his emotion to overcome his intelligence. He then, bewilderingly, went on to suggest that, in his intelligent and informed economic opinion, the NAMA bailout had nothing to do with cuts in public service pay.

Here was the economic guru, whose free-market economic doctrine had created financial chaos and whose only remedy was more of the same poisonous medicine, bizarrely suggesting that an increased national debt could be serviced in any other way other than by government penalising the public in the very manner in which his own report was now suggesting they should do. This had sent quite a large section of the audience into a rage, and McCarthy once more chided them for getting emotional about the prospects of losing their homes, reminding them disparagingly that their "anger was not a policy." The fact that the audience had indeed suggested many policies which might contribute effectively to a recovery based on a more equitable and honest form of capitalism than the one McCarthy had spent his life promoting and profiting from, did not seem to register with either him or the presenter chairing the debate, Pat Kenny. When NAMA had been mentioned as an example of the hypocritical method by which the privileged were being bailed out at the expense of the public, Kenny intervened to effectively cut off that avenue of discussion, remarking that NAMA had been debated and "parked" as an issue and that this debate was restricted to the government overspend of €500 million a week on the provision of public services.

Neatly, Kenny had made use of the well-worn ploy of the free-market capitalists in situations – "we are where we are" – when called to account for some of the more displeasing elements of the economic charade. Kenny was, of course, the most highly remunerated of all our media 'stars', a man who had publicly acknowledged that his pension fund had taken an enormous hit as a result of the collapse in banking shares. Surely, his support of NAMA could not possibly have been influenced by the fact that those banking shares could conceivably rebound to previous high valuations once the banks were devoid of their toxic debts? Similarly, his unconcern for the massive financial burden that would consequently accrue to the ordinary tax-payer could have nothing to do with the fact that he, like many of the privileged in private industry, could benefit from the massive €3 billion in public subsidies for private pensions to avoid paying tax on upwards of 80% of their salary?

This perfectly legal method of avoiding tax was conveniently set up by our public representatives with the deliberate intention of assisting the privileged to benefit from the public purse. In any event, Kenny's assertion that the NAMA had effectively been 'parked', could not have been more apt a description. With eerie echoes of the Enron scandal, where all massive debts were effectively 'parked' to enable those who were orchestrating the scam to protect their personal profits, the government were proposing to effectively 'park' all the outrageous debt of the Ireland Inc. ruse at the doorsteps of several generations of tax-paying citizens.

In another eerie demonstration of how the government was continuing to follow the catastrophic business practices of the Enron model, they subsequently created a distinct company, a so-called Special Purpose Vehicle (SPV), to own and manage the NAMA loans. This SPV, which would be 51% owned by private investors, was effectively set-up, like Andrew Fastow's scheme at Enron, as an accounting manoeuvre to 'park' the €57 billion and keep it off the State's balance sheet so that that enormous figure would not count towards government debt. Worryingly, this was approved by the European Union statistics agency Eurostat. Pat Kenny's inadvertent use of the term 'parked', in the context of NAMA, came not, however, from any profound understanding of what was occurring in the world's economy, as he, like most of our well-paid media 'stars', had remained blissfully ignorant of such matters during the boom.

The *Irish Times* chief political correspondent, Stephen Collins, took up the question the following weekend. In his column, headed 'Self-interest has brought us to this sorry pass', Collins argued that the self-interest which had brought the country to crisis was that of the public representatives who refused to entertain thoughts of public sector pay cuts. In a powerful defence of the economist whose doctrine of free-market capitalism was the true 'self-interest' at the heart of our economic woes, he unbelievably charged that McCarthy had been the victim of "a bad-mannered assault by a range of vested interests on Frontline," and that this showed "just how difficult it is to have a rational debate about public spending." He then went on to admonish TDs on all sides in the Dáil, who "seem to have no idea of the kind of decisions that are required to rescue the public finances from disaster." Riding high on his wave of indignation, and warming to his task, he warned that it might take an election or two to "wake the electorate up to the real peril facing the country, but politicians could at least make a start by focusing their energies on the national interest rather than their own self-interest in the weeks and months ahead."

The self-righteous tone of his condescending diatribe might perhaps have been forgiven, had this not been the same Stephen Collins, a political correspondent for over thirty years, whom I had witnessed in the Dáil the night the government extended the disastrous guarantee to our insolvent banks, blissfully ignorant of the calamitous decision they had just taken. The vision of him nonchalantly making his way into the Dáil without an apparent worry in the world, as I frantically attempted to gain access myself, will remain long in my memory. How someone with his experience and contacts in the Irish political world could be so ill-informed regarding an issue of such national concern, while someone who had given up on Irish newspapers some five years previously could recognise the seriousness of the situation we were facing, surely poses difficult questions for Stephen Collins, the political correspondent. However, it would be unfair to single out Collins, as he was but one laughable member of a media circus that contributed to its own reputation's destruction by its complicity in the Celtic Tiger sham.

The journalists I saw that night in Dáil Éireann, cosily ensconced in relaxed conversation with politicians, brought to mind the 'bedded-in' journalists of wartime situations who appeared thoroughly compromised and subservient to their political masters. An article printed in the *Irish Times* the same day that Stephen Collins ranted against the public sector gave cause for even greater concern. In the same week that Denis O'Brien tried to take control of INM, an acquisition which would see him add five major newsprint titles to his already extensive media portfolio, he launched a startling broadside against journalistic standards, opining that standards were "in decline", that some journalists were "anti-business and anti-enterprise," and that "there was a very real onus on communicators, and indeed educators, to encourage, support and endorse enterprise and innovation," as an enterprise culture would, he boasted, "lift this country out of its current difficulties." That these difficulties had, in fact, been created by the worst excesses of the free-market ideology, of which he himself was a devout disciple, he conveniently overlooked.

This was the man who had acquired the second mobile phone licence, a public asset, in controversial circumstances, from a public representative, Michael Lowry, who himself was later found guilty of tax avoidance. The former Fine Gael politician was also found to have accepted a gift of over €300,000 euro in an unrelated case from businessman Ben Dunne. O'Brien subsequently sold the mobile phone business ESAT for over two billion euro amassing a personal profit of some €313 million in the process, a sum on which he could, by virtue of measures which the government had introduced, legally avoid paying tax on. This episode perfectly illustrated everything that was wrong with the free-market system. A publicly owned asset had been cheaply disposed of so that private individuals could line their pockets. When one considers that the public lost out by virtue of the cheap sale of the asset, the costs accruing to them from acquiring products from the company, the provision of sites on public land for the erection of controversial phone masts, the billion euro profit denied them from the re-sale of the asset, and the loss of tax receipts from that sale, it amounted to a fivefold rap for the people, inflicted by the government's decision to favour private industry over public welfare. That people such as O'Brien and Stephen Collins could continue to disseminate such patent nonsense only went to show how omnipotent they had become.

At this juncture it is also worth casting a critical eye over the role of the leadership of the Trade Union movement during this unprecedented period of exploitation. That their leaderships played a pivotal role in delivering their workforces to the altar of free-market capitalism through the partnership method of national wage agreements has already been discussed. Having completed their role in the scam, delivering the workforce into the slavery of thirty and forty-year mortgages, Union leaders then benefited from the indecently generous remuneration that was available to those who contributed to wealth creation, as their treacherous efforts undoubtedly had. Union leaders' annual salaries, at a time when four-year national wage agreements negated their requirement to deal with much of their mandated work in industrial relations, simply rocketed. That their members were falling deeper and deeper into debt was of no apparent concern to them. The cosy relationship between Union leaderships, employers and government insured that the free-marketers were given free reign to exploit the workforce and gorge themselves in profit making.

How Union leaders, such as John Carr of the INTO, could justify earning over €170,000 a year and at the same time hope to properly understand and represent the concerns of primary school teachers, many of whom were earning in the region of €30,000, is highly debatable. Carr was the leader of a primary school teachers' union that was almost devoid of male members, such was the disparity between wages in the public and private sectors. This irony perfectly illustrated just one of the problems facing the Union at the time. Carr's salary, which was 500% greater than that enjoyed by many of his members, ensured that he inhabited a different world from that of the teachers who directly paid his wages. This was the parallel universe of the privileged, who saw themselves as players in the wealth-creation game, entitled to enjoy performance-related pay which reflected their contribution to the super profits that were being amassed on the backs of the ordinary workers they supposedly represented. The example of Carr could be replicated across the board of Union leaders whose annual salaries were in general significantly higher than €100,000 per annum and far greater than their members' wages whose pay scales their remuneration should in fact have been reflecting.

Union leaders' salaries reflected their performance in delivering their side of the wealth-creating agenda – a salary-capped workforce in a placid and peaceful industrial relations environment – and they were topped up by the bonuses they received from a grateful government in the form of promotions to well remunerated government appointed public positions. Peter McLoone, the general secretary of the biggest public-sector union, Impact, on a salary of €155,000 per annum, was also on the board of the government training and development agency FAS, until he was forced to resign, due to the board's failure to curb the misappropriate use of public funds. A Union leader colleague, David Begg, General Secretary of the Irish Congress of Trade Unions (ICTU), earned €136,000 and was a member of the boards at Aer Lingus and the Central Bank and a contributor to the Economic and Social Research Institute (ESRI), the supposedly independent economic research body which relentlessly championed private wealth creation. Begg's predecessor as General Secretary of ICTU, Peter Cassells, a strong supporter of the partnership project during his twelve year term with the union, was later appointed Chairman of the National Centre for Partnership, a post that rewarded him to the tune of €67,000 per annum. He also benefited financially from his work for his consultancy agency that specialised in mediation and change and which numbered many State and semi-State bodies amongst its clients.

Union leaders' acceptance of lavish rewards from grateful benefactors amongst the free-market capitalists illustrates how the demarcation lines between employers and employees' supposed representatives had been blurred to the point of erasure. The effect of this mutually beneficial two-step was to be seen in the way the discontent within Trade Unions membership was continually manipulated by Union leaders. The provision of a submissive labour force, they well understood, was the sole requirement demanded of them to ensure their continued enjoyment of largesse and patronage. One extremely disturbing example, which reveals the treacherous extents to which they were willing to go was the manner in which they betrayed the anger of the general workforce when the first attempts were made to force them to pay for the incompetence and corruption of the wealth-creators. Public outrage exploded at the government's imposition of spending cuts, wage levies and pension levies, which targeted the poor at levels rarely previously witnessed. The momentum was gathering for industrial action, which would have enabled the public to demand that equitable measures be taken to address our economic woes.

The seemingly long-forgotten fact that the workers were the ultimate harbourers of power, and that this power could be exerted if they united in joint opposition to the corruption of the free-market capitalists' agenda in a national strike, was dawning on an angry public. When a march against proposed education cuts drew to the capital a crowd of over eighty thousand people, representing all sections of the community, the Union leaders cynically harnessed the rage by agreeing to sanction a national work stoppage in March 2009, only to then engage in subterfuge with the government and employers in order to delay, distract and defuse the situation and finally call off the action – a betrayal of the people for which they should never be forgiven. The Union leaders continuously chose to misdirect the anger of their members at a time when ample opportunity existed to demand that the privileged in our society should not continue to exploit the workers, in both public and private sectors.

Public and private pay must indeed be reduced in order to enable our economy to recover sustainability. However, the question that requires addressing, by Union leaders, is how costs can be eliminated from the real economy to allow for such salary reductions. The Union representatives rarely, if ever, focused their memberships' anger on the economically punitive vehicle of NAMA. Instead, they opposed pay reductions that would pale into insignificance compared to the debt that would accrue to their members as a result of

241

the 'bad bank' being introduced. It was conservatively, in my opinion, estimated that the cost of implementing NAMA would proportionately amount to €12,000 per man, woman and child in the State. In an average family of four, this would equate to the imposition of a €50,000 tax on their incomes which they would be expected to pay on the reduced incomes they would also suffer. The proposal to set up NAMA – in Stiglitz's phrase, "highway robbery" – should have been met with a campaign of stoppages by the general workforce, orchestrated by their Union representatives, which would have damned it to ignominious failure. That not one Union rallied the opposition to NAMA ensured that a public protest held in Dublin attracted no more than a few hundred people. The Trades Unions' leaderships had nailed their colours to the mast of the good ship Celtic Tiger, and in so doing had chosen to reward themselves with business class tickets amongst its privileged passengers, while condemning all others in society to endure the hardships of the real economy class. They were also, as members of that select group, assured of seats in the lifeboats if any disaster was to be visited on their luxurious liner.

Another section of our supposed democracy which similarly decided to protect their own vested interests, rather than those of the citizens in general, was of course the body politic. Accepting the fact that one could have expected nothing less from the Fianna Fáil/Mary Harney axis which had abused its position in power over the preceding twenty years in the exclusive service of free-market capitalism, it is, however, a more worrying concern that all other members of Dáil Éireann were guilty of either unquestioned loyalty to, or passive support for, the Celtic Tiger model. From Fine Gael's loyalty to a free-market liberal philosophy that was their original preserve, and which their support for the government guarantee of the banks acknowledged, to Sinn Féin, the supposed republican and socialist party, who also supported the guarantee, the Irish people seemed inordinately misrepresented by their Dáil deputies. The fact that Sinn Féin were economically illiterate was proved not just by the way they failed to spot that the socialist revolution they claimed to aspire to had been thwarted by the very bank guarantee they supported in the Dáil on 30 September 2008, but also by the words of the party's leader, Gerry Adams, who declared that "Sinn Féin were not against the Celtic Tiger but against the unequal distribution of the wealth that it created."

This was a popular interpretation, which found expression in differing ways but which at heart revealed a total ignorance of what had occurred. Whether it was the angry shareholder who lobbed eggs at the directors of Anglo Irish Bank, or the television programmes that asked who had 'caused the bust', it was a gross misconception that it was only the bust that had been wrong. For years ordinary shareholders had spent their time at bank AGMs lapping up the luxury of increased dividends and wallowing in the delight of extraordinary annual results. It was not, as Gerry Adams suggested and many others similarly believed, the 'bust' that was wrong, but the 'boom' that had preceded it. When republican socialist Sinn Féin decided to join forces with Fianna Fáil, Fine Gael and the Green Party and vote for the government guarantee for the Irish banking institutions, the entire body politic was united in guilt. That the Labour Party decided at the last moment to withdraw support for the bill reflected above all an attempt by its relatively new leadership to sever the strongest of the ties with the right wing parties that it had cosily developed over the preceding decades and establish some credentials as a party that offered a different option. There was certainly no evidence that the Labour Party really wished to rock the Celtic Tiger boat.

The sight of Labour Party deputies, amongst them the former leader, Pat Rabitte, chuckling and chortling at the contribution of the Green Party leader, John Gormley, on the night of 29 September, as he declared his pride in the Green Party's involvement in the preparation of the bill regulating the introduction of the guarantee remains etched in my mind as evidence of their general ineptitude. Here was a unique opportunity for supposed socialists to hold their ideological opponents very publicly to account for the disastrous consequences of their self-serving doctrine of unrestrained avarice. Their inability to recognise the significance of the events shows that these were not passionate supporters of a just society, but typical self-serving politicians.

That virtually all members of Dáil Éireann voted without hesitation for the most disastrously inept piece of legislation Ireland had ever witnessed stands as remarkable testimony to the collective incompetence of our members of parliament. When it can be confidently claimed that not one of the 166 members of Dáil Éireann recognised the disastrous economic situation the State was in, when that reality could have been recognised by anyone with an inquisitive mind, it calls into question the legitimacy of that parliament's claim to be capable of representing the public it was elected to serve. The frightening reality that, had a general election taken place, no-one could legitimately claim to be more competent than the fools who had brought us to the brink of disaster was indeed a sobering thought.

The government, and in particular the Taoiseach, the Tánaiste and the Minister for Finance, had proven themselves conclusively as being incompetent to fulfil their duties and had brought the State to the point of bankruptcy, and yet they were never, not once, called upon to resign. What on earth constitutes a proper reason for public representatives to resign if this didn't? Opposition members of the Dáil apparently feigned apoplectic rage at the incompetence of cabinet members, and then refused point blank to countenance demanding the relevant ministers' resignations. What passed for a genuine democratic process, designed to offer protection to its citizens, seemed to be no more than a charade. If a general election result was to reflect what newspaper polls at the time were suggesting was a complete meltdown in support for Fianna Fáil, then the opposition could well have dealt a fatal blow to their supposed opponents. Worryingly for the main opposition party Fine Gael, though, at a time when levels of dissatisfaction with government stood at over 80%, support for their supposed alternate policies had failed to increase from a mere 31%. Neither the government nor the opposition had any wish to rock the well-established political boat.

The opposition did, however, continue to perform their duties in the charade that passed for democratic debate. Both Fine Gael and the Labour Party proposed alternatives to the Government's 'bad bank' which, though falling well short of the radical restructurings required, were eminently more equitable and effective than the NAMA proposal. The Labour party suggested the complete nationalisation of banks on a temporary basis, as had been successfully done in Sweden when they had faced a similar crisis. This suggestion, with which Professor Stiglitz seemed to agree, was one viable option when he opined that "If you spend money in bailing out banks without taking equity, you will end up having a huge national debt, a liability with no assets to show for it." The fact that temporary nationalisation had previously been employed successfully and that eminent economic experts were recommending its use in Ireland counted for nothing amongst those vested interests whose personal financial difficulties it would not have addressed. Nationalisation, though, would still have left the taxpayers holding the huge liabilities that were on the banks books and The Labour Party's support for this policy suggests, once again, that it did not truly understand the nature of the problem within the Irish financial system. Fianna Fáil's assertion that it was against nationalising financial institutions, as that could lead to the politicisation of the banking system, was as laughable an excuse as one had come to expect. Wasn't it the very politicisation of Ireland's banking system, with 'access only' to members of the Golden Circle, which had been responsible for crippling the country in the first instance?

Fine Gael's proposal that a 'good bank' be established, rather than the bad one envisaged by Fianna Fáil, had much to recommend it. This would have seen the country taking on loans to establish a new 'good bank' which could then proceed to lend into the real economy. It would have achieved what all parties, Fianna Fáil included, had claimed was the aim of all proposals: to re-establish an effectively functioning financial system which would re-activate the real economy. It would also have left the well-established banks that had caused the collapse through their culture of reckless business practices, in possession of their enormous self-induced debts. Had that caused their complete collapse, the evidence existed, as Professor Stiglitz amongst others had suggested, that in the long term this would cause less hardship for people than the NAMA proposal would inflict on them. This, though, was the nub of the whole matter.

Chapter 15

Look Back in Anger!

The Fianna Fáil proposal to establish the National Asset Management Agency had nothing to do with protecting the citizens of the State from economic hardship and suffering, but everything to do with protecting the members of the Golden Circle. The counter-proposals from both main opposition parties perceived that this ulterior and self-serving motive lay at the kernel of the Fianna Fáil NAMA proposition and took on board the proposition that the people should not be punished for generations to come for the sins of the privileged. One might therefore have expected that all possible avenues open to the opposition would have been used to ensure that this 'highway robbery' of the citizens did not occur. However, the incandescent outrage one would have expected against the NAMA never in fact materialised. Countless options were available to the opposition to thwart the government's intentions, and yet those opportunities were allowed to slip past by the Fine Gael and Labour parties, in particular.

The first, and possibly the finest, of those opportunities arose with the staging of the second referendum on the Lisbon Treaty. With the government mired in controversy over its handling of the economy, and its standing within the electorate at an all-time low, the prospect that they could successfully negotiate victory in a referendum they had so ignominiously lost a year previously was unsustainable. The fact that a referendum that had been supported by 161 of the 166 Dáil deputies the previous year, when the worst effects of the economic crisis had still not been felt, had been defeated highlighted the enormous task that faced the government on this occasion. Over 60% of the electorate had gone against the expressed political wishes of a nigh-on complete majority of the parliament – a worrying reminder to the political classes of the power of the people to act when given the opportunity to do so. This, then, was the backdrop when those self-same political powers joined forces once more to persuade the people to pass ostensibly the same Lisbon Treaty only one year after they had comprehensively defeated it.

The Taoiseach, and indeed the opposition, having refused to accept the expressed democratic wish of the citizens, continued to claim that the ratification of the Treaty was of fundamental strategic importance to the development of the European model, which Ireland's economy, and therefore its citizens, had benefited so enormously from. The difficulty that faced the government, though, was that their credibility was in tatters with those self-same citizens, and the chances of their obtaining a 'yes' vote was miniscule. Given the the political opportunity that presented itself, the main opposition parties could and should have threatened to withhold their support for the Treaty, unless the government withdrew their proposal to establish NAMA. This threat would have sufficed either to stop NAMA in its tracks or, in the event of Fianna Fáil attempting to proceed alone, to defeat the Lisbon Treaty. That would have triggered a general election, which would have given the public an opportunity to express their opinion on the 'bad bank' proposal. In the event, both Fine Gael and the Labour Party provided the required support for a self-evidently incompetent and corrupt government to continue its inequitable and unjust governance by enthusiastically supporting, and indeed leading, the 'Yes' campaign to a successful conclusion, a fact which the Taoiseach, Brian Cowen, acknowledged when he profusely thanked them in the aftermath of the referendum victory.

The manner in which the most incompetent government in the history of the State was permitted to continue its abuse of power by an opposition that appeared strangely reluctant to challenge its governance was illustrated once more by their innocuous attempts to engender support amongst the public against the NAMA proposal. If the 'bad bank' concept proposed by the government was as immoral and economically flawed as their public pronouncements appeared to suggest, why then was no effort made to coordinate a united response by mobilising public anger? Instead, the opposition limited its opposition to reserved and relatively dispassionate parliamentary debate.

The Labour Party, in particular, stands condemned. Having been to the forefront, in conjunction with the Trade Union movement, in organising mass public demonstrations against a range of diverse issues, such as the Iraq War and the Irish Ferries dispute, on this occasion it chose to allow Union leaders to embark on their distracting and divisive campaign aimed at protecting public sector wages from further cuts. Both the Trade Union movement and the Labour Party should have recognised that the real issue was not unwillingness amongst the public and private sector workforces to contribute to a solution to our economic woes by accepting salary cuts, but outrage at the fact that the wealthiest in society, those who had caused the crisis, were not being penalised to anywhere near the same extent. That the Trade Union movement and the opposition parties were willing to allow a vindictive campaign of naked hatred to erupt between sections of society that had been the true victims of free-market capitalism, rather than organise those victims in united opposition to those responsible for their plight reveals once more the fundamental nature of their complicity in the entire sham.

Fine Gael and the Labour Party's decision to restrict themselves to dispassionate debate and resigned acceptance of the numerical advantage enjoyed by government in parliament ensured that NAMA would be passed and that, when it failed, as it undoubtedly would, they could absolve themselves of blame and take their turn centre-stage in the game of charades which purported to be democracy. The fact that a united people ultimately hold power in any State and that a series of national strikes would unquestionably have halted the NAMA proposal, raises the question once more why the opposition did not seek to organise such resistance in these exceptionable circumstances. Instead, they put forward over a hundred amendments to the NAMA which could have no actual effect on the bill. In any event, the tame debate over the NAMA was to be rendered inconsequential. When not one, but two, ex-leaders of the Fine Gael party, former Taoiseach, Garret Fitzgerald and Alan Dukes, publicly supported the proposal by Fianna Fáil to set up NAMA and cast doubt on their own party's proposed 'good bank', any meaningful debate came to an end.

Alan Dukes's support for the NAMA legislation came at time when he was serving, as a government appointee to the recently nationalised Anglo Irish Bank, a position which remunerated the former leader of Fine Gael to the tune of €100,000 a year. He had been leader of the Fine

Gael party in an interesting period. Succeeding Garret Fitzgerald as leader, Dukes was faced with a dilemma, as Fitzgerald had effectively won a longstanding debate on economic policy with the incumbent Taoiseach, Charlie Haughey, to such an extent that Fianna Fáil effectively decided to implement a Fine Gael agenda. Dukes took what many consider the brave decision, though it was difficult to see any other option open to him, to keep the Fianna Fáil government in power as long as it continued to implement the right-wing agenda proposed by Fitzgerald. The Tallaght Strategy, which had banished any remaining semblance of difference between the two main opposition parties, should have resulted in the end of historic opposition between two parties that were completely at one in philosophy. Instead, Dukes himself was the only casualty, as his removal as leader was orchestrated by members of Fine Gael who realised that their own privileged positions were threatened by the possibility of the public recognising that there was now no fundamental difference between the two major parties in the State.

Dukes' appointment to the board of directors at Anglo Irish Bank by Fianna Fáil was due recognition for the former opposition leader who had displayed such moral courage in choosing to put the welfare of the State ahead of personal political gain. His support for the Fianna Fáil NAMA proposal, which contributed in no small manner to the ending of the debate, could therefore be considered further evidence of this willingness to put the country's welfare before allegiance to his party – or, perhaps, a more worrying allegiance to the welfare of the privileged section in the State over other considerations. His support for Fianna Fáil's adoption of Fine Gael's right-wing agenda had, after all, ensured that his own political doctrine of free-market capitalism was given free reign to proceed unhindered in the State, which was to bring the country to the verge of economic catastrophe. It therefore should have come as no surprise that a former leader of one right-wing political party should come out in support of another when it chose to implement policy which would benefit the privileged few over the majority. The real shock was not that he chose to support the NAMA proposal, but that he publicly betrayed his party, thereby shattering the illusion that needed to exist to ensure the continuation of the two-party charade that existed to insure that right-wing policies continued uninterrupted.

The public support which former Fine Gael Taoiseach, Garret Fitzgerald, provided for Fianna Fáil's NAMA legislation was undoubtedly the most important in effectively ending debate and opposition. Not only did he support the NAMA proposal: he also moved to cast doubt on the counter-proposal of a 'good bank' by his former colleagues in Fine Gael. This was seized upon, not just by the government, but also by supporters of NAMA from the vested interests who would benefit from its implementation. At a stroke, these ex-Fine Gael leaders had ensured that NAMA would be accepted as 'the only game in town'. Fitzgerald's endorsement of the NAMA proposal came from a respected and well regarded former Taoiseach, a former leader of Fine Gael who had excellent credentials as a fierce opponent of the worst excesses of Fianna Fáil's management of the State's finances, particularly during the period of Charles Haughey's leadership.

The son of Desmond Fitzgerald, a founding member of Cumann na nGaedhael, a party which later became Fine Gael, Garret first encountered the man who would become his political nemesis, Charles J Haughey, when they both attended University College Dublin in the late fifties and early sixties. Fitzgerald's abilities, particularly in the areas of mathematics and public oratory, were such that he was approached by the leader of Fianna Fáil at the time, Sean Lemass, with a view to his joining the party, an offer he refused. He subsequently joined the party his father had helped found and, after serving as a member of Seanad Éireann, he was elected to the Dáil in 1969. When he was appointed Minister for Foreign affairs by Liam Cosgrave in 1971, assuming a position in cabinet that his father had held under Liam Cosgrave's father, William T Cosgrave, in the 1950s, the political fortunes which seemed the indelible right of the progeny of former members of parliament in Ireland had been sealed in its usual satisfactory manner. When Garret Fitzgerald eventually succeeded Liam Cosgrave as leader of Fine Gael, the scene was set for the epic series of debates with his former college colleague, Charles J Haughey, who himself had taken a somewhat less fortuitous route to become leader of Fine Gael's main opponents, Fianna Fáil.

Charles J Haughey was the son of northern Irish parents, Co Derry-born Sean Haughey and his wife Sarah. A republican who moved across the border to join the Free State army, Sean Haughey was a commandant when he resigned at the age of 29 in 1928. Having initially moved to a farm in Co Meath, the Haughey family, in which Charles was one of seven children, finally settled in the relatively modest area of Donneycarney in the early thirties. The house in which they lived was a former corporation built dwelling on the outskirts of Dublin City. It was from this relatively modest background that the most controversial politician in the history of the State was to emerge, acquiring power which would eventually enable him to become the owner of one of the great estate houses in Malahide which lay a few miles beyond the area of his modest childhood home. It was during his period in University College Dublin that Haughey, whose own father had no association with Fianna Fáil, began to first establish links with the party. It was there that he first met Maureen Lemass, daughter of the Taoiseach, Sean Lemass, whom he would subsequently marry.

After graduating, Haughey was eventually recruited into the Fianna Fáil fold in 1947 by friends Harry Boland and George Colley, both of whom were sons of sitting members of parliament for the party. Ironically, some ten years after he joined the party Haughey was to repay George Colley's generosity by unseating his father, Harry Colley, in the general election and taking his seat in Dublin North Central. Haughey's ruthless determination to climb to the top of the political ladder had been given a public airing for the first time. His appropriation of his one-time friend's father's seat in the Dáil could be interpreted as a direct challenge to the previously sacrosanct right of progeny to inherent their ancestors' positions of privilege and only added to the suspicions many in the establishment already held towards this blow-in from outside the usual confines of power. When Haughey, the outsider from the wrong side of the privilege divide, was subsequently to scorn the accepted protocol of political privilege by brazenly usurping ultimate power in the party, he was to face the full fury of the combined forces of the country's vested interests. Assuming control of Fianna Fáil in 1979 and elected as leader ahead of George Colley, to whom political protocol would have given precedence, Haughey rocked that ancient code of convention to its very core.

The most public expression of the resentment felt by that golden circle of the politically powerful came from a significant source. As Haughey stood in the Dáil in 1979, his 79-year-old mother watching proudly as her son from such a modest background was declared the sixth Taoiseach of the Republic of Ireland, she was to witness a vindictive verbal assault on her son which was unparalleled in the history of the State. When Garret Fitzgerald, the leader of the opposition rose to speak, the opprobrium and contempt which the privileged members of Irish society hold for those who would dare to challenge their rightful positions at the pinnacle of power in the State was given full vent. "I must speak," Fitzgerald haughtily began, "not only for the opposition but for many in Fianna Fáil who may not be free to say what they believe or to express their deep fears for the future of this country under the proposed leadership, people who are not free to reveal what they know and what led them to oppose this man with a commitment far from normal. He comes with a flawed pedigree." It was this reference to 'flawed pedigree' which revealed the true nature of Fitzgerald's contempt for Haughey, a man who had had the temerity to gatecrash the corridors of power and deny the rightful heirs their just desserts at the high table of privilege.

It was Haughey's subversion of the unwritten law of political patrimony, in my view, that had inspired Fitzgerald's onslaught on behalf of all those across the political divide of privilege who were affronted by his impudence. Fitzgerald's own dogged pursuit of this privileged position, which had led to Liam Cosgrave calling for the expulsion of "the mongrels" he suspected of wishing to usurp his authority, amongst whom it is thought he counted Fitzgerald, was now in danger of being thwarted by this upstart. It could be argued that this was what inspired Fitzgerald and indeed a majority in the political world to wage a war of attrition against the undeniably corrupt Haughey. That war continued long after Fitzgerald had easily won the political debate with Haughey over the chaotic state of the nation's finances. This unsustainable economic situation had been brought about by unrestrained public spending by consecutive Fianna Fáil governments, who showed no appetite to acknowledge this fact until Fitzgerald convinced the public in a series of public debates with Haughey of the veracity of his argument.

When Fine Gael finally came to power in the early eighties, years of Fianna Fáil governance had resulted in an economic crisis similar to the one they have created in the past ten years. The country's national debt in 1985 stood at 104% of Gross National Product. 17.3% of the workforce was unemployed. Anybody in employment whose personal income was above £7,300 per annum was subject to tax at over 60%. Four years of Fitzgerald's stewardship of a Fine Gael/Labour Party coalition government, encumbered by its inevitable philosophical tensions, had failed to significantly address the extraordinary deficit in the public finances. Disillusionment with the democratic system itself was compounded by the fact that the only option left to the public was to return to power the Fianna Fáil party which had brought the country to this unedifying position in the first place. This particular option seemed all the more unpalatable as that party was very publicly wracked by infighting, the result of the continuing efforts to displace the usurper, Haughey by a core cabal within the party. Those considered to have the correct pedigree for such a privileged position included George Colley, who had seen Haughey snatch the ultimate prize so insolently from his grasp, and Des O'Malley, son of a former serving cabinet minister, Donagh O'Malley. These two, in particular, were perceived to be possessors of the correct lineage to aspire to the highest position of privilege which leadership of Fianna Fáil essentially guaranteed.

O'Malley, with the support of a rump in Fianna Fáil who refused to accept the democratic will of its members, and bolstered by vested interests outside the party, made repeated attempts to dislodge Haughey. With the party in total disarray, with the threat and reality of physical violence a near-regular occurrence between party members, the prospects of them being considered a viable option to the prevailing hapless government were remote indeed. The democratic system itself, which had been the preserve of the privileged few who dominated both Fianna Fáil and Fine Gael to their mutual benefit, was in danger of disintegrating. Public disillusionment with the two-party system, which was to all intents and purposes governance by the privileged for the privileged, and which had resulted in catastrophic economic distress, had created a political void and deep disenchantment amongst the public. A passion for political change amongst the electorate was steadily increasing and required only the appropriate leadership to turn the anger into a powerful political force.

Had that appropriate leadership emerged, it would have provided the opportunity to effect real and positive change in our political system. The image of Ireland, a republic in name and by nature, which offered citizens opportunities to escape from the clutch of the privileged classes who had led them to the point of economic ruin, was an eminently appealing one to an ever-increasing proportion of the population. Conversely, it was the most appalling prospect that the privileged classes could ever have imagined and was met with fierce opposition. But, as always in the intricate and elaborate charade that passed for the democratic process in Ireland, this opposition would be by deceit and sleight of hand, rather than by brute force.

When, in 1985, Des O'Malley failed in another attempt, directed on this occasion by backbencher Charlie McCreevey, to remove Charles Haughey from the leadership, an event that would have been sold to the public as evidence of a fresh start in politics in Ireland, another, more inconspicuous coup was staged that would subsequently be inflicted on an unsuspecting public. With the support of the cores of vested privilege, O'Malley, who had been expelled from the Fianna Fáil party for supporting Garret Fitzgerald's government in a vote liberalising the sale of contraception in the State, announced that he was quitting Fianna Fáil and setting up a new political party, offering a radically new and refreshing option to the public. This announcement was greeted with a fanfare of unrestrained approval by the powerful, and the media in particular lavished praise and publicity on the 'new' party. That the 'new' party was comprised of the same 'old' faces from the two parties that had brought the State to the brink of financial ruin did not seem to concern people to any great extent. The fact that a groundswell of support that had been growing into a positive force for change in the country had just been usurped by the democratic deceit which had been played out in the State since its foundation did not raise even an ounce of critical comment in the media, thus revealing the extent to which they were complicit in this insidious duping of the public.

Fianna Fáil's Des O'Malley, Mary Harney, Bobby Molloy and Pearse Wyse were joined by Fine Gael's Michael Keating and party activist Michael McDowell as sitting members of parliament in this 'new' party, the Progressive Democrats. Their 'radically' new outlook offered the public the opportunity to support their free-market liberal agenda. Concurrently, they were also promising to fulfil a role as 'moral watchdogs' over others in the system who might seek to abuse their positions of power for financial gain. That these two stated agendas seemed to incontrovertibly contradict each other again rang no alarm bells in media circles. That those who would support the concept of a market free of government regulation would then be of a disposition to rein in those who would seek to exploit those conditions to the detriment of the citizens was simply incredible. How one could argue for 'small government', on the one hand, a process that would remove interference in business completely, and, on the other hand, assure the citizens that they would, or indeed could, interfere in the market to ensure that citizens were not exploited by those who would seek inordinate personal gain, seemed an irreconcilable proposition. However, the corruption the Progressive Democrats wished to eliminate from the system was not this underhand support of the privileged in society over the public, but the corruption they associated with Haughey, which they regarded as the corruption of the privileged class by an insolent member of the public.

Haughey's corruption was of the more blatantly distasteful 'public' variety, as opposed to the refined and sophisticated chicanery the established members of privileged society practiced. His habit of indulging in overt extortion was perfectly illustrated by the manner in which he unashamedly demanded financial rewards from those he presumed would be expecting his political patronage at some future date. Shortly before he was first elected Taoiseach in the late seventies, Haughey, who had enormous debts which threatened to bankrupt him and thereby preclude him from serving in the Dáil, was embroiled in bitter discussions with Allied Irish Bank executives, who were concerned at the million pound overdraft he had at the time. Despite the fact that Haughey had five different accounts that were overdrawn to the tune of the same amount, AIB decided to loan him a further £350,000, an enormous amount at the time. When his overdraft eventually reached over one million pounds, the bank demanded that he return his cheque-book and cut down his extravagant spending.

Haughey's reply, that he could be a "very troublesome adversary," had the required effect. When he was elected

Taoiseach in 1979 AIB agreed to settle the million pound overdraft and sent the newly incumbent Taoiseach a letter congratulating him on his promotion to the highest office in the land. They somewhat remarkably added in the correspondence that they "had faith in his ability to succeed in restoring confidence in this great little nation." The man whose own personal finances were in a shambolic state had just been given a vote of confidence by his largest debtor to turn around the fortunes of the State that was in the throes of a catastrophic economic crisis. Haughey, in return, informed the same financial institution that they had not heretofore made use of his "influential position." This whole shoddy episode reveals the extent to which Haughey, and indeed the banks, were willing to go in order to ensure the continued mutual benefit of both parties from our democratic system.

This was just one example of the type of undignified and overtly self-serving political corruption which Haughey indulged in and which horrified the public at large when it finally came to light in the tribunals which were set up to investigate corruption in the late nineties. Though it had long been suspected that corruption of this nature was endemic in political circles, it took the advent of the tribunals, set up on the recommendation of the 'new' political blood of Bertie Ahearn and Mary Harney, to bring to light the hard evidence which would confirm the public's worst suspicions. Harney and Ahearn were some of the staunchest supporters of the method of investigation by tribunal, though many of the public would rather have witnessed these investigations conducted in the courts, where criminal prosecutions could eventually have sent corrupt politicians to State prisons. The sceptical amongst the electorate, who doubted that one politician would ever be incarcerated for one of the most heinous crimes imaginable, the corruption of the democratic system itself, were repeatedly assured by Mary Harney, in particular, that she would stand as moral watchdog and guardian of the process of public representation. Her position in cabinet, as Tánaiste and leader of the Progressive Democrats, ironically supporting former Fianna Fáil colleagues in a Coalition Government, would be dedicated to ensuring that those who might seek to harm the democratic system would be held to account. She would, she assured the nation, pursue this moral agenda to the bitter end and guarantee that those who were guilty of criminal behaviour would serve their punishment behind prison bars.

However, as the tribunals of inquiry dragged on, the sceptics' view that they were little more than the optics required to defend the bona fides of the democratic system gained credence. The one clear cause for optimism – that someone would eventually be held to account for this odious betrayal of democracy – was that an abundance of evidence was being collected to demonstrate that Haughey, in particular, had been guilty of corruption and fraud on a grand scale. Included in the utterly damning evidence that emerged regarding Haughey was the fact that he had received payments totalling over eight million pounds between 1988 and 1995 from a variety of benefactors. Amongst those who contributed to his personal political fund, which financed his extravagant lifestyle, was businessman Ben Dunne, who gave him £1.3 million. Dunne was subsequently found to have benefited from a reduction in his capital gains tax bill to the tune of £22.8 million, as a result of a meeting Haughey had organised with an official in the State department. However, despite the incontrovertible evidence, it appeared that the penalty Haughey would be required to pay was not imprisonment, but merely public censure and dishonour.

However, just when it seemed clear that membership of the Golden Circle had spared yet another of it members,

Haughey was charged with trying to obstruct the work of the McCracken tribunal. This charge, which carried a mandatory prison sentence for those found guilty, brought some hope that finally a politician who had corrupted the democratic system and defrauded the citizens for his own benefit would serve a prison sentence as a punishment and a deterrent to others. Haughey's defence focused, not on his innocence, but on the weakness that had been apparent with the tribunal system from the beginning. Claiming that the evidence that had been publicly aired at the tribunal's hearings would impair Haughey's chances of receiving fair and unbiased treatment before a court of law, it was argued that any criminal charges should be dropped. His legal team reiterated this claim at every opportunity and launched a court appeal against the commencement of the case on the grounds that it would be impossible to empanel an unbiased jury. The public awaited with bated breath a decision that would either confirm their worst suspicions or restore their faith in justice and democracy.

With one of their own, however uncouth and reviled they perceived him to be, facing the prospect of prison, the vested interests of the privileged sector of society would have to rally to his cause. Had he been sacrificed and allowed to face the penalties and punishments previously reserved exclusively for the ordinary citizens, a dangerous precedent would have been set which would most definitely be visited upon other members of the elite at some future date. They were therefore left with no option but to consider rescuing the man they had previously considered an incongruous upstart who had usurped power from the privileged in society to such an extent that he and his family were now incontrovertibly indentified as fully fledged members of the Golden Circle. With the case against Haughey being prosecuted by the judiciary, the usual avenues employed by the powerful to 'insure' that relevant decisions went their way were to all intents and purposes closed to them. The only possibility of saving Haughey from prison seemed to be the line of defence being pursued by his legal team that argued that their defendant could not receive a fair trial as a result of the volumes of publicity his case had already generated in the national media.

This very important issue was in the throes of being considered – with the judge in the case acutely aware of the delicate balance that existed between the general public's demand that Haughey's privileged position in society should not protect him from the full rigours of the law and Haughey's natural right to a fair trial – when an unexpected intervention from a very unusual source changed the whole course of events. In an in-depth, exclusive interview with the *Irish Independent*, a paper that had pursued a vicious campaign against Haughey over the preceding years, Mary Harney declared that she thought Haughey, "should be convicted." Coming at a time when the question of Haughey's ability to receive a fair trial was being appraised by the courts, the effect of these injudicious remarks was inevitable. When the judge ruled that Haughey's trial was to be indefinitely postponed, "following prejudicial comments made by the Progressive Democrat leader and Tánaiste Mary Harney," the privileged in society had managed to demonstrate yet again that they inhabited a universe in which the common laws of the land simply did not pertain to them. The fact that it was Haughey's avowed enemy and sworn watchdog of morals in the political world that had come to his rescue, however inadvertently, served to refute any possible suggestions of impropriety in the affair, an assertion that was generally accepted by the public.

Thereafter, the alleged corrupt dealings of politicians, businessmen and all others in the privileged sectors of society returned to the safer haven of tribunal investigation, where the normal penalties of criminal behaviour could not be applied. This, indeed, was the reason for their establishment in the first instance. There, weeks of interminable investigation grew into months, and finally years, with no obvious sign that anyone would pay for their deviously corrupt actions. When one considers that solicitors operating in tribunals were earning upwards of €2,500 a day for their efforts and that the combined costs of the various tribunals was estimated at over one billion euro, one can appreciate why some would consider these government-funded investigations as the perfect symbol of free-market capitalism. In what was, in effect, a privatisation of the criminal justice system, public funds were pilfered by the privileged sectors of society though, in truth, there was no evidence that any real service was being provided to the public.

This helps debunk the myth of divergent 'public' and 'private' sectors. Members of the legal profession, who became millionaires as a result of the tribunals, claimed to be members of the private sector, whilst benefiting from direct remuneration by the State. Similarly, aren't those in the so-called private sector who are employed by multi-nationals that chose to operate in Ireland due to 12.5% corporation tax, enjoying the benefits of their generous salaries as a result of society's willingness to make up for this shortfall in tax receipts? Were the Progressive Democrat members who founded the management consultancy firm, MRPA Kinman, and who then benefited directly from the Department of Health's decision to invest €2.75 billion dollars in the biosciences sector not, in truth, on the public payroll, though claiming to be in the private sector? Are those who work for consultancy agencies employed by the State to promote the questionable business ethics of the 'private' sector to its 'public' equivalent not in reality

Government employees? Were those property investors who benefited from State-subsidised tenants servicing the mortgages on their property investments during the boom years being remunerated by the public or the private purses? Is Denis O'Brien obscenely wealthy due to his exceptional entrepreneurial skills in the private sector, or to the fact that the State provided him with a mobile phone licence, the property of the public, at a knockdown price, and by his then profiting from legal tax avoidance measures introduced by the people's representatives, the government? Are members of the private sector of the medical profession not being directly or indirectly remunerated by the State on a consistent basis? Once again the myth of opposing or divergent 'public' and 'private' sectors is exposed as the illusion it so evidently is. The truth is that the privileged sections of society in Ireland combine to ensure that the trappings of wealth which accompany their positions of power remain their exclusive preserve, out of reach to the general public from both public and private sectors.

This, indeed, is the underlying principle which lay at the heart of the Ireland Inc. scandal. It was also, as we have seen, at the very core of the Enron scandal, which had brought that giant corporation crashing to its knees nearly ten years previously. More worryingly still, it continues to form the basis of the thinking of the same economic experts who created the Ireland Inc. disaster as they ineptly attempt to rescue the country from the chaos they created. Ireland's 'bad bank', or NAMA, proposal is Enron re-incorporated. All those with vested interests in the privileged sections of society whose personal wealth and power would be endangered should the NAMA bill fail to proceed through parliament have combined to ensure that nothing would be allowed to hinder its introduction. The enormous private personal wealth that was created during the boom will be transferred to the public purse, now that it has turned into debt. By employing, and outrageously abusing, the accounting technique which had been fundamental to the Enron scandal, Ireland's legislators, in conjunction with all the vested interests in this crime against the State, propose to 'park' or 'hide' the debt once more and just continue on their merry way.

The proposal of NAMA supporters to pay over the current market price for property assets and then hope that those assets will recover some of their previous 'bubble' market valuations is yet another example of the abuse of the discredited 'mark to market' accountancy manoeuvre which was fundamental in causing the collapse of Enron. This will save the privileged – as it did Jeff Skilling, Kenneth Laye and their privileged co-executives and directors in the Enron Corporation – from facing up to their liabilities and will permit them to continue fraudulently manipulating affairs for their own benefit. It will, however, eventually cause a catastrophic collapse which will burden millions of innocent Irish citizens with crippling debt for generations to come. As was witnessed with Enron, the practice of hiding or parking debt can only be sustained for a limited period before it is exposed as the sham it undoubtedly is. That the warning that Enron provided was not heeded in the first instance to ensure that the world's financial system did not replicate its ignominious fall from grace was in itself a shameful indictment of the world's leaders. That the Irish Government, having brought our economy to the brink of collapse, was now intent on repeating these mistakes served only to stress how incompetent they were. The obsession with accumulating vast personal wealth which drove this deceit will one day come back to haunt, not only those guilty of its implementation but, unfortunately, all citizens of this State.

When one considers that, in supporting NAMA, Garret Fitzgerald was offering the Irish banks, and indeed the vested interests in the Ireland Inc scam, an incredible 'get out of jail' card for free, at the tax-payers' expense, when other options existed which would have protected the public's interests far more securely and equitably, one is entitled to question his motivation for doing so. Could the fact that he, like his predecessor before him as Taoiseach, Charlie Haughey, had benefited from an enormous 'write-off' of debt valued at £220,000 from Allied Irish Bank have influenced his decision? That debt had been accrued by Fitzgerald when he sought and was given a £248,000 loan from AIB in 1993 to acquire shares in the aircraft leasing firm Guinness Peat Aviation, only to be left badly exposed when its share price subsequently collapsed. Fitzgerald's claim that he was "an innocent abroad," and "had not read the thing properly" before committing to purchasing the shares, leaves him vulnerable to the suggestion that he was therefore not as eminently qualified to comment on affairs of a financial nature as many would have us believe. The fact that a former colleague in Fine Gael, Peter Sutherland, a former director of Guinness Peat Aviation, was chairman of AIB was surely helpful in ensuring that Dr Fitzgerald was not left vulnerable to share prices on the free-market falling as well as rising, as ordinary punters from the general public would be. That Peter Sutherland, had been appointed Attorney General by Fitzgerald on two occasions and had been appointed European Commissioner by him, as well, only adds to the suspicions that the cronyism which is at the heart of the privileged sections of Irish society played its part in influencing Dr Fitzgerald's decision to support NAMA. The Moriarty Tribunal investigated the matter of Dr Fitzgerald's AIB loan and found that though there had been a substantial discounting or forbearance shown in the case of Dr Fitzgerald's debt forgiveness, no wrongdoing had occurred. Would that a similar forbearance or discounting also be shown in the case of the ordinary citizens of this State who are now expected to service debts which financial institutions such as Allied Irish Bank had recklessly incurred during the profligate years of Celtic Tiger Ireland. Unlike Dr Fitzgerald, or indeed Charles Haughey, both members of the privileged elite who were invulnerable to the customs and duties of normal society, the ordinary citizens and indeed their children are expected to pay up, in full, enormous debts they had not even been responsible for creating in the first instance. Chief amongst those who haughtily lectured the Irish people on how they were duty-bound to repay these immoral debts was the chief executive of investment bankers Goldman Sachs, Peter Sutherland. The fact that many of the Irish banks' bondholders are also clients of Sutherland's employers, Goldman Sachs, was surely of some significance?

Ironically, Peter Sutherland, who subsequent to his periods in public service as Attorney General and EU Commissioner, built an astonishing empire of 'private' wealth, was also Chairman of Royal Bank of Scotland, a subsidiary of which, Ulster Bank, was the first to grant 100% mortgages in Ireland. Royal Bank of Scotland was also to be one of the first English banks which had to be ignominiously bailed out by the British tax-payer because of its reckless lending habits prior to the crash in 2008, all of which occurred under Sutherland's chairmanship. The patently unjust manner in which the free-market is in fact only free from government intervention when share prices are rising, and the scandalously inequitable way in which the incompetence of the wealthy is bailed out when share prices fall, exposes another myth of the free-market ideology. Whether it is the cancelling of Dr Fitzgerald's debt, which was in effect an incompetent gambler's debt – a gambler who by his own admission hadn't bothered to read the 'form guide' – or the British tax-payer's bailout of incompetent lending by RBS under Dr Sutherland, or NAMA's bailout of the privileged in Ireland, it is an unwritten law of that free-market doctrine that market valuations do not carry any risk for the privileged amongst the free-market capitalists.

Further evidence of the manner in which a relatively small privileged sector of Ireland's society wields immense power and enjoys considerable prestige can be gleaned from a cursory look at Dr Fitzgerald's progeny. It also provides the perfect example of the manner in which certain families in Ireland enjoy positions of tremendous influence in our society across a vast array of sectors. In the case of the Fitzgeralds their considerable influence on our nation's affairs extended from business to politics and from economic commentary to the media. However, if one considers the catastrophic nature of the economic state we now find ourselves in, surely it is appropriate and legitimate to question the performance, proficiency and profundity of all those who were our 'self-professed' guiding lights over the past twenty to thirty years.

Unlike most others in the political field, Dr Fitzgerald's sons did not choose to take up their father's seat at the table of privilege that is Dáil Éireann. Instead, Mark Fitzgerald is Chief Executive Officer of Sherry Fitzgerald, one of the prime estate agents in Ireland, a company which cashed in fully on the fruits of the Celtic Tiger property boom but which in 2009 announced losses in the region of €16 million. No doubt Sherry Fitzgerald, would welcome the relief which NAMA would provide for the vested interests of the property sector. This would release their primary customers from the enormous debts they currently hold and enable the estate agents to benefit from their percentage of future business when the banks inevitably lend money to the same developers to buy back property at greatly reduced prices. In an interview Mark Fitzgerald conducted with the Sunday Tribune in 2008 he was quoted as saying that because we were in the process of gaining competitiveness, "what that does is make it look like a very bright decade ahead". It was his expert opinion that "we weren't actually in bad shape when the credit crisis arrived", that "the bottom of the market is in sight" and that "the pace of Ireland's recovery post 2010 will surprise people". Moreover he claimed that he was in agreement with the ESRI that "it is very important that we don't become transfixed with short term difficulties" because "a better decade" economically was on the horizon. Furthermore he was confident that the Irish property market would recover before its English counterpart because "there's enough capital and prosperity in the country to take over the assets. The wealth hasn't gone you know", he continued, "It's just in hiding".

Though that final statement certainly bore an alarming ring of truth about it, the overall analysis provided by this property expert could not have been wider of the mark. Irish property prices were nowhere near their lowest point at that juncture. Unfortunately when they did eventually strike rock bottom the catastrophic loses would be born by the Irish taxpayer and not the property developers who had created them in the first instance. The National Asset Management Agency, the proposed solution to our banking crisis, which Mark's father Garrett so enthusiastically supported would see to that.

Another of Dr Fitzgerald's sons, John, is hewn, as one would quite rightly expect, from the same ideological block as his brother Mark and his father Garrett. As a chief economist with the Economic and Social Research Institute, (ESRI), the supposedly independent but in fact blatantly biased instrument of propaganda for the free-market capitalists' ideology, John Fitzgerald had assumed a significant role in absolving the privileged sector of blame for the crisis and instead apportioning guilt primarily to a public sector which he and the ESRI disingenuously accused of having in some way bled the Celtic Tiger financial system dry of capital. A cursory review of the reports the ERSI have issued relating to the Irish economy would illustrate quite clearly the ineptitude of those involved in their deliberations. In its medium term review for 2008 – 2015 which John Fitzgerald co-authored, the ESRI stated that "the economy has the potential to grow at around 3.75% a year over the coming decade, despite significant short-term problems". Mirroring comments by his brother Mark, John Fitzgerald, as co-author of the report, stated that "when the current global economic slowdown ends, with appropriate policies, the economy should recover quite rapidly". In fact so frequently have ESRI reports, claiming that our economy had 'turned a corner', been proven incorrect, that they have spawned the popular retort amongst observers that we must be back to where we started! In a similar vein, by consistently issuing reports which establish a myth that public sector wages are higher than their direct counterparts in the private sector, the ESRI fulfils its function of nurturing the 'public' versus 'private' sideshow, a conflict which allows the true culprits in the Ireland Inc. scam to escape inquisition and punishment. Simultaneously it also served to support the free-market capitalists' agenda of maintaining their profit margins in a declining market by proposing cuts in public sector wages to match those already enforced at the lower ends of the private sector, while allowing the privileged to escape any form of penalty on their bloated salaries. The support of the ESRI for this method of tackling the crisis could hardly have been more effusive. They, once more, became the cheerleaders in chief for the policy our government chose, to bailout the privileged elite at the expense of the general public, a policy far more callous and merciless than the name they gave it suggests. Austerity.

This phenomenon, which was, to all intents and purposes, a repeat of the 'rank or yank' system employed by Enron to reward their fraudulent bosses, proved once more that no lessons had been learned from the disastrous events of the worldwide economic crash. While right-wing commentators were calling for a 'yanking' of the worthless and disposable employees in both public and private sectors, by a combination of salary reductions and growing unemployment queues, they were simultaneously permitting the grossly excessive profit making, which was a core factor in causing the disaster, to continue unabated. This profiteering by the top echelons of society was the way capital disappeared from the financial system, and this malpractice was to be allowed to continue. One example which beggars belief was that of insurance companies who, at a time when salaries in the public sector were being slashed in an attempt to regain competitiveness, announced that they were increasing their premiums by 10%. This increase, which was sanctioned by government, would greatly increase business costs, as well as pressures on ordinary households, harming the real economy in the process, but it was to be sanctioned, as it would achieve the required increase in profits for one of the privileged sectors of corporate business.

This was just one of many indicators that the government and the economic experts who had failed to see the economic crisis approaching were still shockingly ignorant about the true factors that had caused the crash. That insurance companies, such as AIG and other such corporations which had bled the financial system dry of capital and caused the economic chaos in the first instance, were to be allowed to continue amassing enormous profits on the back of the long-suffering public, and to the detriment of the real economy, illustrated perfectly the incompetence of those charged with masterminding an exit strategy from our particularly woeful economic dilemma. That they were unwilling to admit that cutting and capping profits from the top, rather than the bottom, of the economy was what was required revealed also the extent to which they were personally compromised by their membership of the ruling elite whose wealth would be threatened if the right steps were taken to solve the financial crisis.

Cutting or capping corporate profits, for example in the insurance industry, would have removed the incentive to engage in the reckless business practices which endangered the whole financial system in the first instance. It would also have reduced excessively burdensome costs for the business community in the real economy and society, which would have had enormous beneficial effects on the economic structure. That the State chose to ignore methods of regaining competitiveness, other than the blunt instrument of reducing the salaries of ordinary workers in both the public and the private sectors, shows that government was still exclusively supportive of the demands of big business over the entitlement of the general public they had been elected to serve. That this cap on profits will ultimately be essential if the world's economy is not to succumb to an even more disastrous 'event' than the one which was only narrowly avoided in 2008 is incontrovertibly the case.

Unfortunately, all the evidence suggests that the self-righteous arrogance which had been so evident in those who had brought the world to the brink of collapse is still a major part of the make-up of those charged with preventing disaster. Rather like an unreformed alcoholic who has cheated death and been offered a second chance by dint of being the recipient of some unfortunate donor's liver, only to pathetically return to his previous addiction, these wealth junkies are incapable of resisting the temptations to grossly self-aggrandise. In a similar vein, a cap on corporate profits will eventually have to be accompanied by a cap on excessive personal remuneration, which was another cornerstone of the Enron debacle. Instead of focusing exclusively on viciously slashing the wages of those in the middle and lower sectors of the economy, what is required is that a salary cap be introduced – a 'maximum' wage to accompany the 'minimum' one which already exists.

The evidence is clear that this lesson has not been learnt, as was shown by the refusal by the Minister for Finance, Brian Lenihan, to rule out the payment of a bonus to the person charged with overseeing the implementation of NAMA. One is left in grave doubt that the required levels of State regulation of the free-market will be enforced so as to ensure that the outrageously fraudulent business practices which were a feature of the Enron Inc., Ireland Inc. and indeed the World System of Finance Inc. scams will not be repeated. When it was revealed, at the height of our economic crisis, at a time when half a million people were unemployed and millions of others were facing severe economic hardship, that the head of the Health Service Executive, Bernard Drumm, had written a five-page letter explaining why he had been deserving of a €70,000 bonus for his work in 2007, and that this had been granted to him on top of his €400,000 salary, it reconfirmed the belief that nothing had changed in the free-market capitalists' mentality. Apparently, he was simply being 'rewarded' for his stewardship of what was universally regarded as an appallingly inefficient public health service.

In fact, Drumm was being rewarded for contributing in no small measure to the privatisation of the health service, a policy which was the mastermind of the Minister for Health: the chief architect and propagandist of the free-capitalists ideology of 'small government', Mary Harney. The policy of effectively removing government influence from the affairs of business, thereby creating boundless opportunities for wealth-creating entrepreneurs to amass gigantic personal fortunes, also served the minister well in allowing her to distance herself from decisions taken by the independent HSE. When pressed on whether Drumm was deserving of the bonus he received while overseeing a public health care system that was shambolic, Mary Harney blithely dismissed the question on the grounds that it was the concern of the HSE and that she, as Minister for Health, did not have the power to intervene in the matter. The bizarre, though inevitable, outcome of full implementation of free-market capitalist doctrine had led to a situation where the Minister for Health could not intervene to ensure that an ethically wrong decision, which further undermined the public's perception of our health system, was reversed. Significantly Harney, when pressed as to whether she considered it morally correct for Drumm to apply for, be granted, and accept his bonus, refused to answer, on the grounds that she "did not want to get into the moral issues concerned." That would indeed have been uncomfortable ground for this free-market capitalist who, despite her long-standing propagandising on behalf of her beloved free-market system, knew full well the extent of the moral obfuscation which lay at its heart. Her refusal to entertain questions which attempted to address the moral aspect of political and economic matters revealed how uncomfortable those who had heartlessly ignored less fortunate citizens felt when pressed on this vitally important aspect of the Ireland Inc. disaster.

In this connection, we cannot avoid questioning the role which other institutions of the State played in creating the immoral haze in which the free-market capitalist doctrine flourished. That our schools and universities, supposedly institutions of enlightenment and education, were permitted to indoctrinate a generation of our citizens with the principles of free-market capitalism undoubtedly contributed to its highly successful immoral crusade. The manner in which an unseemly proportion of the current generation of Irish citizens bear unswerving loyalty to the doctrine of the free-market economy over a properly functioning society is proof of the success that the free-market capitalists have achieved in subverting the education system to their own advantage. That the wealth-creation philosophy enjoys devout, unquestioned and unfaltering support, which was more commonly reserved for religious doctrine in the past, is a highly significant aspect of what occurred.

When one considers that just thirty years ago the Catholic Church in Ireland enjoyed not only the trappings of wealth which accompanied the position of power and privilege it occupied in the State, but also the near total support of the citizens, one could have thought that a collective moral compass, which adherence to religious doctrine should imply, would have ensured that the immoral teachings of the free-market capitalists would have been rejected out of hand. Unfortunately, the Church's influence in these affairs was fatally undermined by its own immoral behaviour in choosing to protect its privilege and power, rather than nurturing a moral culture based on ethics and integrity. Significantly, in Ireland Inc., when the Catholic Church was faced with the dilemma of choosing the moral path over the path to financial security, it inexcusably chose the latter. When the Church decided to enter into a contemptible contract of collusion with the State to transfer to the public purse its debts of duty to its unfortunate victims, it was aligning itself wholeheartedly with the free-market capitalists' agenda. As fully-fledged members of the Golden Circle of Irish society, it could exploit all the advantages that accompanied such a powerful position, and when profit turned to debt it too could transfer this outrageous financial burden to innocent citizens to service. Far from driving the money lenders from the Temple, as they told us Christ had done, the Church drove the people away in their droves and elected to enjoy the company of the immoral fraudsters and conmen of Celtic Tiger Ireland.

On the publication of the Ryan Report, which detailed the extent of the systematic abuse of children in Church institutions, and having witnessed the Church's subsequent revolting attempts to avoid paying the financial compensation that was due to its victims, I, like many others I know, vowed never to set foot in a Catholic Church again. However, coincidently or not, as the anniversary of my parents' death approached I realised that I would be faced with the first real challenge to my new conviction. Realising that it could be misinterpreted as an offence to their memory, and also so as to be united with my close family in grateful commemoration of the lives of our parents, I decided to attend.

Nearly a year to the day after the government introduced the State guarantee, and five years after the untimely death of my parents in an unfortunate accident, I sat in the close comfort of my family and relatives and reflected on their lives and their undoubted influence on mine. As I considered the enormous debt I owed them for endeavouring to instil the principles of integrity and ethical behaviour in their children, and the way they railed against injustice, the words being read from the altar began to interrupt my thoughts. As the events of that evening brought back memories of my father warning of the inevitable collapse of the financial system represented by the free-market-influenced stock exchange, I took in the words of the second reading, from a letter by St James: "Now listen, you rich people, weep and wail because of the misery that is coming upon you. Your wealth has rotten, and moths have eaten your clothes. Your gold and silver are corroded, and that corrosion will be a testimony against you." Pulling my young son closer to me on my knee, and acknowledging the glance of wondrous surprise from my wife beside me, I listened with ever more intent to the words echoing around the church which I had attended in my youth with my parents.

The profound influence they had on my life which provided me with a spiritual vision which I believe guided me to the Dáil on the night the Government provided the State guarantee for our corrupt banks, came ever more to mind as the words from the altar resounded about the chapel: "You have stored up treasure for the last few days. Behold, the wages you withheld from the workers who harvested your fields are crying aloud; and the cries of the harvesters have reached the ears of the Lord of hosts." Listening to these words, I thought of the role that educators are obliged to fulfil in ensuring that a vision, based on the principles of liberty, equity and respect for human dignity, is provided for in society. As I glanced around the church, wondering how these profoundly pertinent words were resonating with those present, an alarming 'other truth' was dispiritingly revealed: the church was as good as empty. Apart from the thirty or so relatives of my parents, there were perhaps no more than the same number of regular Saturday evening mass goers to listen to the words of St James. Had they been appreciated fully, they could have helped us to avoid the suffering which the economic crisis threatens to inflict upon all of us.

"You have lived on earth in luxury and pleasure; you have fattened your hearts for the day of slaughter. You have condemned; you have murdered the righteous one who offers you no resistance." The near-empty church stood as a symbol of modern day society, where wise and invaluable counsel, formulated over many generations, is ignored in an undignified rush to accumulate personal wealth. The empty church also stood as a reminder to me of the day I rushed to the parliament to join with other like-minded citizens to protest against the injustice which the government intended to perpetrate against its own people, only to find nobody there. The shocking extent of the public's disengagement from rational debate, the life-blood of any properly functioning society, was devastatingly brought home to me on that day.

Subsequent acquiescence by a submissive public to the outrageously unjust measures which the government introduced to address our economic woes was further evidence of the dysfunctional society which predominated in the Ireland created by the free-market capitalists. When the very public that 'had offered no resistance' to the wealth-creators of Celtic Tiger Ireland, as they "stored up treasure for the last days," were subjected to measures which would effectively see them pay for the sins of the avaricious, the all-pervading control of the free-market capitalists was shockingly self-evident. When the Minister for Finance, Brian Lenihan, could boast in public that other European leaders had expressed "amazement" at the government's ability to introduce these savage measures, directed in the main against those least responsible for the economic collapse, the public's humiliation by their economic masters was complete. When Brian Lenihan could brag that "there would be riots in France" if the government there had attempted to introduce the measures which he and his cabinet ministers had inflicted on the citizens of Ireland, the extent of the absolute power which the government yielded over the citizens became heartbreakingly clear.

The fact that the citizens of the State were willing to accept this public humiliation from a man who, by his insufferable arrogance and outright incompetence, perfectly symbolised the mentality of the free-market capitalists that had brought us all to the very brink of economic catastrophe was somehow ironically appropriate. This, after all, was the man I had heard boast so vaingloriously in the members' bar of Dáil Éireann on the night he introduced the disastrous government guarantee for insolvent Irish banks – a guarantee that left the citizens facing the very real possibility that would have to service a €460,000,000,000 debt – that he was "playing a blinder."

When the Minister was pressed on his inability, and the inability of others, to foresee the economic catastrophe that was to break on an unsuspecting world, he was inclined to fall back on the standard pathetic reply which also serves to confer total absolution for their incompetence. With the benefit of hindsight they would, of course, have done things differently, but – they invariably argue – no-one foresaw the economic crisis that was on the horizon. If it is true that 'nobody saw this coming', as is habitually claimed, then surely we are duty-bound to ask ourselves: Why not?

October 2009

*"It is difficult to get a man to understand
something, when his salary depends upon his
not understanding it."*

(Upton Sinclair)